D1112596

Suicide of a Nation?

Suicide of

An enquiry into the state of Britain today by:

Fairlie	Seton-Watson
Muggeridge	Mander
Rees	John Grigg
	(formerly Lord Altrincham)
Shanks	Connolly
Shonfield	Cunliffe
Albu	McGlashan
Crawley	Elizabeth Young
Cole	Vaizey

EDITED BY ARTHUR KOESTLER

a Nation?

DIEU ET · MON DROIT

THE MACMILLAN COMPANY
NEW YORK
1964

First Published in The United States of
America by The Macmillan Company,
1964

Library of Congress Catalog Card No. 64/11937

Contents

III: TOWARDS A NEW SOCIETY?

Introduction

The Lion and the Ostrich

A CHIMAERA, in Greek mythology, was a monster with a lion's head, a goat's trunk, and a serpent's tail; more generally it meant a composite animal. Throughout the ages, painters and writers of fantastic tales have been fond of creating chimaeras. My own favourite brain-child is the momiphant. He is a phenomenon most of us have met in life: a hybrid who combines the delicate frailness of the mimosa, crumbling at a touch when his own feelings are hurt, with the thick-skinned robustness of the elephant trampling over the feelings of others. I think the sizeable majority of Germans of the last generation who supported the *Fuehrer* belonged to the species of mimophants. They were capable of shedding genuine tears at the death of their pet canaries; what they did at other times is perhaps better forgotten.

The average Englishman is certainly no mimophant. He strikes one as a much more attractive hybrid between a lion and an ostrich. In times of emergency he rises magnificently to the occasion. In between emergencies he buries his head in the sand with the tranquil conviction that Reality is a nasty word invented by foreigners. This attitude is not only soothing, but also guarantees that a new emergency will soon arise and provide a new opportunity for turning into a lion and rising magnificently to the occasion. The collaborators on this issue, a mixed crew ranging from Conservative M.P.s to Labour dons, all share the conviction that in the long run such an attitude must prove suicidal. Hence the alarming title and the hopeful question-mark.

7

THE LEONINE QUALITIES we take for granted; perhaps too much so; mere mention of them is considered in embarrassingly bad taste. Yet it needs to be brutally said that without the lion, France, Germany, and the rest would either still be ruled by *Gauleiters*, or they would have been 'liberated' by the Red Army and shared the fate of Hungary. In either case, Europe would have lost its historical identity: its élites liquidated in serial purges, its active resisters crushed, its passive masses cowed, it could only hope and pray, as the early Christians did in their catacombs, for a miraculous redemption in the distant future. All this is difficult to imagine. The hypothetical state of Europe in the 1960s, after a total victory of either Hitler or Stalin in the 1940s, is hardly ever discussed. Yet there can be no doubt that if, after Dunkirk, Britain had lost its moral fibre, the Americans could not have landed on the Continent, and the fate of Europe would have been decided between two paranoic Caesars.

There can be equally little doubt, however, that if the ostrich had not kept its head in the sand from Hitler's invasion of the Rhineland until well after Munich, the war would have been avoided, the dead would not be dead, and there would be no Iron Curtain studded with minefields, garotting half of Europe. The Battle of Britain was one of the most heroic and most unnecessary episodes in modern history. And let us remember that the tragic responsibility was equally shared by both sides: the Tory appeasers who were struck with blindness, and the Labour demagogues who shouted anti-Fascist slogans, warning against the Nazi menace and in the same breath preaching one-sided disarmament.

It is impossible to look back at the war without sickeningly mixed feelings of pride, pain, and bitterness. This may be one of the reasons why so many ex-R.A.F. men cultivate their moustaches and sign dud cheques. They may not be conscious of it, but they know that it was all so terribly unnecessary.

IT WOULD be comforting to believe that this gratuitous holocaust had at least taught us how to avoid its repetition in the future. The evidence does not bear this out. The conduct of our external and internal affairs was supposed to be guided, to some extent at least, by Ernest Bevin's sonorous warning after the Russians had seized Czechoslovakia in 1948: 'Europe must unite or perish.' Judged by the record, one would think that we tried our level best to promote the second alternative. In 1950, when Britain was invited to join in the European Coal and Steel Community, we refused; in subsequent years, as Europe's economic integration was gathering momentum and repeated attempts were made to secure our participation, we again refused; on various occasions British delegations either walked out in haughty contempt, or tried to wreck the conference—a sorry record which reminds one of Molotov's famous *nyet*, vetoing United Nations resolutions. We did not succeed in preventing the spectacular success of E.E.C.; but at least we had the modest satisfaction of having managed to put Europe at sixes and sevens. (A glance at Appendices 1 to 4 will show the wisdom of this policy.) The painful sequel of 1962–63 is fresh in our memories; but it is amazing how people succeed in forgetting the events of the last decade that led up to it. De Gaulle's trenchant *non* rings in the ear; our icy *nyets* are forgotten, perhaps because the public at large was never aware of what went on. This, of course, is not meant as an apology for the General; Nemesis never was an attractive goddess.

When the war was won, Britain's political and moral prestige in Europe was at an unprecedented height; in less than twenty years, her leaders managed to bring it down to an equally unprecedented low. Within the lifetime of one generation, the ostrich has deprived the lion of the fruit—or meat—of his victory.

These remarks concern a focal aspect of foreign policy in the past; for a constructive approach to the future, the reader is referred to the articles by Professor Hugh Seton-Watson and John Mander.

WHAT 'UNITE OR PERISH' meant to foreign policy, the parallel slogan 'expand or decay' meant to our economy; and here, too, we seem to have plumped for the second alternative. Imagine a visitor freshly arrived from Mars being taken on a conducted tour of Europe—from Oslo to Bonn to Milan to Paris to London and back; and then being asked to guess which was the only country that had lost the war and obviously had not had time to recover from its defeat. One must indeed try to look through innocent, Martian eyes to perceive the bitter irony of it all. Almost daily we read items in the newspapers such as (*Guardian*, April 9th, 1962):

BRITAIN BOTTOM OF THE CLASS

Britain economically came bottom of the class in the annual report published here to-night by the Secretariat of the United Nations Economic Commission for Europe.

Britain has the 'sorry distinction of being the only Western country whose volume of national output was practically unchanged from the previous year', and is 'the one country where the employment situation has seriously deteriorated'.

Appendices 1 to 4 explain how this came about; but since the professional economists writing in this edition took the basic facts for granted and are only concerned with their causes, I must quote a few salient figures which characterize the situation.

First, Britain's share in world trade had been steadily declining from the end of the last century to the second World War (from 33 per cent to 22 per cent in round figures); then rapidly declining to approximately 15 per cent. This means that within the last ten years our percentual share in world trade has shrunk by as much as in the course of the whole previous half-century.

Next, compare our exports in the post-war period with those of our neighbours. In the five-year period 1950–54, British exports increased by 6 per cent, those of the Common Market by 76 per cent. In the next five years, British exports rose by 13 per cent, Common Market exports by 63 per cent. In the last three years, up to and including 1962, our exports increased by approximately 10 per cent, those of the Common Market by approximately 50 per cent.

One need not be an economist to find these figures disconcerting. But there is a struthonian answer to them (from *struthio* the Latin for ostrich). Your Old Struthonian will start with some disparaging remarks about statistics in general, and probably quote to you that old chestnut about statistics being like bikinis ('what they reveal is suggestive, what they conceal is vital'). He will then explain that Britain started the Industrial Revolution, and that accordingly it is only natural that her growth-curve should flatten out and that other nations, which started later, should grow at a faster rate. This argument would be debatable if those newcomers on the industrial scene were still in the process of catching up with us; in fact, however, the youngsters have not only caught up with, but are rapidly outgrowing us. In terms of productivity (*i.e.*, real product *per caput*), the U.S.A. outstripped us in the 1880s, Canada before the first World War; and in the last few disastrous years we have been left behind by Sweden, Denmark, Norway, Germany, and France. To quote Anthony Crosland in a recent House of Commons debate:

> ... I want to register a protest against what I think is the very dangerous habit of saying that [other] countries are only growing faster than we are because they started from a point further behind. I think that this is a very fallacious argument. I think it impossible to reconcile with the fact that ... European countries with practically the same standards of living as we have are still going ahead a great deal faster than we are.... I think this is an argument which proves a great deal of complacency.[1]

I MUST APOLOGIZE for having bored the reader with economics. But I do not think the majority of readers study publications like O.E.C.D. reports or the *Economic Review*—nor do I, unless forced to do so, as on this present occasion. Hence we know vaguely that all is not as it should be, but we fail to realize the full extent of the country's economic decline, in the long-term perspective over the last century, and its alarming acceleration in the course of the last few years. There is indeed no reason why the average citizen should pore over export curves or G.N.P.C. percentages. But for heaven's sake don't let's listen to the Old Struthonian who tells us to be Greeks to the Romans, to let the Germans sweat and bustle while we

---

[1] *Hansard*, April 4th, 1963, p. 695.

recite poetry to each other at the fountain on the *agora*. We would certainly all prefer to be Greeks, but Piccadilly is no *agora*, commuter trains are not chariots, and Lord Russell is no Socrates, though he has been trying hard to earn his glass of hemlock. Since not only the Germans but the French and the Italians too had their economic miracles, proving that *joie de vivre* and cultures by no means inferior to ours can happily combine with an economy expanding at the rate of 6 per cent *per annum*, the Graeco-Roman analogy has become arrogant nonsense or, to be more polite, just plain silly. We cannot evade the economist's drab curves, because they are mirrored in our living standards, the prospects before our children, and the rate at which we develop stomach ulcers. The curves are also reflected in some recent surveys which show that between 40 per cent and 60 per cent of young people under twenty-five would like to emigrate if they could. Young people want to 'see the world', perhaps live a few years abroad; but for half a nation's youth to wish to leave their country and have done with it, is a different matter altogether.

AFTER A BRIEF prelude in which two highly idiosyncratic authors seem to be engaged in a kind of blind man's buff, the present issue divides into three sections. The first is devoted to analysing the root causes of our economic plight, the second to foreign policy, the third to education and culture; but the divisions are not rigid and the subjects overlap. The primary aim was diagnosis rather than therapy—for the simple reason that agreement on diagnosis must precede therapy. Since the diagnosticians who were called in differ in their party allegiances and personal opinions, it was to be expected that they would also disagree in their evaluation of the symptoms. However, it will be seen that while the contributions vary in accent and emphasis, there is a remarkable degree of unanimity among them regarding basic causes.

In the first place, there seems to be general agreement that we are faced with a 'functional' rather than a 'structural' disorder. Structural diseases have objective, material causes, functional diseases have subjective, psychological causes. Thus our diagnosis runs counter to the principles of materialistic philosophy in general and Marxist philosophy in particular. According to the tenets of the latter, the economic facts of life provide the 'sub-structure' which determines the 'super-structure' of cultures and ideas. We hold, to the contrary, that psychological factors and cultural attitudes are at the root of the economic evils—*not* the loss of empire, *not* the huge sums we must spend on armaments, *not* the misfortune that the steam engine was invented by an Englishman. 'We are at the moment dying by the mind,' wrote Ian Nairn, 'it is the mind which must will the change.'

It is true that we have lost the capital influx from overseas investments, and that 'the Continent will not suffer England to be the workshop of the world'. (This warning, incidentally, was not uttered by Tony Crosland, but by Disraeli in 1838.) But it is equally true that fifteen years ago West Germany was truncated, lying in ruins and flooded by several million refugees; that France too lost its empire and has only just emerged from its seven years' war with Algeria; that even little Austria, a torso from which all four limbs have been amputated, is running merrily about in its self-propelled invalid chair. What ails Britain is not the loss of empire but the loss of incentive. We hear the news at nine o'clock, but where are the eagles and the trumpets?

SOME OF THE CAUSATIVE factors of our economic, political, and cultural maladjustment are mentioned independently by several contributors; they crop up like *leitmotifs* from a *Götterdämmerung* re-written by Gilbert and Sullivan. Among these are: fixation on (a) the glories, (b) the miseries of the past, affecting both the upper and lower classes in opposite but equally deleterious ways; and the resulting perpetuation of class-barriers and class-resentment. We are constantly being assured by wishful thinkers that these are on the wane. In fact the Welfare State has dulled some of the more glaring economic inequalities, but not the psychological *apartheid* between the bourgeoisie and the proletariat—to use these good old terms which the English dislike, perhaps because they fit the situation here better than anywhere else, and describe it in too precise, explicit terms. It is still true that only exceptionally bright young people of proletarian or lower-middle-class origin are able to cross the barrier; and most of them still carry a traumatizing chip, or cross, through life. It is a remarkable feature of the English progressive that privately he knows of more than one of these chipped case-histories in his circle of acquaintances; whereas in public, or in print, he will quite honestly pretend that all this is a matter of the ugly past.

A further *leitmotif*, directly related to the previous one, is what one might call 'rule by mediocracy'. The cult of amateurishness, and the contempt in which proficiency and expertise are held, breed mediocrats by natural selection; the too-keen, the too-clever-by-half, are unfit for survival and eliminated from the race in which the last to pass the post is winner. Old Struth-onians are Amateurs and Gentlemen; they fight valiant rear-guard-actions in the merry civil war between Eggheads and Engineers; and they see to it that their sons are educated in the same spirit, by becoming thoroughly immersed in Homer's universe, but not in the universe of Newton. Thus equipped, they may hope for a place in the sun, and add their voices to the 'plaintive treble from the Treasury Bench' (more Disraeli). As for the rest of the world, beyond the golden sand of our beaches where the ostrich meditates among the litter of paper bags and discarded contraceptives, our ancient words of wisdom remain as true as ever—that English is the only sensible language, 'because a knife, for instance, is called by the French *couteau*, by the Germans *Messer*, and so on, whereas we English call it a "knife", which is after all what a knife really is. . . .'

A.K.

Publisher's Note

AT THE beginning of 1963, *The Observer*, London, published a series of articles on 'What's Left For Patriotism?'. The concluding article in the series was written by Arthur Koestler. It had such wide repercussions that the Editors of the monthly *Encounter*—Stephen Spender and Melvin J. Lasky—invited Koestler to act as a guest editor for a special issue on the state of Britain today.

To explain to their readers this unusual invitation, the Editors of *Encounter* wrote:

> In 1940 when France collapsed ARTHUR KOESTLER, at thirty-five a veteran of Europe's prisons and concentration camps, made the decisive choice of his life: instead of accepting the hospitality of the United States which had not yet entered the war, he made his way to England. He was sent to Pentonville as an illegal entrant, but released after a few weeks and allowed to join the Pioneer Corps to 'dig for victory' (as the posters said). 'To be born into this world as a British citizen', he later wrote, 'involves neither effort nor an act of choice. To become British by naturalization involves both . . . Pentonville was my prep school, the Pioneer Corps my Eton.' In the twenty years since, he has been dividing his time between his London home and Europe. He feels thoroughly critical of our ways when in England, but 'thoroughly British when abroad'.

Encounter Magazine accepted Arthur Koestler's idea for a special number and he accepted in turn their idea that he should edit it. In a slightly different form, this provocative and searching analysis of the state of Britain today, which originally appeared as the July, 1963, special issue of *Encounter* is now published in book form.

Blind Man's Buff

No ENGLISH SCENE would be complete without its practitioners of the cult of eccentricity, as ritualized as the Zen-master's KOANS—without the Buccaneers with tousled locks out of *The Forsyte Saga*. Henry Fairlie, invited to write on the State of England, wanders off to denounce all State-of-England writing. And Malcolm Muggeridge, asked to indulge this time in the more creative aspects of his well-known despair, relapses into his darkest, most destructive mood. Mr. Fairlie is angry with *The Times*, the mores, and Mr. Muggeridge. Mr. Muggeridge is thirsty for dragon's blood. They represent opposite extremes in the familiar range of Anglo-Saxon attitudes: one a proud, sulky retreat from the crowd's ignoble strife; the other a lashing-out at all and sundry with impartial gusto.

We publish their contributions (or rather *antributions*, in the sense of the physicist's anti-matter) as a prelude to this inquiry—because no contrast could be more fitting to mark the opposite poles in between which we must try to wend our way.

Perhaps we ought to have been more conscientious and appended a glossary of the more obscure terms used by the authors. For instance: 'when Mr. Muggeridge says "you look like a pig" he only means that you have a rosy complexion'; or: 'when Mr. Fairlie speaks of "liberty" he means pre-Keynesian *laissez-faire* economy, and when he berates "State-of-England writing" he means what used to be called social criticism. . . .' But in this free and kind country it would be most unfair to prevent anybody from hitting as far below the belt as he can stoop to conquer.

On the Comforts of Anger

Henry Fairlie

ANYONE WHO WRITES a fair amount (and we all, these days, write far too much) about political and social issues is always in danger of writing what may briefly be called 'State of England' pieces: editors, for one thing, like them; and they are, for a second thing, easy to write. You only have to make a certain kind of noise. Elsewhere, I have called them 'Wurra-wurra-wurra-wur-aw-aw-aw' articles, for that is the noise which the lions make in *The Rose and the Ring* when they gobble up Count Hogginarmo; to this I have little to add, except that I have since discovered that Tigger makes almost exactly the same noise, 'Worraworraworraworraworra', when he suddenly pulls the tablecloth off in *The House at Pooh Corner*.

All 'State of England' writers remind me irresistibly of him:

... he jumped at the end of the tablecloth, pulled it to the ground, wrapped himself up in it three times, rolled to the other end of the room, and, after a terrible struggle, got his head into the daylight again, and said cheerfully: 'Have I won?'

This is exactly how most articles on the 'State of England' are written.

I am aware, of course, that this is a 'State of England' collection of essays; but it is just this grotesque fact which has prompted the moderate thoughts which follow. I was asked to discuss the current vogue of 'almost nihilist criticism'—the phrase, I may be allowed to say, was not mine—and the more I have thought about it, the more I am convinced that the fault (if fault at all there is) lies here: right here, in the ceaseless articles, books and special numbers about the 'State of England', which we keep writing and others keep publishing. I can hope only that this collections of essays will kill the subject.

'STATE OF ENGLAND' PIECES (of whatever length) are pre-occupied with England, with decline, and with crisis. Since we live in England, it is in decline, and it is buffeted by crises, this may not seem surprising. But what ought to be matters of interest change their character when they become obsessions. Problems which are real and manageable become part of a Problem which can never be tackled but only constantly written about. Changes which need to be quietly made are presented to us in terms of Decision, demanding the exercise of some kind of national will.

Moreover, we allow these obsessions to grow only because we ignore so much of what is real around us. The most important facts about England are that it is as free and orderly and kindly a country as any in the world. I can see no reason why it should not remain so: and I am not sure that I wish it to be anything more. Before I can share the concern of the 'State of England' writers, therefore, I need to be shown what it is they wish to alter in our society or, to use their own language, what it is they wish to inject into it. If they reply, as they usually do, 'vigour', or 'dynamism', or 'efficiency', or 'greatness', I then need to be shown that these words do not conceal attitudes hostile to the kind of liberty I am accustomed to enjoying and the kind of order I am prepared to tolerate.

THE FIRST QUESTION to ask, when confronted by any 'State of England' writing, is what we are being asked to exchange for what. I agree that the price to be paid for the kind of liberty and order we know may, to some, seem high. It probably means that our society will have less efficiency than economists would like, less sense of purpose than moralists would like, less simple priorities than sociologists would like, less doctrine than theologians would like. To these, unable to shape us as they please, it is no doubt all a little alarming: to the rest of us, less so. At least, it means that we still have some chance left of doing what we ourselves want to do, and not what they want us to do. To me, this seems a civilized state of affairs, if not the only civilized state of affairs.

A free society is necessarily an untidy, uncomfortable, and apparently inefficient affair; and I suspect that one of the troubles with 'State of England' writers is that they cannot bear the whole anxious process.[1] As the American conservative, Fisher Ames, said: 'Monarchy is like a splendid ship, with all sails set; it moves majestically on; then it hits a rock and sinks for ever. Democracy is like a raft; it never sinks but, damn it, your feet are always in the water.' 'State of England' writers seem to me not to like getting their feet wet: it makes them jumpy company on a raft.

It is my belief that England's feet are no more than ordinarily wet; but, since this is not a 'State of England' article, that is beside the point. What I am concerned with here are the language and attitudes which have helped to create the stereotyped impression (which may end up by acquiring substance) that, sitting on our raft, we are about to sink, unless we take drastic and unusual action: that we face some unique Crisis of Decision. Unless this language and these attitudes are challenged, we are in danger of acquiring other attitudes which should have no place in the thinking and aspirations of a fortunately free and orderly people.

THERE ARE SUCH ATTITUDES about. Here, for example, is a passage from a leading article in *The Times* of April 10th, 1963, entitled 'The Kindly Dinosaur':

> The British, a naturally kindly people, are coming increasingly to believe that kindness is all that matters. Hardly any major modernization or rationalization can be proposed without protests that it will inflict hardship, particularly on the infirm or the elderly. That is considered reason enough for its abandonment. It is not enough. The dinosaur, for all we know, was good to its aged and did not eat its young. It may

---

[1] A 'stop-and-go' economy is both unavoidable and even proper in a free society. Certainly, it is no reason for creating an 'atmosphere' of emergency: which is then used to justify restrictions of freedom.

well have been the most benevolent giant that ever was. That did not prevent its lack of adaptability enforcing its extinction.

The argument seems innocent enough. In fact, it could be used to justify, in the alleged interests of society, the deliberate and callous neglect of the interests of any minority: especially, so it seems, the weak and the aged.

It needs to be extended only a fraction to justify, again in the alleged interests of society, any inhumanity: lack of adaptability to the supposed characteristics of the species sent a fair number of people to the gas ovens. It is this primitive Darwinism in the argument used by *The Times*, the lurking assumptions about the 'survival of the fittest', which make me suspicious. The Pathetic Fallacy crops up in political as well as in other kinds of writing and, as our generation should know better than any other, it usually leads to nasty results. Before asking us to consider the dinosaur as a warning, *The Times* might have stopped to recall that nature is careless of the single life: *homo sapiens* usually claims not to be.

Arguments which, like this one, derive from false parallels with biological species or races are far too dangerous not to be recognized for the nonsense they are. It may therefore be worth quoting from *Fossil Amphibians and Reptiles* by Dr. W. E. Swinton, of the Natural History Museum:

Thus the factors that led to extinction are many and complex. No one theory, no single event, can explain the disappearance during the closing stages of the Cretaceous and the dawn of the Eocene of groups that had hitherto had a long record of dominance. It may be, perhaps, that dominance itself is impermanent, for the organisms that have survived for the longest periods of geological time have usually been, like the brachiopod *Lingula*, obscure and unobtrusive.

The case, then, would seem to be for becoming ourselves obscure and unobtrusive, a small nation, brachiopod *Insula*: then we would survive. Heavy weather, all this may seem: but it is to such balderdash that almost all 'State of England' writing, with its canting about 'survival', can fairly be reduced.

A SECOND QUOTATION needs to be put beside the one from *The Times*. It comes from a letter which Mr. Corelli Barnett wrote to the *Spectator* after I had expressed my doubts about the current cry for 'leadership' and 'sense of purpose'. He took me to task for what he called my 'talk of open and free societies'. I was, he said

> faithful to nineteenth-century humanism, liberalism, and parliamentarianism. All these are luxuries possible only to a world empire with a huge navy, a vast bank account, and few rivals. What faces Britain today is the more basic matter of survival, and survival in terms of developments in technology (with all their colossal sociological consequences) that our political traditions simply do not encompass. What Britain must think about is Power. . . . Without it, you simply do not count.

Mr. Corelli Barnett is not uncharacteristic of today's tough young realists. He throws humanism, liberalism, and parliamentarianism into the dustbin. We can hardly complain that we have not been warned. By the time we grow infirm and elderly, clinging to our out-of-date humanism and liberalism, what place can there be for us in the society which he and *The Times* appear to envisage?

These quotations could be matched by many more over the past twelve months, especially from leading articles which have called for 'leadership' and a 'sense of purpose', and have sought to re-introduce the awful distinction between the 'useful' and 'useless' members of society. (This distinction is most easily resisted by assuming that one is among the 'useless' members.) I have given these quotations attention because they help to underline the carelessness about liberty—about the actual liberty which we enjoy in this country—lying behind almost all 'State of England' writing.

Its motives can be seen most clearly in the writings of the economists and of those who have set themselves up as spokesmen of the technocrats. Their trick is an old and familiar one, which has been most recently described, in another context, by Sir Isaiah Berlin:

It is one of the stratagems of totalitarian régimes to present all situations as critical emergencies, demanding ruthless elimination of all goals, interpretations, forms of behaviour save for one absolutely specific, concrete, immediate end, binding on everyone, which calls for ends and means so narrowly and clearly definable that it is easy to impose sanctions for failing to pursue them.

We are, of course, nowhere near a totalitarian régime in this country, but we are daily getting nearer to using totalitarian arguments to justify another large encroachment on our liberty: or, rather, on some of our particular liberties.

IF THIS SEEMS to be pitching it too strongly, it is worth noticing that the currently fashionable criticisms[1] which are made of the amateur and the politician are merely the old and insidious managerial criticisms of politics presented in a new jargon. Like Lord Reith, their dark prophet, they ponder the deadly question, whether it is

> undesirable to have elected representatives associated with the management of public services? Log-rolling; ears to the ground; fear of the electors; everything submitted to the criterion of the vote. Timidity, compromise, mediocrity—are these the inevitable concomitants of democracy . . .?

The voice of the manager then, now the voice of the technocrat, proclaiming, as does every opponent of free institutions, that, freed from the necessity to consult ordinary people, he could run their lives for them far more efficiently and beneficently than they can themselves. It is time that, against their evil doctrine, we re-asserted our right to be inefficient.

DO I EXAGGERATE the dislike which our 'new men' have for our liberties? I do not think so. The clearest proof is in their most familiar comparisons. We are invited by them to contrast our own economic performance since the war with the 'economic

---

[1] These criticisms have become, in Orwell's phrase, one of the 'smelly little orthodoxies' of our time.

miracles' of Germany and France. This point deserves, one day, to be refuted in detail. Here, I must be satisfied with bald assertions.

1. I am extremely doubtful whether we have anything to learn from either the Fifth Republic in France or the Federal Republic in West Germany about the manner of ordering and sustaining a free society; I am not even sure whether we have much to learn in the matter from the French and Germans as peoples.

2. I am extremely doubtful whether either the Fifth Republic or the Federal Republic will survive. I hope that they will develop—and so survive. But, for the moment, I am prepared to wager fairly heavily that our own social and political arrangements will outlast theirs. Any takers?

3. I am convinced that the strength of our society lies in the spontaneity of its social decisions. They are decisions taken by responsible and independent societies within our society. The process is slow, but the experience goes deep.

4. I do not expect Continentals to understand this. But I do expect Englishmen and even Americans to understand it. We have ways of conducting our affairs which provide our society with huge reserves of energy when it is needed: in a crisis.

The result is in history, and I think again will be. I am not one who is apt to confuse *vox populi* with *vox dei*, but the one thing which the people of this country have shown they can do, over a number of years, is sort out their long-term aspirations. This is their wisdom; and they are wise also in knowing that so ticklish a task cannot be left to the professionals, by whom I mean all those extraordinary people who are always wanting to do extraordinary things to us. Mr. Simon Raven may seem an unlikely character to find voicing the instincts of the common people, but, when faced by the fashionable cant of Mr. Anthony Sampson's *Anatomy of Britain*, he burst out that he had no wish to be efficient, especially at the price which seemed to be being asked. In this, I believe he represented a deep and proper instinct in the English people.

I SIMPLY DO NOT believe—and this is the point I would most like to be answered by the 'State of England' writers—that either the French or the Germans have sorted out their long-term aspirations. I do the Germans the credit not to believe that they will for ever be satisfied with the material satisfactions of the 'economic miracle'. But that only leaves the alarming question where they will turn when their energy is once more united to a spiritual hunger. I do the French the credit not to believe that they share (although they may enjoy) the superb fantasies of President de Gaulle. But that only leaves the alarming question where they will turn when his magnificent but irrelevant personal influence is removed.

On the whole, I am prepared to rest again on an assertion: that the English people are working their way, far more clearly and calmly than those who preach at them, to a quite realistic estimate of their changed position in the world and also, which is much more important, to the kind of body of common sentiments which makes a people conscious of itself as a people. It includes all kinds of rum things: but, above all, there runs through it an insistence that consideration for the weak should never too little inform public policy. (This was the dreadful mistake which the Conservatives made in 1959.) To the charge that they think that only kindness matters, they would probably assent. It would be appalling hypocrisy, but there are many worse images for a people to hold of themselves.

'STATE OF ENGLAND' writing, however, would never have obtained its hold if there did not lie behind it something even more serious than an ignorance of the quality of English society: an ignorance of the quality of the whole of our civilization. It is essential to take one quick look, and one lusty swipe, at those who set themselves up as the popular scourges of our civilization (and therefore of this country as part of it). Like Gregory of Tours (but with considerably less reason) they cry, 'Woe to our times.' They stand in a long and distinguished line, but I think it is necessary to see where their gloomy spirits take them. Here is the familiar rasp of Mr. Malcolm Muggeridge:

Such is liberalism; the disease, not the cure, of our sick civilization, a major destructive force in an age of destruction. The winds of change on which it rides blow over a charnel house, and carry a stench of death; its liberating armies, marching as to peace, rape, kill, and enslave on their way.

I am the last to dispute that the promises of liberalism have been among the great delusions of modern man. But the daemonic force of liberalism has always been released by men using exactly the kind of language which Mr. Muggeridge himself uses. If the world and its institutions and its doings are so evil, then scorch its earth.

Whether it is Luther, or Mr. John Osborne speaking through the mouth of his make-believe Luther, the fury is equally destructive: even if, as in the case of Mr. Osborne, only self-destructive. The violence, in turn, provokes counter-violence; the reformation, counter-reformation; and the moderate man is left, querulously calling with Erasmus: 'If the dove of Christ— not the owl of Minerva—would only fly to us, some measure might be put to the madness of mankind.'

I WAS THINKING of Mr. Muggeridge's words as I walked along a platform at Paddington on the Monday morning after they appeared. At the end of the platform stood a large white van. I had to step to the side to get round it, and I stopped to watch. One by one, railwaymen were going into it, and coming out of it. On the sides of the van were the words: NATIONAL HEALTH SERVICE: MASS RADIOGRAPHY UNIT. How many railwaymen (and miners and factory-workers) would waste with T.B. without this service? It is at this point that one stops finding the age peculiarly vile, and our society peculiarly evil. Savonarola, I suspect, would not have thought much about that van. He would have been fretting about the follies and wickednesses of Ascot.

I am not saying that services like these are enough, only that they take us a long way along *one* of the roads that we ought to be travelling, and glad that we are travelling. In so far, then, as 'State of England' criticism is part of a chastising (self-chastising) criticism of our times, I think we should be very careful that we are not led into a blindness to the humanity and compassion around us, lest we should thereby be led into a rejection of the opportunities to extend those areas of humanity and compassion. This is the worst form of obscurantism. Indulging the kind of despair to which Mr. Muggeridge gives popular expression can lead much too easily to indifference and lethargy about sending just one more medical unit to the Congo.

UNTIL WE AGAIN THINK of ourselves individually as members of an enlightened Western civilization, whose values, methods, and sense of direction we trust, we will never learn how to look at our own society as a member of it. We will become insularly preoccupied with things which scarcely matter a whit: with stops and goes in the economy; with evidences of a class structure which are more imagined than real, and which are anyhow breaking down; with tea-break strikes; with demarcation disputes; with an unimportant Communist Party and an equally unimportant monarchy; with public opinion polls on this, and mass observations of that; with traffic jams; with Mr. Marples; with Mr. Anthony Wedgwood Benn's title.

For it is the lack of sense of proportion in 'State of England' writing that most depresses me. Perhaps it is because the Critic has for the first time become a well-paid member of society, expecting services from it which were previously given only to the most privileged. I sometimes have the impression that all their criticism comes from a bad digestion. The thing most likely to set them off is a tasteless *bisque d'homard* in a luxury hotel, or the inability to obtain a meal when they reach Ballachulish after 10 p.m. It is all very affecting. But I do not really think that you can begin a reformation by nailing the *Good Food Guide* to the door of a provincial hotel. And there, I suspect, is the cause of it all. Our oligopoly of 'State of England' writers (beside them, satire is only a home-loom industry) are consumed with guilt at what they consume from society.

So let it be, but I wish they would chastise themselves in private and, if they wish to record it all, put it into novels, or poems, or autobiographies, and not pretend that they are engaged in an objective concern for the 'State of England'.

England, Whose England?

Malcolm Muggeridge

EACH TIME I return to England from abroad the country seems a little more run down than when I went away; its streets a little shabbier; its railway carriages and restaurants a little dingier; the editorial pretensions of its newspapers a little emptier; and the vainglorious rhetoric of its politicians a little more fatuous. On one such occasion I happened to turn on the television and there on the screen was Harold Macmillan blowing through his moustache to the effect that 'Britain has been great, is great, and will continue to be great'. A more ludicrous performance could scarcely be imagined. Macmillan seemed, in his very person, to embody the national decay he supposed himself to be confuting. He exuded a flavour of moth balls. His decomposing visage and somehow seedy attire conveyed the impression of an ageing and eccentric clergyman who had been induced to play the part of a Prime Minister in the dramatized version of a Snow novel put on by a village amateur dramatic society.

We like to persuade ourselves that our leaders betray the trust imposed in them and distort the aspirations of those who elect them. Actually, they represent us all too exactly. The melancholy tale of our Prime Ministers, from Lloyd George and Baldwin, through Ramsay MacDonald and Neville Chamberlain, to Attlee and Anthony Eden, provides a perfect image of our fate. No one is miscast. Each left the country appreciably poorer and weaker, both spiritually and materially, than when he took over, giving an extra impetus to the Gadarene rush already under way.

Churchill may be separated from the others in that he was

29

confronted, in 1940, with an evidently desperate situation to meet which he invoked desperate remedies. Yet it may be doubted whether the overblown rhetoric he fed the English, in the written and the spoken word, was, in its ultimate consequences, appreciably different from MacDonald's exuberant incoherence or Eden's relentless banalities.

Macmillan, in any case, has provided a symbolism which is perfectly appropriate. The crofter and the ducal connection; that antique rig with its faint flavour of burlesque, grouse-moor spats, and evenings wreathed in cigar-smoke and rich with port; those meandering disquisitions, Trollopian, historical, floating loose, as it were, upon some aimless and inexhaustible tide—who could more fittingly direct our affairs in the mid-twentieth century?

Never can I forget him in Kiev during his visit to the U.S.S.R. and Mr. Khrushchev. He was dressed in a tweed ensemble suitable for rural occasions, worn, I should suppose, at many a Conservative garden fête. His speech, delivered with old-style elegance, referred to how in the eleventh century a Ukrainian princess had married into the English royal house. Might not this union, he went on, be regarded as a happy augury for future relations between two countries whose history and traditions had so much in common? The crowd, as is usual on such occasions in the U.S.S.R., consisted largely of government officials, with a top dressing of plain-clothes police; solidly built, grey-faced men in issue suitings, containing ample room for a slung gun, and with wide trouser-ends. I studied their granite expressions as the Prime Minister's oratorial flow washed over them. In just one or two of their faces I thought I detected a faint trace of wonderment; a tiny flicker of an eyelid, a minute fold of incredulity round the mouth. The others remained inscrutable, their pleasure in their former princess's London nuptials, if any, well under control.

As Macmillan walked away, seemingly well pleased with himself, with little Selwyn Lloyd trotting along behind him; tall white fur hat perched on his head, and something crustacean in his gait; I realized that these two had gone about the troubled world before; in the parched plains of Spain, the one mounted on the lean mare, Rosinante, and the other on a donkey, looking for wrongs to redress and maidens in distress to champion. Unmistakably, they were the living image of Don Quixote, Knight of the Woeful Countenance, and Sancho Panza, his squire.

As in cervantes' masterpiece, one feels today that things are out of sync. The conductor is working from one score and the orchestra from another, with consequent total confusion in the resultant performance. The players have learnt their lines from a play other than the one which is being performed; they make false entrances and exits, stumble over unfamiliar scenery, and turn in vain to the prompter. There is no correlation between word and deed, between the aspirations ostensibly entertained and what actually happens, between (to use Blake's dichotomy) what is seen with, and what is seen through, the eye.

Such is the prevailing impression when I look back at what has happened to and in England during the last five decades, since, that is, the outbreak of the 1914–18 war. I have a vivid recollection, at the age of thirteen, of going to Brixton after the first Zeppelin raid, and seeing crowds of people collecting, by way of mementoes, fragments of metal from the macadamized roadway. Most of these fragments were motor-treads, and had no connection with the raid, but were no less zealously collected for that. It was an episode over which I brooded long.

On Armistice Day my father astonished us all by producing a minute Union Jack when he returned from the City, and fastening it to the porch of our small suburban house, where it rather absurdly fluttered. In our socialist-pacifist household this action was as staggering as if he had announced that he was to be ordained into the Anglican Church, or that he had joined the Primrose League. The Union Jack covered the chairman's table at Conservative gatherings; it was waved on patriotic occasions; it embellished pernicious leaflets. It was not for us.

I spent Armistice Day going on the top of a motor bus to its Woolwich terminal and then back to South Croydon. It was the first time I had seen human beings released from restraint; climbing on to the roofs of taxis, shouting, reeling, and clasping one another; dancing, and grimacing, and exchanging hats. In those days there was no radio to tell us about what we were doing and feeling; no television to show us ourselves. We had to make do with the *Daily Mail*, in which I read about the celebrations I had witnessed on the way to and from Woolwich. I think, therefore I am; it was in the *Daily Mail*, therefore it happened. The microphone and the television screen, and other popular newspapers and magazines, were to make such propositions infinitely more actual in the years to come. I turned to the *Daily Mail* in preference to the *Daily News* with some trepidation. It was owned, I knew, by Lord Northcliffe, whose name my father used to pronounce when he drew a piece of string tightly round his finger like a noose.

My father's explanation of so astonishingly flying a Union Jack from our porch was that it signified on this occasion, not national pride, but national redemption; the ending of a war to end war, and the ushering in of the League of Nations, a land fit for heroes to live in, a world safe for democracy; the fulfilment of all the promises and prognostications dredged up out of Woodrow Wilson's Princetonian virtue, and Lloyd George's Welsh cunning, and the fathomless French duplicity of Clemenceau. It was, and to some extent still is, the fashion to complain that these promises were all broken and the prognostications all unrealized; my father soon, metaphorically speaking, lowered his flag to half-mast.

YET HOW MANY housing estates have been built for heroes to live in! Hear old Beveridge's sheep's voice enumerating the benefits which Lloyd George aspired towards, and Attlee brought to pass! As for making the world safe for democracy, when has it ever been safer? Democracy in India, where millions go to the polls, choosing between Elephant and Lotus Flower in the maturest possible manner. In the U.S.S.R. and the People's Democracies, where polls of 95 per cent and more are regularly registered. In the U.S.A. where, thanks to television, rival candidates become personally known, a Real Presence, enabling the electorate to discriminate nicely between a Kennedy and a Nixon. In the upper reaches of the Nile, where tall naked electors standing on one leg register their votes, and in our own boroughs and counties where votes are similarly registered by electors for the most part clothed and standing on two legs.

Never, it is safe to say, has there been so much voting, on so broad a franchise, since the world began.

And the war to end war? After 1918, there was not, as it happened, another war, but only the same one, which is going on still. Admittedly, in that sense, the 1914–18 war might be better described as a war to begin war than as one to end war. In any case, the League of Nations duly came to pass. How well I remember it: that windy Quai Woodrow Wilson, and Ramsay MacDonald and his friends, and Anthony Eden idealistic behind his moustache, and Aristide Briand asleep behind his ampler one, and the Café Bavaria where journalists assembled to drink and dream up inside information. If some champion of the League like Lord Robert Cecil or Mr. Noel-Baker heard complaints that it was somewhat ineffectual in actually terminating hostilities in Manchuria or Abyssinia, the reply always was that in other directions, like white slavery and narcotics, it was extremely effective. Thus, in August, 1939, the codification of level-crossing signs came up for consideration. The discussion was suspended when the Russo-German invasion of Poland began. Whether it was ever taken up again at the United Nations, and if so with what result, I do not know.

The books about the war, Graves, Hemingway, Aldington; the poems about the war ('They have not died in vain'); the plays about the war, *Journey's End*, men in trench-coats, tin hats, marching, singing; Edmund Blunden, Herbert Read (Sir); Lawrence of Arabia, *Seven Pillars*, Ross, and all his lies, which, if anything, only ministered, and minister, to the cult, grisly, shrinking, scruffily self-assertive prototype of all the scruffily assertive resistance fighters and fighting resisters to come, filling the deserts and the maquis and the mountains with authors in search of a hero; the other Lawrence (D. H.), Leavis his prophet, on the side of life, Saint Chatterley and all the Devils, in blissful sylvan union with her gamekeeper, though, according to perceptive Warden Sparrow, by the back passage. The clergymen of the war, Woodbine Willie, Tubby Clayton, Dick Shepherd, mine hosts at the sign of the Lamb of God; poppies, graveyards with all the little identical gravestones stretching to eternity, the Prince of Wales fingering his tie; *All Quiet on the Western Front*, Old Contemptibles and Old Bill, cockney humour, to come in handy again in the underground shelters. ''Arf a mo', Kaiser! 'Arf a mo', 'Itler!' with good old *Punch* throwing in its blessing all the way; minstrel boys, their wild harps slung behind them, who to the war will not go, Peace Pledge Unionists, Peace Balloters, never to fight again—never, never, never, never.

What a spectacular! What (as the reviewers say) a crowded canvas! What a yarn or slice of life, with Good Companions (Honest Jack) bringing up the rear, and, in the vanguard, the torch of culture borne aloft; Rare Tom Eliot with his Wasteland, Squinting Jim Joyce with his vocabulary, Yawning Bill Yeats with his hive for the honey bee, and, coming along, Charlie Snow, Dilly Thomas, Johnny Osborne, Kit Logue, and Ken Tynan's Wolf Cub Troop, all wearing their accredited badges as State Registered Satirists.

A REPEAT PERFORMANCE of the 1914–18 war was called for, and was duly put on, under the direction of the Old Impresario himself, his stage cigar stuck in his mouth; siren-suited, jutting-chinned, a bulldog breed straight out of Cruft's if ever there was one. Some of his fellow-players in the original production had to be discarded for their creaking joints and stiff delivery, but there was plenty of new talent coming along; for instance, genial Monty, with two badges in his hat and a heart overflowing with 'binge'. Soon the long, long trail was again a-winding; the home fires, thanks to the *Luftwaffe*, were kept burning, lighting such a candle by God's grace in England as (I trust) shall never be put out. Russian blood and American money sealed the glorious victory, and soon there was again a new and better world to be built.

See the three Architects, met to de-limit its frontiers, shape its destiny, decree the punishment of the guilty and the reward of the virtuous; the Four Freedoms on their breath, the Atlantic Charter about their heads, enfolded in the luminosity of a common cause, a common dedication to life, liberty, and the pursuit of happiness for all mankind. Roosevelt with his large expanse of sirloin face, neon-smile lit; Churchill, British-warmed, fur hat rakishly awry, cigar rakishly jutting; and Stalin with his wary, slit eyes, staring, like some Mongolian shepherd, at a distant prospect, brooding on loot and murder and vast metal statues of himself to be erected in distant places. Imagine his heartfelt delight when Roosevelt, with the ingenuity of a Talleyrand, managed to slip out 'Uncle Joe'; when Churchill, shrewdly shaping up to Stalin's simple peasant shrewdness, demonstrated with match-sticks how his kingdom might be enlarged and his subjects increased, scribbling on a piece of paper the simple arithmetical division of their respective spheres of influence, and illuminating their discussion with primitive peasant imagery about not stuffing the Polish Goose too full of German food to the point of bursting. By way of preparation, he, too, had thoughtfully lighted such a candle by God's grace in Dresden as (I trust) shall never be put out.

Great was it in that time to be alive, but to be old was very heaven. The Four Freedoms reigned; in the rubble of Berlin and other demolished cities displaced persons picked their way, and constructed weird little caves or shelters to live in; cigarettes for currency, calories for food. In Nuremberg the fallen tyrants were brought to justice, Ribbentrop hanging his head and confessing to his Soviet judges and accusers that he had partitioned Poland. Thus was the majesty of international law upheld.

It fell to two newcomers to the stage of history, Harry S. Truman and Clement Attlee, to make a momentous decision. The mice laboured and brought forth a mountain. Reading from a typescript, in a mechanical, expressionless voice, stumbling, childlike, after the words too eagerly to discover the sentences, President Truman announced the dropping of atomic bombs on Japan. Mr. Atlee likewise informed Honourable Members in the House of Commons, who rustled their Order Papers to indicate excitement, approval, and perhaps concern. Thenceforth the mushroom cloud adorned all deliberations. ''Arf a mo', Krush!' But would there even be that much time? Millions now dying will never live. Ah! bearded, duffle-coated, twanging, chanting, Nuclear Disarmers; ah! Canon Collins in your belted cassock, and old philosopher Russell; ah! ten-gallon-hatted Jacquetta, and all you resolute matrons and tousled girls, your souls go marching on.

Civilization has already been saved twice, once by Lloyd

George and once by Churchill, and is now again in hazard. Who will save it this time, so that consenting adults may go on joyously consenting; Cancer, Kama, and Chatterley continue to edify the young, delight the mature, and solace the old; no colour prejudice any more, from Bow Group to Bow, no class prejudice either; an Empire now on which the sun never rises and a Commonwealth on which it never sets, great acts of statesmanship performed in withdrawing here, there, and everywhere; no poverty any more, bumper to bumper down to the sea in cars; our moral influence in the world mightier than ever before, though, let's be frank, our military strength diminished (God who made us feeble, make us feebler yet); we Greece to America's Rome, and, 'Your Royal Highness, Your Grace, Your Excellencies, My Lords, Ladies, and Gentlemen, as long as we, the two great English-speaking Democracies, stand together . . .' with cigar-smoke billowing upwards and brandy-fumes billowing downwards; Here! here! Here! here!

The New Towns rise, as do the television aerials, dreaming spires; the streams flow, pellucid, through the comprehensive schools; the B.B.C. lifts up our hearts in the morning, and bids us good night in the evening. We wait for Godot, we shall have strip-tease wherever we go. Give us this day our *Daily Express*, each week our Dimbleby. God is mathematics, crieth our preacher. In the name of Algebra, the Son, Trigonometry, the Father, and Thermodynamics, the Holy Ghost, *Amen*.

PART I

Cold Class War

RISING wages, improved housing conditions, washing machines, and television sets have gone a long way towards providing the top layers of the working class with the external trappings of middle-class life. But, except in the minds of wishful thinkers, the rift between the two main divisions of the nation shows no sign of healing; it has, on the contrary, hardened into a cold class war which exerts its stifling effect on economy and morale. The six articles in this first part attempt to analyse its manifestations and causes from different angles; and, also, to suggest some possible remedies.

Amateurs and Gentlemen

or the Cult of Incompetence

Goronwy Rees

THROUGHOUT our present society, there is dispersed a class of men who perform the kind of function that was discharged, in earlier ages, by the feudal lord, the landed gentleman, or the *entrepreneur*: that is to say, the function of providing the system of direction and control which is essential if a society is to conduct its affairs with any degree of success. Today, the class of men who exercise this function is composed of *the managers*, the men to whom, in industry, in the Civil Service, in administration, society has directly or indirectly entrusted the task of exercising authority over its affairs. But in an advanced industrial society like Britain's, this exercise of authority is so dispersed and so diversified, and the members of the class which perform it have become so numerous, that it is exceedingly difficult to identify them and even more difficult to say what they have in common. Perhaps that is why, today, any discussion of the problems of management fairly quickly degenerates into generalizations with so wide a field of reference that they cease to have any meaning at all.

I have before me a recent book on management by an able, intelligent, and successful British business man, who quotes with approval from *Printer's Pie*, as the fruit of twenty-five years of experience, the following rules for success in business:

1. Do one thing at a time.
2. Know the problem.
3. Learn to listen.

4. Learn to ask questions.
5. Learn to distinguish sense from nonsense.

One wonders if the author believes that there is any form of human activity, except perhaps the higher mysticism, to which these rules do not apply. How does one succeed in anything if one cannot distinguish sense from nonsense? But what is more significant is that men at the head of large and important concerns should read such books as these, and encourage their subordinates to read them, in the hope of finding some light in the darkness in which they operate.

IN RECENT YEARS, an attempt has been made to identify the class of managers with a body known as 'the Establishment'. It was a term which enjoyed a considerable vogue for a time, though it has now declined into the name of a night club which specializes in the sick humour which is itself a manifestation of the sickness of the society which it pretends to satirize. Perhaps this is a sign of how quickly British attempts at self-analysis and self-criticism work themselves out before the body relapses into its normal condition of inertia.

The concept of 'the Establishment' was essentially a false one. It was based on the idea that authority was exercised by a kind of secret society, bound together by strange rites and customs, a genteel Mafia, operating in obscurity and vaguely connected with the public schools and the older universities. Such an idea, even if it may once have been true, was already an anachronism when 'the Establishment' was invented by an enterprising journalist; though something like it has been given a new life by such books as Anthony Sampson's *Anatomy of Britain*, with its assumption that if you look just under the surface of British society you will find a neatly articulated managerial structure. This is the gossip columnist's view of society and it only adds to the confusion about who in fact conducts Britain's affairs today. There are pressure groups, but without co-ordination or common purpose; there is no neatly articulated structure, hidden as the bones are hidden beneath the flesh; nor is there a conspiracy of faceless men, working in the dark, who control the effective levers of power. If there were, things might be a good deal better than they are, for it is at least better that a country's affairs should be administered by a secret society than by no one at all.

Before the war, Dr. Thomas Jones, who was for many years secretary to the Cabinet and had a keen sense of how power is actually exercised, could state with confidence that the three most important men in Britain were the Prime Minister, the Governor of the Bank of England, and the Editor of *The Times*; a triumvirate of Mr. Baldwin, Montagu Norman, and Geoffrey Dawson. In a sense one might agree that Dr. Jones was right, even if one might argue about the particular instances he had chosen to illustrate the thesis that in Britain there are easily identifiable centres of authority and power, not necessarily identical with its political constitution, which direct the overall functioning of the system.

Today no one could, with any plausibility, attempt to identify such centres, because in fact they do not exist; they are like those Trotsky-Zinovieff centres which once so inflamed the imagination of Stalinists. What we have instead is a widely diffused and dispersed aggregation of individuals who each in their own sphere of authority, large or small, exercise the function of management with little or no reference to each other, and with no sense of a common purpose.

For the idea of 'the Establishment', working blindly but instinctively towards its own secret ends, we should substitute the idea of a vast and unwieldy committee of management, something rather like the Polish *Seym*, in which each member exercises an effective veto on the activities of the others. The characteristics of the members of this committee are that they are now so numerous as to constitute a social class of their own; that, even though perhaps one might identify them individually if one had sufficient industry and the right books of reference, it is almost impossible to discover where responsibility among them actually lies; and that in fact by today most of them do not know what they are supposed to be doing, to such an extent indeed that it is only the exceptionable ability of a few of their outstanding members which enables the system to function at all. We are in the hands of a committee of management that has ceased to manage; and perhaps the greatest shock which any modern Balzac might suffer, who tried to explore the jungle of British affairs, would be to penetrate to its darkest secrets, its most sacred altars, and find there—nothing at all.

I DO NOT THINK that anyone would wish to doubt the existence or the significance of the managerial class in Britain today; it is, after all, one of the most characteristic products of the age through which we have to live. Equally, I do not think that anyone would say that, in this respect, Britain is any different from other advanced industrial societies; if anyone did say so, one would only have to point, for example, to the part which the managerial class plays in two such widely different, but industrially advanced countries as the United States and the Soviet Union.

Yet the moment one did so, one would also have to admit that in respect of the part played by their managers, and the attention which is paid to them, both these countries resemble each other more than either resembles Britain. For some people in this country this is a reason for self-satisfaction and self-congratulation, for a *Schadenfreude* which rejoices in the absurdities which sometimes arise out of the existence of a kind of managerial priesthood in both these countries. Others may find in it one of the reasons why this country has so conspicuously failed to keep pace with the rate of industrial advance which both these countries have been able to achieve since the war.

In both the Soviet Union and the United States, the dominant characteristics of the managerial class are that it is homogeneous, that it is technically competent, and that its members are subjected to a careful process of selection, training, and indoctrination before they are admitted to the privileges of the position they occupy. In the Soviet Union, these effects are achieved through the vast and elaborate apparatus of the Communist Party; the Soviet manager is a man who from an early age has been deliberately selected and trained for the tasks which Soviet society requires him to perform, and has been given the intellectual equipment which will enable him to perform them.

In the United States, the same effects are obtained by other means, but the efforts devoted to achieving them are no less serious and no less intensive; indeed, the care and attention invested in ensuring that the managerial class shall have common standards of education, of training, of ability, even of deportment and behaviour, may often strike us as wrongheaded and even more often as naïve and ludicrous; they are the counterpart of the ceremony with which every American child salutes Old Glory before he starts school every day. As Mr. Vance Packard has pointed out, the American manager has little chance of success unless he is a WASP (*White, Anglo-Saxon, Protestant*), has a university degree, if possible from the Ivy League, and is preferably over six foot tall and of lean physique ('We like them lean and with us they stay lean'); others have added that he should be slow of speech, impressive in appearance, and totally without any sense of humour.

WE MAY DEPLORE the abject degree of conformism which such standards succeed in imposing on the managerial class both in the United States and in the Soviet Union; we may think that they produce efficient and competent managers only at the cost of destroying human beings; we may object that the managerial types which these societies choose as their ideal are not those we should like to imitate. What we must recognize, however, is the enormous, sustained, and organized effort which both societies devote to creating the type of manager which they think will be of use and value to them. It is the kind of effort which is designed to ensure that the managerial class shall be composed not of amateurs but professionals.

In comparison with such efforts, British methods of selecting, educating, and training its managers seem designed to achieve a precisely opposite effect, that is to say, to produce a class composed of amateurs instead of professionals, and they seem to succeed very well in doing so. An American commentator on British management says mildly: 'In Great Britain the talented amateur with a grounding in the arts rather than the sciences is likely to be esteemed. . . .' We do indeed have elaborate social and even educational tests for screening candidates for entering into the managerial class; but they are largely a matter of historical accident, and are in no way related to the kind of abilities which will one day be required of the managers or to the kind of knowledge which they will one day need.

43

We are perhaps today, tardily, beginning to realize that anyone who can reasonably aspire to exercise, in any field, a managerial function must have a certain minimum of technical knowledge and intellectual discipline, and that on the whole this can best be acquired by a university education. But the universities themselves show little realization of what is expected of them. Their syllabuses still remain a curiously old-fashioned farrago of specialist courses which, so far as they have any purpose except a purely academic one, have been moulded by ideas and ideals which have no conceivable relevance to the functions which those who pursue them will one day have to discharge.

Nietzsche once wrote a magnificent essay called *Vom Nützen und Nachteil der Historie für das Leben* (The Uses and Disadvantages in Life of the Study of History). The idea that the study of history, or indeed any other university study, can have practical uses, and may have serious disadvantages, as a preparation for life would strike our present-day universities as inexpressibly vulgar; and so far as it would not, the kind of world for which they would accept that a university education could be a useful preparation is a fantasy world in which the ideas of Jowett and T. H. Green are a vital and dominating influence.

BY THEIR FRUITS YE SHALL KNOW THEM. I am at this moment irresistibly reminded of a scene from business life which once used to be repeated at frequent intervals for my benefit. It seems to me to show some of the characteristic effects of the wildly haphazard and irrational system by which Britain today selects and trains, or does not train, its managers.

It used to take place in the office, richly furnished with thick carpets, an Annigoni painting, and extremely expensive antique furniture, of the chairman and managing director of a large engineering firm which I will call Amalgamated Castings, Ltd. The chairman was a friend of mine and used frequently to ask me to lunch, usually ending his invitation with the words: 'Just drop around to my office about half past twelve.'

When I arrived, the chairman of Amalgamated Castings was in conference with his fellow-directors; their deliberations were sweetened by draughts of gin-and-tonic drunk out of beakers of cut glass. The discussion followed no conceivably rational pattern; a large part of it was invariably taken up by the sales director's amatory reminiscences of the world capitals he had most recently visited, and by fantasies of expansion that were not within the wildest dreams of possibility. There were frequent interruptions, by telephone, from the directors' wives, who each had various social and domestic problems to solve, and by the entry of secretaries with letters to be signed, and explanations of why the original dictation had had to be altered in the interests of sense. At one-thirty, the conference adjourned for large dry martinis and lunch at the Dorchester, where we sat surrounded by other directors who looked as if they had spent very much the same kind of morning. At three-thirty, my friend and his colleagues returned to their office, where their chauffeur-driven cars were waiting to return them to their homes in the stockbroker belt and the bosoms of their families. It had been a long, hard day.

I refrain from elaborating some of the more bizarre details of these occasions, or from dwelling on the conspicuous waste, the expense-account extravagance, with which Amalgamated Castings ran its affairs. I do not say that in these respects Amalgamated Castings was typical of British industry as a whole, and I do not believe that Mr. Paul Chambers or Dr. Beeching work a six-hour day of which a large part is spent in eating and drinking at the Dorchester; even so, anyone who has had much experience in business will have come across companies whose methods of management were not unlike those of Amalgamated Castings. Nor would I wish any political implications to be drawn from the scene I have described; there are working men's organizations which are managed with precisely the same kind of fecklessness as Amalgamated Castings.

IN ANY CASE, these are relatively trivial matters. What was truly dismaying and depressing about Amalgamated Castings was that none of its directors had any of the technical knowledge, the trained skill and competence, required in their particular position. They had arrived where they were by the normal hazards of business life, which is rather as if a professional football team were chosen by drawing from a hat eleven

45

names out of a thousand chosen at random, and no one could have given a rational or plausible account of how this had happened.

No doubt, since they were making and selling delicate, complicated, and expensive pieces of machinery, there must have been somewhere in the organization skilled and competent men who knew what they were doing, or the company could not have continued to exist for a moment; but the members of the board, on whom fell the specific function of management, were in the strictest sense of the words amateurs and dilettanti. In this they were not unrepresentative of many boards of management in Britain today, even though few, perhaps, push feckless-ness to such an extreme. Thus it is not surprising that, for instance, one very large retailing organization should have found it necessary to form its own production engineering department, precisely in order to teach and assist its suppliers to run their own factories efficiently.

There exists at this moment a fantastic wealth of new scientific and technological knowledge, of new techniques and new processes, which if applied to industry would revolutionize Britain overnight. In this sense it is not true to say that Britain's problems are primarily economic ones; the means already exist by which those problems can be overcome. But it is true to say that the great majority of those who form the country's grand committee of management do not have the knowledge or the understanding to apply them.

In this, business and industry should not be blamed too much, for they simply follow the example of those who should know better. The country's financial affairs, for instance, are man-aged by the Treasury, and among other things the Treasury is responsible for allocating scarce national resources both to the country's universities and to a large part of its programme of scientific and technological research. Yet there is not at the Treasury a single member in the administrative grade who is a natural scientist or has any but a theoretical acquaintance with the methods and procedures of natural science.

At least, I was assured that this was so by one who was in a position to know and had good reason to deplore the fact. But when I tried to obtain confirmation of it from a brilliant young Treasury official, I was told, with that ineffable air of mingled complacency and fatuity which makes brilliant young Treasury officials so intolerable: 'It's not precisely true. At least, we have just appointed a young natural scientist in the administrative grade. It's true, he's not a very good scientist, and he's in a very unimportant department, and he's never very likely to amount to very much, poor fellow. But at least no one can say that the Treasury doesn't have its own tame scientist any longer. . . .' *Quem deus vult perdere, prius dementat.*

WE ARE AT THIS MOMENT in the middle of the 'National Productivity Year', the British committee of management's grand campaign to revivify British industry, establish new standards of efficiency, and inaugurate Britain's entry into the twenty-first century. There are times when the National Productivity Year reminds one of nothing so much as the great 'Collateral Campaign', in Robert Musil's novel *The Man Without Qualities*, which, in Vienna in 1914, when the shadows were beginning to close on Austria-Hungary, was to be 'a magnificent demonstration of the spirit of Austria', 'a lofty symbol that would be at once an admonition and a signal for a change of heart . . .' Like the National Productivity Year, the Collateral Campaign was under the most august patronage and had the support of all classes in society, though even its originator, Count Leinsdorf, did not know exactly what it was meant to achieve; its vagueness, says Musil, 'stirred him, as he himself felt, more intensely than anything definite ever could have . . .'

Again, like the National Productivity Year, the Collateral Campaign had that quality of whistling in the dark which is so appropriate to people who do not even know what they fear. To quote Count Leinsdorf: 'As Cromwell said: "A man never rises so high as when he does not know where he is going" . . .' How much Count Leinsdorf would have enjoyed the National Productivity Year; how much he would have admired that television programme in which it was inaugurated by Prince Philip with the startling news that time-and-motion merchants were to be introduced into Buckingham Palace. That was indeed a lofty symbol after Count Leinsdorf's own heart.

I imagine that the assumption which is common to all the contributions to this reprint of *Encounter* is that Britain is in the course of a crisis which, *if it is not overcome within the not very distant future, will lead to her permanent decline*. When I reflect on this assumption, which I share, I am reminded that it was not so long ago, in 1939 to be precise, when Britain was faced with another crisis, which threatened her not merely with decline but with total extinction. There are some aspects of that other crisis, and of the ways in which it was overcome, which are so relevant to the present one that they are worth some consideration.

DURING THE FIRST YEAR of the war, Britain discovered that she was facing an even more formidable enemy than she had imagined. She also discovered, with some dismay, that her armed forces were in no condition to fight on land with any prospect of success, and after Dunkirk she had her first opportunity of seeing what a defeated army looks like.

One reason, and a decisive one, for the inadequacy of the army to its task was that it was officered by men who had been commissioned, or had achieved promotion, for reasons which had no relevance to the conduct of a modern war. They were not properly trained for the task, they did not have the basic knowledge or skill that was required to discharge it, many of them, because they had been selected for other reasons, were unfitted by character and temperament for command in modern war.

In the years that followed Dunkirk, the army, while still suffering further defeats, carried out a comprehensive programme of reform in its methods of selecting, training, and promoting officers, designed to create a system of command which would be adequate to the actual conditions in which the war had to be fought. And since, in modern war, command cannot be exercised unless those who are commanded understand what they are being ordered to do, the army also had to carry out an intensive programme of education for all ranks. In this its zeal outran its discretion to such an extent as to invite a stern rebuke from Sir Winston Churchill, who felt that educating private soldiers was really going too far.

By such methods the army created a class of officers who were, by comparison with those who held command in 1939, professionals and not amateurs; and partly as a result of this, the army was in a condition, by 1944, to carry out, in the invasion of Normandy, one of the most difficult and complicated operations in the history of war.

To achieve this result required the abandonment of many ancient prejudices and traditions; it meant recruiting officers from entirely new sources; it involved developing new ideas of training and education; it meant acknowledging that the art of war had been revolutionized by science and technology, and that those who practise it must have some knowledge of how their techniques should be applied. One cannot say that the army was completely successful in its efforts to reform itself; one can say, however, that by the end of the war the average British officer was professionally and technically the equal of his counterpart in any other army, and that he was fit for the job he had to do. And one could add that this result was achieved without the sacrifice of those virtues of which the British Army has always had most reason to be proud.

I DO NOT BELIEVE that war has many lessons which can be applied in peace. But there is a useful analogy between the crisis in which Britain found herself in 1939 and the crisis in which she finds herself today; and because, in 1939, the question of command, which is the military equivalent of management, was a vital one, there is also an analogy between the methods which Britain employed to solve her problems then, and those which are required of her today. The analogy is all the closer because of the time element involved. Just as, in 1939, we had very little time in which to reform our ways, so we have now if we are to avert the decline which threatens us.

If this is to be done (and no one can yet say whether it will be done) one of the first and most urgent requirements will be a serious and sustained effort to create a managerial class of equal professional competence, technical knowledge, and seriousness of purpose to its counterpart in other advanced industrialist countries, with whom we are after all in competition. This does not mean that we should necessarily adopt either their judgments of value, or their modes of procedure, or their style of life and behaviour. It means simply that Britain, as a nation, must devote to the problem of management the same serious thought and study as it has been given elsewhere.

For in this respect we appear to be incurably frivolous, and to believe that the well-tried methods of the past will be sufficient to carry us through the present. It may seem curious to name frivolity as a characteristic vice of our sad island today. But this is not the frivolity of the *chasse au bonheur*, which after all is a serious matter; it is the frivolity of people who will not take serious problems seriously, because they somehow believe that they do not really apply to them.

Most of all, it is necessary that the problem of selecting, educating, and training the members of the managerial class should be given an attention which it has hitherto been denied. Like most of the problems which face Britain today, its problem of management is fundamentally one of education. It now seems that the university of Oxford is considering the possibility of establishing a school of business management. This is, in itself, admirable; yet it is singularly late in the day. For how long will it take for such a school, or other schools, to establish a discipline, evolve a doctrine, acquire a prestige, exercise an influence, comparable to those of the great American business schools of Harvard, Massachusetts, or Michigan, often in the face of the contempt and derision of our own universities; and who is to say that such a school will not fall into the hands of those who, like the managers of our new universities, still fundamentally believe that the only education worth having is one which was designed for the production of pro-consuls?

It seems sometimes, today, as if the grand committee of management which has for so long conducted the affairs of the country has at last become conscious of its failure and seeks desperately for a cure. Hence the 'lofty symbols', the 'admonitions', the 'signals for a change of heart', which we are offered daily. But how are our managers to cure themselves, and where, in the short time that may be left to us, are they to discover either the knowledge and competence, or the powers of will, energy, and creativeness, which today so many of them conspicuously lack?

The Comforts of Stagnation

Michael Shanks

THE FACTS of Britain's economic stagnation are now so well known that it would be tedious to repeat them. Both in its consequences and in its causes the problem transcends economics. In a sense all our other national problems—our declining stature in the world, our bitter social antagonisms, the defects of our public services, and so on—flow from, or are aggravated by, our central economic weakness. It is not goodwill that is lacking in Britain, but the basic wherewithal to get things done; our reach persistently exceeds our grasp.

Equally, it is useless to look to the economists for a complete solution. There is no single economic panacea for transforming Britain from a country that grows at 2 per cent per annum to one that grows at 5 per cent per annum. It would be nice if we could find some way of winding up the sterling system, and so getting out of a situation in which our international liabilities exceed our reserves in a ratio of about three-to-one; it would be nice if we could persuade the Americans, or the Six, or the International Monetary Fund, or some other charitable organization to underwrite the expansion of the British economy. But policy must be based on realities, not dreams.

It is not true that the basic failing of the British economy is 'too little investment'. There is no necessary correlation between the proportion of national income invested in industry and the strikingly high ratio of investment to gross rate of growth. What matters is the *return* on investment, and this in turn depends on the direction and the nature of the investment. To put it bluntly, worth-while investment depends on good management. If the management is bad, then one can waste more money more quickly on capital investment than in almost any other way; and the outstanding fact about Britain's post-war investment programmes is not that they have been too low, but that they have yielded a remarkably poor return in terms of national productivity.

THERE ARE MANY REASONS for this—all rather discreditable.

First, a great deal of investment has been misdirected. Much of the £1,500 million or so invested on railway modernization in the pre-Beeching era was, frankly, money down the drain. Our investment in nuclear energy was, equally, based on a staggering misjudgment of the extent of fuel supplies available in the world. Over the bulk of our investment in defence it would be kindest, perhaps, to draw a veil. All countries make these mistakes, but in post-war Britain they have been on a bigger scale than most—for reasons which we shall see shortly.

Second, British industry has not invested enough in labour-saving equipment or in the newer, more sophisticated areas of industry. Professor Barna of the University of Sussex has re-vealed the extent to which our export structure is still based on comparatively old-fashioned products and industries—where we are becoming increasingly vulnerable to competition from lower-wage countries like Japan.[1] Mr. J. R. Sargent has shown[2] how our capital stock per employee has grown faster than productivity, whereas in most of Western Europe (other than Norway and Belgium) the reverse has been true. For various reasons, in fact—poor management, bad policy decisions, bad labour relations—a depressingly large part of our capital in-vestment in recent years has been ineffective. Too much of our money has been invested in the wrong things in the wrong way, often at the wrong time.

WHY? The first, simple answer is that the quality of the people who direct our economy—in industry and in Whitehall—is simply not high enough, and until we can improve it we will not get anywhere. No economic policy or combination of policies can give Britain growth without inflation until the

[1] See *The Times*, April 3rd, 1963.
[2] Fabian pamphlet, '*Out of Stagnation*' (February, 1963).

52

structure and the leadership of industry itself become more efficient. This is not to say that better economic policies can do nothing to help us. Of course they can do a great deal. But they can only help *by operating on the structure of industry, and on the social attitudes and values which govern this structure.* Everything else is, in the last analysis, gimmickry—which may help in the short term, but can do nothing in the long.

There are two obvious ways in which the quality of the leaders of industry can be improved—by competition and by training. Neither has been working as it should in post-war Britain.

British society has become, over a very wide field, remarkably uncompetitive since the war. Everybody pays lip-service to the need for 'growth' and 'change', but there is an extraordinary reluctance to accept the price. British society is based on a very delicate and intricate balance of forces, and anything which upsets this balance is highly unpopular. The essence of growth is that it upsets the existing structure, by introducing disparities and 'distortions'. But this is precisely what the British in their present mood find hard to accept. It is impossible to bring in the tax reforms which are needed to galvanize our economy, because any change in the tax burden will be 'inequitable'—that is, it will alter the existing balance. It is impossible to speed up the adjustment of industry to the modern world because the social conscience demands that sick industries be protected—at the expense, of course, of the strong. It is impossible to introduce an incomes policy or to achieve a more rational distribution of labour because to do so would involve interfering with traditional differentials and traditional collective bargaining practices. And so on.

The depressing thing about Britain is that the forces supporting change are so weak. The issues that really arouse the British people are not issues of national efficiency but issues of 'social justice' or 'fair play'. We are unwilling to advance if it means that anybody is going to get hurt. This means, of course, that social justice has to be defined almost exclusively in terms of the past. Each section of the community stakes out its appeal, before the court of public opinion, by reference to what it has traditionally expected and enjoyed. The very niceness of the

British, the national desire to 'do the decent thing', uninformed by any rational calculus of what constitutes the common interest, has become an enormous force for *immobilisme*. We grumble over unofficial strikes and restrictive practices, but what we really get excited about is whether nurses are being paid a fair wage. This is in many ways an admirable trait, but it is a sure recipe for national decay.

I WAS READING the other day an extremely intelligent book by the anthropologist Mary Douglas about the Lele.[1] The Lele are an amusing, cultivated, intelligent Congolese tribe who have conspicuously failed in recent years to advance their economy as have their neighbour tribes. Mrs. Douglas traces the reason for their stagnation back to their distinctive tribal customs, which are based on avoiding what is felt to be the humiliation of old men losing power and becoming dependent on their juniors. To prevent this, the Lele have built up an immensely complex system of checks and balances, in which the old men are given a virtual monopoly of wives and the right to cultivate the fields. The younger men are kept in a state of what amounts to prolonged idleness and avoidance of responsibility, so that they will not infringe on the prerogatives of the elders. In this way a delicate equilibrium has been achieved, but at an enormous price in efficiency, since the most vigorous section of the community is prevented from playing any effective part in it. Because of its artificial nature, the balance is continually on the point of breaking down, but it is always shored up by increasingly complex conventions.

The British, I am afraid, are in danger of becoming the Lele of Western Europe.

ONE EXAMPLE of what looks like a national 'failure of nerve' is provided by the recent history in this country of resale price maintenance—the system by which manufacturers dictate the price at which retailers sell their goods. R.p.m. is eminently 'fair'—it protects the manufacturer from having his goods sold at different prices in different shops, it protects the housewife from inadvertently making a 'bad buy' by going to the wrong

[1] *The Lele of the Kasai* (Oxford, 1963).

54

shop, it protects the small shopkeeper from price-cutting competition by the big stores. It is exactly the sort of system which a society that believes in stability and 'fair shares' tends to support. It is also, quite obviously, a major obstacle to dynamism and efficiency, because it limits competition and keeps prices up. It is hardly, therefore, a system which should commend itself to a society which wants to grow.

As competition has grown more severe, r.p.m. has come under pressure in almost every Western country. Cut-price or discount stores have sprung up everywhere, from the U.S. to Japan, bringing prices down and introducing an element of cut-throat competition into the staid and overcrowded retail trade. In the U.S. and on the Continent, the price-cutters and the discount traders are on the offensive and gaining ground—in France at least with Government blessing. Only in Britain are they at present in retreat.[1]

One can see the same national tolerance of inefficiency, the same laudable desire not to be beastly to one's fellow-men however mediocre their performance, in almost every sector of industry and public life. Men whose career in Whitehall or Westminster has been an almost unbroken catalogue of failure are allowed to continue in high office, or to move from key Civil Service posts to positions of eminence and power in industry or the academic world, laden with all the tributes which a status-loving society can bestow. And it is the same in most of the board-rooms of big industry. We accept the theory of 'equality of opportunity' and '*la carrière ouverte aux talents*', but we do not recognize that if there is to be room at the top for the

---

[1] The sad story is told in a recent article in the *Financial Times* of March 28th ('The Tightening Grip of R.P.M.' by Patrick Coldstream). The paper's Commercial Editor points out that a departmental committee under the President of the Board of Trade recommended the abolition of r.p.m. in the interests of greater efficiency and lower prices some six months ago, and the original draft report of the National Economic Development Council echoed this recommendation. But, he goes on, the Board of Trade report was never published, and 'legislative change now looks unlikely'.

The moral is simple and depressing. Faced with the challenge of greater competition, British industry—with tacit Government support—has taken a step back towards cartellization and 'stability': a policy of retreat in which as a nation we are almost alone.

bright young men (and Britain, thank God, does not lack these), somebody has got to create that room; mobility has to be downwards as well as upwards.

TRAVELLING ON THE CONTINENT, I am struck by the extent to which Britain has become a gerontocracy. We have not experienced the social revolution which took place after the war in most of the leading Continental countries, and which catapulted young active men into positions of power which, here in Britain, they are still for the most part waiting impatiently to occupy.

But there is more to it than that. One of the reasons why we in Britain pay a greater respect than do most of our competitors to age and experience, and correspondingly less to energy and sheer talent, is that our educational system encourages us to do so. During the Common Market negotiations last year I spent some time travelling between London and the Continental capitals, and the contrast between Whitehall and Paris, in particular, I found profoundly depressing and disquieting. It was not just that France's plans for Europe were totally different from, and inimical to, Britain's. That we now know—and it was this, not a whim of General de Gaulle's or anything that happened at Nassau, which dictated Britain's exclusion from the Community. Nor was it the sense that France's 'Establishment', giddy with success and national pride, constitutes a menace to the rest of the Community and to the West as a whole. Rather it was the contrast in atmosphere and in efficiency between the two power-centres of Western Europe, between the products of the two countries of the Western world which deliberately set out by their educational systems to produce a governing élite.

To anybody who examines the present record the conclusion is inescapable that in terms of the needs of modern industry and society the French system works and ours does not. The governing élite in France—the men who occupy the key decision-making posts in the administration, the planning commissions and industry—are increasingly the products of the *grandes écoles*, the specialized institutes originally set up by Napoleon which today occupy the top place in France's educational pyramid. The *polytechnicien* is the intellectual aristocrat of modern France, the nearest thing to a 'meritocrat' in the West today. These men move freely between the administration and industry, in a way which is almost impossible in modern Britain. To a remarkable extent their educational background enables them to bridge the gulf of the Two Cultures. The planning system which is France's greatest contribution to the art of post-war economic management—of which Britain's N.E.D.C. is an adaptation—is essentially the creation of the technocrat; and France's dramatic rate of economic growth—between two and three times as fast as ours—is a proof of its succses.

The point is that the free movement of top personnel between Government and industry, and their common educational background, ensure that each side speaks the same language and understands the other; and this is plainly essential if planning is to work, or economic policy to be effective and intelligent. Moreover, the education system ensures that the makers of policy have at least some understanding of the technological basis of modern industry. The technocrat may not be an altogether admirable person but there is no doubt that he is efficient. Every time I have visited Paris I have come back impressed with his faith in the future, his sense of purpose, and his deep understanding of what the modern industrial system is all about.

IT IS PRECISELY these attributes that are lacking in Whitehall today, as well as in large areas of British industry. In Whitehall one can almost smell the atmosphere of failure and bewilderment, the sense that every possible plan has been tried and every one so far has failed—the feeling that the task of projecting Britain successfully into the 'sixties is probably impossible for sane, civilized, democratic men and women (which British civil servants overwhelmingly are).

What are the reasons for this? One reason undoubtedly is the extreme *compartmentalization* of British public life. We recruit our civil servants to an overwhelming degree direct from university or college, and once in the Civil Service one has very few opportunities to acquire detailed first-hand knowledge of industry, trade, or the professions. Civil Service seniority provisions and salary differentials make it very difficult to achieve the same freedom of movement between industry and Government as exists in France. The same compartmentalization applies outside Whitehall. There is less contact between the universities and technical colleges and industry in Britain than in almost any other advanced country, particularly on the engineering and scientific side.

But the second thing which is wrong with Whitehall is its overwhelmingly non-technical intake in the administrative class. Of the 280 recruits to the Civil Service administrative class between 1957 and 1962 only nine had a scientific background and four a mathematical one—95 per cent of the intake, in other words, was non-scientific. Outside the Treasury and the Ministry of Agriculture, there are only four full-time economists in Government service. Among the key policy-making departments which do not boast one are the Board of Trade, the Ministries of Transport and Housing, and the Inland Revenue. The shortage of scientists and engineers in Whitehall is equally acute. The Treasury has one scientist at its disposal, and the Ministry of Science also boasts just one.

THE AVERAGE SENIOR CIVIL SERVANT, in short, is not only without any practical experience of modern industry but also without any technological training. When one considers that more than two-fifths of all the money spent in Britain is spent in the public sector, this lack of expertise is fantastic! Even in the key policy-making department, the Treasury, the number of economists is less than two dozen, and most of these are on short-service engagements. Even here, the vital policy decisions are almost invariably taken by people without economic training.

The concentration of power in Whitehall in this single department greatly complicates the problem. For of all the major departments of State, the Treasury is traditionally the most introverted, the most withdrawn from the daily current of life. This is understandable when one considers that its historic role has been to regulate a strictly static economy, and to control the spending policies of the other departments. But the qualities which made it a good regulator of public expenditure, a useful brake on the enthusiasms of the 'spending departments', are singularly inappropriate in the new role into which it has gradually moved since the war—namely, the power-house of an economy bent on growth in an age of dynamic technological, social, and economic change. In such a world and in such a role the Treasury, as it is now constituted, is frankly and hopelessly lost.

The defects of the Treasury—its lack of understanding of or contact with the outside world, its monastic character—are shared, in somewhat lesser degree, by the other Ministries (whose average intellectual calibre is well below the Treasury's).

WHAT ARE the results? *First*, an appalling vacuum in economic and industrial policy. To give just one example out of many, the lack of economists in the Ministry of Transport has meant that Britain has no overall transport policy, and no mechanism for relating the sectional requirements of the railways, for example, to road transport and other aspects of the nation's general needs. The Beeching Plan, instead of being treated as part of an integrated process, has to be debated *in vacuo*—and what is in fact a fairly routine technocrats' exercise is greeted either as the unveiling of the tablets from Mount Sinai or as a diabolic interference with the liberties of the citizen, according to taste.[1] There is a similar vacuum as regards regional planning, fuel policy, the distribution of industry and land use generally, and the promotion of research and industrial efficiency. One reason for the general absence of effective planning is the Government's lack of interest in enforcing the collection of meaningful statistics from industry.

Second, there has been an almost total failure to make Government itself efficient—to use the techniques of business management in Whitehall itself, and to ensure that decisions once taken can be quickly and effectively implemented. The nature of the Whitehall machine has thus become a serious brake upon change.[2]

Third, there is a lack of communication between the civil servant and the industrialist—and *a fortiori* between the civil servant and the trade unionist. This is what lies behind

[1] All Dr. Beeching has done is to apply the standard tools of operational analysis to an industry which has hitherto lived in the accounting Stone Age.

[2] Reforms in the taxation system which are almost universally agreed to be desirable are held up because the Inland Revenue—which is seriously under-staffed—claims that the new taxes would be 'too difficult to administer'; though in almost every case they are already widely in operation abroad.

industry's persistent complaints about the 'stop-go' nature of Government economic policy.

It is unfair to blame all this on the civil servants themselves; they are, in fact, among the ablest men and women our educational system produces. While Whitehall and the learned professions may have lost a little of their glamour *vis-à-vis* industry and business for the top graduates of our universities, they still retain a very high place in the pecking order, and still attract a large share of our best academic brains. If the men are not to blame, then, what is?

The answer must be, I believe, the education system itself—and by this I mean the dominant humanist tradition of our public and top grammar schools, and Oxbridge.

What I am criticizing about the education of our rulers is its amateurish, non-professional character. There is a popular illusion in Britain that any scientist or technologist is *ipso facto* a specialist, while every humanist or 'arts' man is *ipso facto* an 'all-round' man who is fitted by his education to command, to take the broad view, to grapple with all questions *sub specie aeternitatis*. This is, I am afraid, an illusion. The average 'arts' graduate from university is just as much a specialist as the scientist or engineer, with the difference that his specialism is probably more remote from the needs of industry. The curse of British education is its premature and excessive specialization, which hampers scientist and non-scientist alike and prevents either from fully comprehending the other's world.

The curse of amateurism must therefore be tackled at its root, in the schools themselves. The education given there must be more genuinely broad-based, and we must get away from the idea that one can only learn the 'important things'—management, craft skills, and so on—'on the job'. The result of this fixation is to make industry more conservative and inbred than it should be, and to slow down the infusion of new ideas and techniques.

IT IS NOT JUST that we need to train still more technologists. Much more urgent is to get more technologically trained people into positions of power. It is no good having experts on tap if those who take the decisions do not know the right questions to ask them and do not know how to evaluate the answers they get; yet that is the position today in much of industry and Whitehall. This does not mean that we should forthwith turn over all the top places to engineers and scientists. The narrowness of British education today affects technologists as much as it does 'arts' men, and unfits most of them for decision-making. What we need—and this is hardly a new thought—is more literate scientists and more numerate humanists. The need is for balance, but in most of British industry today the bias is heavily in favour of the non-technical man. The cult of the amateur, the distrust of the 'specialist'— always, in Britain, taken to mean the technologist—runs very deep, as any study of the structure of boards of directors in Britain, compared to the U.S., France, or Germany, will confirm.

British industry has paid, and is paying, dearly for this bias. A slow response to technological change—witness the reluctance to exploit the resources of the British electronics industry, the slow development of British inventions like the Hovercraft, the 'brain-drain' of Ph.D.s to America (which, *pace* Lord Hailsham, reflects the fact that their talents are better recognized and used in U.S. industry as much as it does the pay differential); a lack of commercial drive; poor direction of investment; a general under-valuation of human skills: these have been among the main characteristics of British industry since the war, and they reflect directly the character of the people who have had the running of it.

IT IS SIGNIFICANT that Britain has been among the last countries in the industrial world to take seriously the possibility of teaching management techniques at university level or after. The sort of mobile business *corps d'élite*, trained to move from one enterprise to another, with skills which are readily transfer-able, which the U.S. enjoys through the Harvard Business School or M.I.T., or France through the *grandes écoles*, is largely non-existent in Britain. Here management is still largely trained 'on the job', and in consequence managerial mobility is much less than in most other industrial countries.[1] A Dr. Beeching, who successfully applies the lessons of one business to another,

[1] The growth of management consultancy in Britain is, fortunately, beginning to make this less true than it was.

is still a considerable rarity in British industrial life. This is, I believe, a major reason for our industrial conservatism.

Another is the remarkably continuing isolation of much of industry—particularly small industry—from the mainstream of our educational, and indeed our social and political, life. The visitor to Britain is often astonished at how much of our traditions and our standards of values still dates from a pre-industrial world.[1] The fact that the Industrial Revolution occurred in the North of England, while the centre of our cultural, social, political, and commercial life has always been in the basically (until very recently) rural South, no doubt explains why we have been able for so long to ignore the needs of industry.

PROBABLY IN NO OTHER industrialized country does the industrialist as such enjoy such a low standing in society. Nowhere else in the industrialized world are trade and manufacture regarded to such an extent as means to better things—to politics, to land-ownership, to culture, to a position in the City. In other countries the land-owning aristocracies, by excluding the *nouveaux riches* of the Industrial Revolution, ensured their own impotence and decline. The British aristocracy, less rigid, embraced the rising *entrepreneurs* and infected them and their children with its own standard of values; and the quality of industrial management has suffered in consequence. The pursuit of prestige rather than profit has done great damage over the years. Talents have been distorted. Even within industry there are subtle gradings of respectability. It is more meritorious to produce than to sell, better to make steel than soap. Better than both is to be a man of culture, a landowner, or 'something in the City'.[2] Other Countries have their absentee landlords. Britain suffers more from absentee managers.

[1] Anthony Sampson, in *Anatomy of Britain* (1962), has well described the Court and Oxbridge as 'fairylands in the heart of modern Britain'—and the essence of the magic is that it is pre-industrial. Apart from their other attributes, these institutions (and other less worthy ones) testify to the extraordinary capacity for escapism and nostalgia of the modern Briton.

[2] It is interesting that, when professions need to be socially upgraded, it is done by the use of semantics. Thus 'selling' becomes 'marketing', while advertising acquires status by becoming 'creative advertising'. Perhaps before long we shall have 'creative manufacture' or 'creative public relations'.

Among the most instructive pieces of social literature in modern Britain are the advertisements of the socialist estate agent and chronicler of contemporary *mores*, Mr. Roy Brooks. I remember one recent example in which an eligible house-selling couple were described thus: 'She paints. He dabbles in insurance.' In that simple inversion can be traced the sickness of contemporary Britain. Thus has effortless superiority declined into effortless inferiority; thus has the catholicity of Renaissance man dwindled into dilettantism. The hard-headed (and often hard-hearted) mill-owners and steel-masters of the North have bred—if I may borrow a phrase from Arthur Koestler—the little flirts of Chelsea and Kensington. It is gay, it is madly amusing, and it carries with it the smell of death.

EVERY BOSS CLASS gets the working class it deserves.

Last autumn I visited Sweden with a delegation of British electrical and engineering manufacturers, as guests of the Swedish engineering industry. In this industry Swedish labour costs exceed ours by around 25–30 per cent, yet their prices have been and remain exceedingly competitive. We soon found that the Swedes' secret does not lie in the existence of managerial supermen or revolutionary forms of automation or production techniques; nor, so far as we could tell, does it lie in hidden State subsidies. The secret lies almost entirely in the fact that Swedish labour can be used with a degree of flexibility that is unknown in Britain, and that the unions encourage managerial innovation as a means of paying the very high wages the Swedish worker demands. Swedish executives admitted freely that the constant pressure of the unions for higher wages, coupled with a willingness to give management as free a hand as possible in altering production techniques to pay those wages, is one of the biggest stimuli to change and efficiency in the Swedish economy today.

In this respect the attitude of the Swedish unions is in complete contrast to that in Britain. In Britain the worker's instinct is to put security before higher income, and to oppose changes in working methods and techniques. In Britain innovation has to be 'sold' to the unions, and far from being an accelerator the union structure operates as a major brake upon change.

When this mammoth force of inertia is thrown on to the scales on top of a generally cautious, conservative-minded and in-expert management, and a public opinion which is, at best, ambivalent in its approach to change, it is hardly surprising that Britain lags behind other countries.

In Sweden the union movement is not only overwhelmingly powerful but feels itself to be so. As one of the leaders of the L.O. (the Swedish T.U.C.) put it to me in Stockholm:

> In this country we control 90–95 per cent of all industrial workers and 70–75 per cent of all white-collar and profes-sional workers. What political force could stand up against us? And why, given this strength, should we bother about outdated methods of defence like demarcation rights and so on?

This, I believe, is the outstanding fact about the Swedish experiment—that it works because the unions are strong and supremely self-confident, and therefore not defensive-minded.

It is in this basic psychological approach that the British worker and his union representatives are so painfully different. During my talks in Stockholm I was reminded of a previous set of meetings in the North of England the previous winter, when I was discussing with audiences of rank-and-file trade unionists whether or not the T.U.C. should join the N.E.D.C. The attitude of the trade unionists was overwhelmingly that their leaders should have nothing to do with Neddy, despite their approval of planning in principle and despite the obvious benefit to the T.U.C. of direct access to the decision-making machinery. The reasoning was simple. Since it was proposed by 'them', it must *ipso facto* be against 'our' interests. And if 'our' leaders start making common cause with the 'enemy', on however limited a scale, they will inevitably either be out-smarted or seduced into betraying 'our' interests.

The cold class war, in other words, is still very much on; and the attitude of the rank-and-file British trade unionist is still motivated by an overwhelming sense of suspicion—which extends, significantly, to many of his own leaders—and by a marked lack of collective self-confidence. From this one can, I think, draw a number of conclusions.

FIRST, it is not true (as is often alleged in middle-class circles) that what is wrong with the British unions is that they are 'too powerful' and 'too greedy'. Exactly the reverse is true. British wages have not in recent years been rising particularly fast—in fact they have been rising much less fast than in the homelands of almost all our main competitors. And when it comes to fringe benefits and improvements in working conditions the achievements of the British unions have been derisory. The idea that the Swedish unions, or the unions of the Six, are more modest in their demands on employers than British unions will not bear examination for a moment. The truth is that British trade union leaders have achieved remarkably little for their members, given the circumstances of the last two decades; and it has often been the most militant leaders who have in practice achieved the least.

Britain has been and is in trouble, not because our wages have risen too fast, but because our productivity has risen too slowly—and therefore our unit labour costs have been pushed up. One of the main reasons for this slow rise in productivity has been our inability to make effective use of our labour; and while this is partly due to deficiencies in our education system and in the quality of management, the main reason is the poor state of our industrial relations. This is shown in the inability of the two sides of industry to make common cause and to sink their sectional differences (*e.g.*, outstandingly, over such issues as incomes policy, redundancy, or apprenticeships), the reluctance of workers to accept change, and the insistence of most unions on maintaining restrictions on labour flexibility—such as demarcation rights, control of intake of apprentices, etc.

It is a significant fact that most labour disputes in British industry are, from the workers' point of view, defensive operations. Even when the real issue is a claim for more money, the strike is often 'sold' to the workers as a defence of traditional union rights—in this case the right of collective bargaining. And the biggest single cause of unofficial strikes in British industry is workers' opposition to redundancy—an issue which in almost every other industrial country is either covered by collective bargaining machinery or is recognized to be the province of Labour Courts (an institution which we in this country have not yet got around to considering).

The chaos and defensive-mindedness which dominate British industrial relations reflect not union strength, but weakness. From this I draw two further conclusions:

1. If we are to have a more dynamic society we must first have a more *equal* society—not in the sense of equality of income or wealth, but in the sense of an absence of class-barriers, a greater equality of educational opportunity, of status, of power: in a word, social equality.

2. To get this more equal society we need a stronger and more effective trade union movement, one which will give the worker confidence that his interests can be properly safeguarded in a world of change. Only in this way, I believe, can we finally lay to rest the ghost of the 'thirties. It is a remarkable and depressing fact that the experience of the mass depression of the pre-war years should have bitten so much more deeply into the working-class mind here than anywhere else. Other countries suffered more than we from the slump, but in no other major country is it so widely felt among the industrial workers that those days are bound sooner or later to return. Nowhere else are union attitudes so conditioned by the paramount need to prevent people from ever, at any time, losing their jobs—and nowhere else do they take a form more guaranteed, in the long run, to achieve just that dreaded end!

PLAINLY THE PERSISTENCE of these fears is influenced by a lack of confidence in the unions' own strength. And this lack of confidence is certainly justified. By and large, the unions have exercised no discernible influence on British social or economic policy in the last decade, other than to slow down the process of industrial change and growth. They have signally failed to make headway among the rising class of white-collar workers and technicians—the 'new men' who will determine Britain's future social and political structure. They have found themselves increasingly thrown back on a steadily eroding working-class base, concentrated in the older industries (coal, railways, etc.) and among declining craft skills (*e.g.*, shipbuilding). In their own interests, they must break out of the crumbling fortress.

IT IS NOT HARD to see what needs to be done to make British trade unionism stronger and more coherent.

First, the present split between craft and general workers' unions needs to be ended, and the structure of the unions brought into line with the actual structure of modern industry. It is absurd, for example, that union representation in the motor industry should be divided between upwards of three dozen different unions, each with interests outside the industry.

Second, the union members must be persuaded to pay the sort of dues needed to allow their organizations to operate efficiently. Most union leaders today are grossly overworked as well as underpaid; they lack the resources to maintain efficient administrations, to employ specialist advice, or to establish effective contact with the rank-and-file. It is this which causes apathy at branch level, the rise of virtually autonomous shop-stewards' movements, unofficial strikes, suspicion of the remote 'head office', and the failure of British unions to keep up with the new thinking and methods pioneered by their colleagues abroad.

Third, the individual unions should be prepared to combine forces under a general staff which would be responsible to the movement as a whole, which could bargain on behalf of the entire movement and impose discipline on recalcitrant member-unions.

If these things were done, the British union movement would quickly acquire the same degree of power as the Swedish unions —who have in fact adopted this sort of system. That power could be used in two ways. (1) A strong T.U.C. would have to be accepted as a genuine partner in Government—as it is in Sweden, and as is indeed foreshadowed in the structure of the N.E.D.C. In return for co-operation in an incomes policy, the T.U.C. could rightly demand a leading voice in the formulation of social and economic policy. In this way it could do far more to protect and further the interests of its members than it has ever been able to do so far. (2) The unions could do a great deal more to create the sort of equal society which is needed, not only for its own sake, but as a prerequisite for growth; and they could start in industry itself, by attacking the barriers which harm industrial relations, and therefore limit productivity. This means a sustained drive for better fringe benefits to destroy the bogeys of insecurity and inequality. For example, the insecurity which leads workers to go slow when redundancy threatens could be tackled by negotiating redundancy compensation agreements, and by better pension and labour mobility provisions. The sense of inequality as between staff and payroll workers could be eliminated by extending to all workers the benefits now enjoyed by staff—longer holidays, sick-pay provisions, better pensions, and so on. And more, much more, could be done to extend the principle of consultation and workers' participation in the decision-making process in industry.

By such means, at least a start could be made on breaking down the hostile, non-co-operative attitude, rooted in a sense of weakness, which seems to afflict so much of the working class in Britain today. But it can only be done if the union members themselves see the necessity for it, since it is they who must authorize the changes in union structure and pay the extra dues. So long as their psychology is dominated by suspicion as it is today, this is not going to happen.

FOR THE BRITISH WORKER, the Welfare State has proved in many ways a cruel sham. Materially he is, of course, much better off than before the war; but even the British working man does not live by bread alone. He is still as far away as ever from achieving a real partnership of power, or genuine equality of educational opportunity with the other sections of the community. Indeed, in many ways class-barriers have become more rigid in recent years, while each class blames the other for the country's failure to advance socially and economically. The worker feels—not without reason—that he is being asked to exercise restraint while others much better off than he are not; that rewards in our society are not related to effort, that there are big profits to be made on the Stock Exchange and elsewhere by those 'in the know'.

His reaction is to adopt a general 'dog-in-the-manger' attitude, to get what he can—and it is not much in all conscience —from the general pork-barrel. What he needs to be told is that if he will only exercise the potential power in his hands, through a revitalized trade union movement, he can achieve infinitely more than this. When one travels round the big industrial cities of the North, one cannot help but feel that *this is simply not a tolerable way for people to be made to live in the mid-twentieth century*. No amount of washing machines or television sets—not even Mini-minors—can compensate for the squalor in which we still expect a majority of our people to live; and this applies also to the conditions—physical and contractual—in many of our factories, and to many of our schools and hospitals. When so much needs to be done, it seems intolerable that the energies of our workers should be concentrated on fighting phoney issues, and that their objectives should be so pitifully limited. Somehow or other, we have got to find a way of mobilizing the energies and the enthusiasms of all sections of the community for the enrichment of Britain.

IF WE CAN DO THIS, there is no reason why Britain should not achieve her own economic 'miracle', just as, two decades ago, she achieved a near miracle in the war. I have been critical of many of our institutions and attitudes, and nobody who knows what the British people are capable of can feel other than sad and alarmed at the present state of affairs. But there is a brighter side. The abilities of our younger generation—particularly the young managers in industry—compare, in my opinion, favourably with those of previous generations. The talents, the will, are there—if they can be activated and guided into the proper channels. At present they are not. A working class whose horizons are limited to the currently fashionable consumer durable; a middle class intent on refining the caste marks distinguishing it from those below; industries concerned to limit competition; a trade union movement seeking only to shield its members from the impact of change; a Civil Service dedicated to avoiding the awkward parliamentary question.

These are the hallmarks of a society which has embraced stagnation as a way of life.

The Plaintive Treble

Andrew Shonfield

'. . . *amid the rumbling terrors I heard the plaintive*
treble of the Treasury Bench.'

> DISRAELI (House of Commons,
> February 13th, 1851)

THIS LINE OF THOUGHT began on a train to Birmingham.
I had been delighted at St. Pancras when getting into the new
model British Railways Pullman by the high standard of comfort and by the treatment of passengers; inside there was an
approach to the physical standard of American trains, which
are much the most comfortable in the world, and as for the
staff, I was thinking complacently that they were noticeably
better mannered and nicer than they would have been in any
metropolitan centre in the United States. Then, as we pulled
away from the station, I turned to look out of the window, and
found myself staring at an accumulated coating of grime so
thick that it seriously interfered with the view. It also made the
whole business of looking out faintly disgusting—a disgust
which was somehow aggravated by the shiny and well-appoin-
ted comfort inside.

A small matter really—an oversight—don't indulge yourself
and go on about it! I began to read my newspaper. Then I
recalled the treatment given to trains in New York and in other
stations in the United States, when they were about to leave on
an inter-city run. Invariably before their departure someone
came along with a pail and a very wide, efficient brush at the
end of a long handle, and with a few energetic movements

scrubbed the outside of the windows clean. It seemed such a simple operation; why had nobody thought of introducing it here? As I considered the question, it was borne in on me that this belonged to a wide category of minor gestures of a graceful character which in Britain consistently fail to get organized. The real reason why the grimy windows had suddenly produced such intense feeling in me was that they were an integral part of a definite and well-understood attitude—an uncreative attitude towards simple amenities. They went with the chipped cups in cafés, the uncertainly cleaned plates, the squalid waiting-rooms of National Health Service doctors, and also with the terrible need to gird oneself in readiness for a quarrel, or at least for a sulky exchange, whenever one wished to assert that some small service for which one was paying was not coming quite up to scratch.

'Why make such a fuss about it? Fuss, fuss, fuss!'

There is an obnoxious bossiness on the part of those who provide services towards anyone who dares to assert rights—whether it is a conductor on a bus, a waitress in a café, or a nurse in a hospital. What is behind it? These people are not unkind: far from it. When they take full charge of you, if you happen to be in trouble—and so have no rights to assert—they are often capable of real solicitude and active generosity. In an emergency, I have no doubt that I would prefer to be looked after by a British driver or pilot of an aeroplane; and I know many other people who share this feeling. But we also know that the emergency treatment stands entirely on its own; it is felt to be personal and special; once it is over there is nothing left to build on for other occasions. Ordinary, small, simple services reliably performed are much more difficult to come by.

ONE RESULT OF THIS is the shoddiness and uncertain standards of inspection of British goods. The latter have become an international scandal; they are certainly one of the factors which help to explain why during the unprecedented boom in international trade which has lasted right through the 1950s and the early 1960s, Britain's share of world exports of manufactures has gone down consistently by a bit more in every year. It used to be fashionable to blame this failure on full or 'overfull' employment in Britain—until in the 1960s we achieved a higher ratio of unemployment than any other European industrial country except Italy; and still our share of world trade went down.

THE ATTITUDE that I am trying to describe is not simply slackness: it is more complicated than that. Nor is it confined to the working classes. On the contrary, I believe that the ethos which leads to an extraordinary national resistance to the provision of small reliable amenities takes its original source from something which is distinctly an upper-class phenomenon. For behind it there is an overwhelming pride in refusing to learn a drill about how to be nice to people. Being nice is something that either comes—or doesn't. Very up-stage this; and it can be extremely pleasing when it is successful, so that casual encounters acquire the meaning of a subtle personal relationship. But most of the time one is aware that the British lower-middle and working classes have been given a set of manners which are too sophisticated for them to handle with charm. The manners depend on an ability to make lots of small, half-spoken, throwaway gestures. When these are absent, the performance too easily becomes wilful and gruff. It is as if people had been trained to constrict their throat muscles to make it difficult to sing simple tunes. In Britain the ritual artificial smile of the American girl at the cashier's desk, when you pay your bill and she says she 'hopes you will come again', would appear as a kind of personal dishonesty. It seems to me characteristic that the British are one of the few nations which do not have a standard response from a giver, when the receiver says 'Thank you'. American boys and girls are taught to say, 'You're welcome,' and to smile.

UPPER-CLASS MANNERS—and it is these manners which set the tone for the whole community in Britain—are unsympathetic to the crudity and explicitness of a performance of this type. Things are understated or delicately hinted; good manners consist in implying one's own belief in the sensibility of other people. Here surely is one of the causes of the widespread cult of the implicit, which is such a marked feature of English culture. It is not by any means confined to tricks of speech or manner. There is a pervasive national hostility to the whole business of spelling things out; and the obverse of that hostility is the inhibition on the asking of difficult or awkward or persistent questions. Public authority too easily escapes the extensive pressure of people demanding full explanations for this or that piece of inefficiency—because there is a readiness to believe that there are unstated problems behind public statements, and beyond that unstatable understandings which are much more important than the meanings of the words actually used.

Once one begins to trace the cult, one discovers its influence in all sorts of unexpected places. In industry it is not just that there is a resistance to the establishment of explicit and therefore precise standards of inspection. There is also the myth of the craftsman with his incommunicable skills. This in turn helps to explain the extraordinary refusal to bring the British system of apprentice training into line with twentieth-century needs. The failure to do so is not for want of being told about the way that other countries in Western Europe have tackled the problem. Britain is almost alone today in insisting on a standard five-year period of apprenticeship, whereas Continental European industry trains its people successfully in three years, and also in refusing to impose any publicly authorized test of efficiency in different trades which a worker must pass in order to call himself 'skilled'.[1] The whole method of training here is still guided by a romantic craftsman's mythology, which sees the young lad learning his trade, through his pores, by sheer physical propinquity to an older experienced man whom he watches and apes throughout the day.

Apart from certain unpleasant authoritarian overtones, this method as practised in the traditional style in the smaller British firms turns out to be a sure-fire formula for acquiring, with the maximum expenditure of time, the technology of the generation before last. At the very least the older man, who is usually educated in little else besides his own particular skill, will tend to communicate to his young pupil a scepticism, if not

[1] See Gertrude Williams, *Apprenticeship in Europe* (Chapman & Hall, 1963).

73

an outright hostility, towards new-fangled methods of production. Naturally the very notion of an examination designed to demonstrate by means of verbal answers to questions, as well as practical tests, whether a trained man knows what he is really about, is scoffed at. The trade unions seem to be especially vigorous in the struggle not only to avoid the introduction of tests, but also to assert that a particular skill for which a man is qualified must be defined as narrowly as possible. Of course they have their own practical motives: it is only in this way that the lines of demarcation can be kept rigid between different trades. If any man who was able to prove ability could take employment in a skilled operation, the present system of self-contained and all-powerful trade union fiefs would soon collapse. But what is interesting is not that the leaders of craft unions should wish to behave as if they had a mystery to guard against all comers, but the national attitude of mind which lends an acquiescent ear to their pretensions. As Professor Gertrude Williams points out:

> . . . This is the only European country in which the unions believe they are protecting their members by refusing to allow one worker to undertake the jobs normally done by another. . . . In other countries it is the industry and not the craft which provides the common identity of interest, and consequently unions are anxious for their members to have as wide a training as possible, so that they have greater security of employment by the ease with which they can move from one branch of the work to another. . . .

THE RESISTANCE of British workers when anyone tries to introduce clear-cut standards of any kind is an old story. F. W. Lanchester, the pioneer motor manufacturer, was compelled when he started to manufacture cars in England in the late 1890s to produce his own standard range of screw threads for his vehicles, because of the difficulty of getting work done to standard specifications. He said:

> When a body-builder was asked to work to drawings, gauges, or templates, he gave a sullen look such as one might

expect from a Royal Academician if asked to colour an engineering drawing.[1]

The end result was that Lanchester's attempt to manufacture the components of his car on an ingenious system of interchangeable parts 'proved intolerably expensive' and had to be given up. Circumstances like this helped to keep Britain well behind America in the development of an efficient motor industry. As late as 1913, W. Morris (later Lord Nuffield) could not persuade British firms to supply him with standard components on the scale that he required, and so he had to import them from the United States.[1]

Where the craftsman principle cannot easily operate, it is replaced by the leadership principle. The London bus conductor is the nearest example which comes to mind. In no other country with which I am acquainted do conductors assert quite so vociferously and constantly that they are in command. A remarkable aggressiveness takes hold of nice and mild-mannered people once they are put in this situation. '*Hurry along there, please!*' they shout roughly on every possible, or impossible, occasion. Watch what happens if anyone suggests, however politely, that the conductor may be charging him the wrong fare. The usual reaction is that of a captain faced by an act of insubordination on his ship. Indeed it is as captains of a vessel that these men and women seem instinctively to see themselves. I remember once in conversation with a friendly bus conductor telling him that I had had a dispute with a colleague of his on the same route who had in fact charged me the wrong fare. His reply was immediate: 'He shouldn't have let you argue with him. After all, it was his bus, you see.'

I FELT TEMPTED to tell my conductor about the behaviour of people doing similar jobs to his own in other countries. I recalled the relaxed and not very efficient Italian sitting at the receipt of custom near the entrance of a bus or tram, occasionally shouting laconically '*Avanti, per favore!*' before closing the automatic doors. The British double-decker bus seems in fact

[1] See H. J. Habakkuk, *American and British Technology in the Nineteenth Century* (Cambridge, 1962).

to have been designed by someone who was determined to put the maximum strain on the collector of tickets: he has to stand and can never claim a seat of his own; he is responsible for the movement of passengers on and off at each stop, but he cannot close the entrance or exit with an automatic door. I can only conclude that the London Transport designer (who has inspired most of the other bus companies in the country) was dominated by the ideal of a bus commander, a man who would pull through by the sheer force of personality. Some bus conductors really do.

LEST MY EXAMPLE of the bus conductor be thought to be eccentric and exaggerated, I shall refer to another familiar figure who powerfully supports my thesis: the hospital nurse. Where else in the world are patients, and even more the relatives of patients, who inquire into the causes of the illness or the progress of the cure, treated with such curt authoritarian answers? Temperature charts, the names of medicines or their purposes—all these are mysteries which no self-respecting nurse will reveal in order to satisfy the mere curiosity of the persons subject to their ministrations. Here the nanny principle is added to that of the commander. One is left in no doubt that it is bad manners, indeed evidence of a serious lack of character, to ask for explanations at all.

In a British hospital I am sometimes reminded of Whitehall. There is the same underlying assumption that the real business of government is none of the public's concern. Admittedly things are not quite so bad as they were a few years ago, immediately after the war; a more lively and aggressive press, and, even more important, the pressure of television have slightly dented the image of those inviolate offices in Whitehall. But anyone who has tried it knows just how uncomfortable it can still be made for a questioner—even an invited questioner at a press conference—if he persists in pressing an official spokesman on a matter which he prefers to have left vague and obscure. All the techniques of the wink and the nod between gentlemen are brought into play on such occasions. There is the implication that the questioner is being a bore, that he is overstepping the bounds of good manners, and even occasionally the dire hint that his probing is not in the national interest. Of course none of this need deter the questioner who is really bent on obtaining an answer—or alternatively a revelation of the incapacity to provide an answer. But in order to do so he will have to husband all his resources of aggression, and then go through the unpleasant ritual of insisting that yes, he (he alone, stopping other people from putting questions meanwhile) wants a full and explicit statement (in spite of the fact that repeating a lot of this elementary stuff will be wasting his own colleagues' time) on what is after all a fairly minor point.

Characteristically, foreigners or quasi-foreigners, Englishmen of one-generation vintage or those with a foreign parent, seem to come through this psychological obstacle race more easily than the full-fledged native journalist.

THE FINAL EXCUSE for avoiding detailed explanations on difficult matters of public policy is that this is the business of Parliament. There is no getting past that. The pretence that all the decisions that matter are made in Parliament in full public view is essential to preserve the independence of the civil servants, while they get on with the real job of looking after the country from day to day. The Minister must answer for the decisions which they make in his name; and unless an official is very unlucky the public will not be able to touch him. It is fair to say that this inviolability is rarely, if ever, used as a cover for despotic decisions on policy. Rather the great official in Britain knows that the condition for his immunity from public inspection is to refrain from overmuch policy-making. This rule does of course leave out of account the fact that policy can be made just as effectively by default. But what it does mean is that British civil servants are loth to engage in 'positive government' in the style of French and other Continental bureaucracies.

In particular they see it as none of their concern to interpret the intentions behind various pieces of legislation and to ensure that they add up to some kind of coherent administrative practice. Questions of this kind are not supposed to be asked. Laws are what they say in the text—no more and no less—and it is the business of the courts to interpret their meaning. In France by contrast there is the *Conseil d'État*, the supreme court of the Civil Service, with its splendid weapon of 'annulment for wrong use of administrative power' (*annulation pour excès de pouvoir*). In deciding whether an administrative decision, which may have been taken some time back, is null and void (with the consequence that all the official acts which followed from it become illegal), the *Conseil* is guided by what it thinks the legislators who made the law under which the administration acted, *intended* to achieve. This has, incidentally, proved awkward for General de Gaulle recently.[1] The *Conseil* in its capacity as the supreme court of the Civil Service, watching over its relations with the public, has expressed its concern at the recent practice of French Governments in validating arbitrary administrative actions *post hoc* by passing legislation which makes these actions legal. It proposes that the administrative courts should compel the Government to pay heavy damages to citizens who can claim to have been harmed, whenever an investigation has shown that some action by a provincial Prefect or some official of a Ministry went beyond the purposes of the original legislators. All this is only possible because there is an institution and a procedure which compels the French Civil Service to ask itself awkward questions about its own actions, and to do so in public.

EVERY NOW AND THEN a small crack is opened up in the British system. People peer through it, and although it is still pretty dark inside they can, if they go on staring, sometimes see enough to start asking some irritating questions. This was what happened with the annual Economic Survey, which used to be issued by the Treasury just before the Budget. It was not much use as a guide to policy, but it did give a few useful hints about the kind of advice on the outlook for the year ahead which the economists in the Treasury were giving the Government. It did not begin to compare with the U.S. President's annual Economic Report, which spells out each January the doubts and the probabilities which emerge from a study of the best information available by the Council of Economic Advisers. But all the same the Treasury felt it was too much; and the reason why it felt this resides in the very nature of the intellectual

[1] See *Études et Documents, Conseil d'État* (1961).

process. The creative aspect of any explanation, however meagre, applied to complicated facts is that it suggests further questions to be answered; and then the need to prove the inner consistency of the story leads to still further explanations. Even the Soviet statisticians have found this. Moreover—and this was the blood-chilling fact for Whitehall—it was impossible to pretend that all these complicated calculations and economic predictions were the single-handed responsibility of the Minister, who would bravely take the blame if they went wrong. The threat of public accountability was creeping up on the Treasury officials. Each year, it seemed, they might be asked to explain a bit more.

So they decided in 1963 to suppress the Economic Survey after it had been running for sixteen years. And what did they put in its place? Characteristically the Chancellor of the Exchequer was given the task of explaining to Parliament how *he* saw the situation, as part of the background to his Budget speech in April. The Treasury for its part went back to the safe business of producing a deadpan recital of what had happened, closing its story in December of the previous year. The final outcome is that the one serious piece of economic reporting by the Government which reached professional standards has now been turned into a meagre and hurried Ministerial commentary attached to the tax changes announced on Budget Day.

IT WOULD BE a mistake to suppose that the motive for decisions of this kind is simple anti-intellectualism. In fact the Treasury thinks hard about its problems, and it has a lot of able people working on them. The excuse for refusing to reveal the assumptions behind official policy is ultimately that to give the public this chance to pry merely makes it more difficult to carry on the task of government. No gain is seen from imposing on the administrator a more rigorous examination of his own thinking by the pressure of public argument. Indeed to argue is thought to be a waste of time. And the reason is that administration is seen as being essentially an art. Once administrators are viewed as artists, it is plainly wrong as well as useless to ask them to communicate the reasons for their decisions to people without the unspoken understanding that comes from shared experience.

Now, there is clearly something in the contention that certain aspects of the work of government cannot be adequately explained to people who have absolutely no feeling for the difficult business of governing. But the facts about the incommunicable skills, involving decisions which a rational and well-informed man would fail to understand, are relevant in a much smaller area than administrators like to imagine. One recalls the extraordinary performance of Montagu Norman as Governor of the Bank of England in the 1930s, who when asked to explain the methods and the policy which guided him in the management of the nation's finances, in the midst of the economic depression, replied roughly that it was all a matter of intuition and feel. The Bank of England today still has a strong propensity to murmur '*Fingerspitzengefühl*' whenever it is asked an awkward question. People in Whitehall do not do that. The Threadneedle Street habit is no doubt partly the heritage of Norman, who was the apotheosis of the English cult of the administrator as artist-leader—a kind of *Künstlerführerprinzip* which sees the only means of satisfactory communication in the action itself.

IT WOULD BE EASY to multiply examples of the evil consequences of relying excessively on the implicit agreement, the unwritten constitution, the imprecise undertaking with no dateline attached to it, the argument that was not pressed to its logical conclusion, the understanding that was never fully understood.

Yet one should not overlook, on the other side, the satisfactions that go with living in a firmly rooted society like Britain where the assumption of an unspoken consensus on a variety of matters is so strong. For one thing it makes it possible for policemen to move about unarmed. The assumption, which is confirmed in frequent instances, is that ordinary people will join together and help the police against a law-breaker once he is known to have a gun. There are other subtler pleasures which derive from the existence of a certain type of allusive shorthand in literature. To have a language in common use which readily carries such a load of implicit meanings provides the opportunity for exceedingly rich aesthetic experiences. This, it should be noted, is not just the English language itself; it is literature produced in an English context. Too often I have the feeling that some ultimate literary delicacy is absent in modern American writing, because of the all-pervading cult of the explicit which rules in the United States.

For all that, and in spite of the various consolations of life in Britain, I believe that we must deliberately set out to borrow a large draught of this American explicitness. It is, among other things, an essential ingredient of a mass society which is managing to keep up with the contemporary pace of innovation in industrial life. It is also an instrument for putting pressure on public authority of all kinds, and making it more responsive to rapidly changing needs. It should be an invariable rule, as it is in other European countries, that any regulation made by any law-making agency should have a clear set of reasons for the administrative decision attached to it. The blanket postscript 'By Order', and the bland ministerial assertion, '*Not in the public interest*', should be publicly banned.

People in authority should be forced to explain themselves fully—and not only why they have made certain decisions, but, perhaps more to the point, why other decisions have gone unmade for so long.

Taboo on Expertise

Austen Albu

'INEFFICIENCY' and 'lack of drive', the two most common faults of which it is accused, are not new characteristics of British management. It is many years since the first critics began to issue their warnings that, unless British industry became more scientific and efficient, it would inevitably decline. These warnings—the year is 1867—started after the Paris Exhibition, where the comparison between the exhibits of Britain and other countries showed such a startling contrast with the glories of the Great Exhibition of 1851. They led to innumerable enquiries and to reports by Select Committees; it was still necessary for them to be repeated by Lord Haldane and others before and after the first World War. Since 1945 working parties galore have studied British industries and their managers, and some of the criticisms have even become a shade sharper as our economic plight has become more frightening.

The causes of the failings of which British industrial management is accused must, therefore, be sought in social and historical roots going back at least into the middle of the last century. It was at this time that 'the amateur tradition', which is so prevalent in most branches of public and business administration in this country, became firmly established. It finds expression in the opinion that 'the general education of a gentleman is the best background for the making of decisions'; that the specialist should be 'on tap and not on top', and that if there is 'character' there need not (except in the higher ranks of the Civil Service) be brains. Developing from the Northcote-Trevelyan reforms in the prevailing nineteenth-century atmosphere of Manchester School economics, the British Civil Service adopted the view that its main function was the making of policy and not the executive action which required special knowledge. It was not the civil servant's job to be *expert*, but to be *fair*. Initiative and action should come from private individuals and if (as in the Colonies) there was no indigenous initiative, then law and order ruled over economic stagnation.

THUS CIVIL SERVANTS came to resemble university dons, and industrial managers, in the days when Britain became the workshop of the world, were *entrepreneurs* and 'practical men'. They did not have and did not need much education; if they had learnt their trades they had done so as apprentices; they were frequently themselves inventors. The professional and intellectual classes (educated in the revived classical tradition of the universities) despised such practical men, who were in any case far removed from the aristocratic ruling classes. Only the great speculative nineteenth-century booms of canal and railway building gave to the engineering *entrepreneurs* a certain heroic prestige.

During the early eighteenth-century heyday of British industrial predominance there had been a lively interest in technology and invention among the middle and lower middle classes who were forming the new entrepreneurial class. Even some members of the aristocracy (for example, Sir George Cayley, now recognized as one of the chief inventors of the aeroplane) spent their lives in experiment and invention although their social origins prevented them from applying themselves to 'trade'. But in time, as the American sociologist Reinhard Bendix has pointed out, the progress of technology became the special ideology of the business class in its battle with a hostile land-owning aristocracy who held it as, at best, a necessary evil.

The attitude of the members of this new social class towards the aristocracy was, however, ambivalent. On the one hand they resented the contempt in which their occupations were held by the aristocrats; on the other, they envied the latter's dominant political and social position. It was the well-known political flexibility of the English ruling class (and the less-recognized *mobility* in English society) which in the end undermined the thrusting, innovating, entrepreneurial spirit of British manufacturers. The combination of a sharply divided class society—and the possibility of rising from one class to another held in greater esteem—meant that the ambition of the sons of many manufacturers was to leave their family businesses and to become land-owners (or, at least, 'professional men'). The early manufacturers despised education, and it is an attitude which has largely persisted so far as higher education is concerned up to the present day. But to be fair the only educational channels open to them were the few old-established grammar schools or what are now called the 'public' schools and (in England) the two old-established universities. When they sent their children to these institutions it was for social recognition and not for useful education. Of the 5 per cent of Cambridge undergraduates who came from business families between 1800 and 1849, *none* went into business themselves. To be classical dons, doctors, orchestral conductors, or simply country gentlemen—these were their aspirations.[1]

THE EARLY SUCCESS of the 'practical men', coupled with the *laissez-faire* attitude of British governments which delayed the establishment of a public system of education until the end of the nineteenth century, led them to a contempt for formal education as it then was in Britain. This was the beginning of the tradition of vocational education by evening classes. It was the lack of education for the working and lower-middle classes which made necessary the foundation of 'Mechanics' Institutes' for this purpose, where courses suitable for those working in industry were provided. These were the precursors of the 'technical colleges' providing evening and part-time day classes by which alone so many of those who work in industry (even as professional engineers) acquired—and to a considerable extent *still* acquire —the scientific and technical knowledge necessary for their jobs.

When the new middle class began to take an interest in general education they made precious little attempt to adapt the system that they found to their own occupational needs. Britain was now growing richer and becoming more and more

---

[1] In Prussia, on the other hand, where social mobility did not exist, but a system of public education did, the business class established its own prestige system and the aspiration to leave the world of trade and industry was, therefore, weaker.

of a *rentier* in the world; the industries of other countries were beginning to take a growing share of world trade. The children of the founders of Britain's industrial prosperity increasingly adopted the standards and outlook of the aristocratic classes. They gradually lost the self-confident business enthusiasm of their forefathers. They sent their own children to the fashionable 'public' schools, the numbers of which were growing fast, and (to a lesser extent) to the universities, where there were few opportunities, until late in the nineteenth century, for the study of such industrial subjects as applied science and engineering. There they learnt to become *gentlemen*, but nothing so *vulgar* as how to practise any trade or profession.

When the industrialists of the nineteenth century acquired any formal education for their jobs it was frequently abroad. Tom and Albert Vickers (the second generation of the great armament and engineering firm who were mainly responsible for its early expansion) were sent to Germany for their technical education. Many chemists also received their education in Germany. Several of the most scientifically managed firms in Britain in the nineteenth century—as again today—were founded by foreigners who had received a scientific education on the Continent. These included such well-known names as Hans Renold, Alfred Mond, John Brunner, and Sebastian de Ferranti. Even when they were not technically qualified themselves, foreign industrialists who established themselves in Britain tended to look more for formal professional education among their employees than their English competitors.

THE HISTORICAL DEVELOPMENT of the British middle class thus led to a split between general and professional education from which we are only now beginning to recover. Even the old-established professions (such as medicine and the law, not to mention accountancy and architecture) relied—and still to a large extent rely—on 'apprenticeship methods', with the contempt for research that such methods imply. As for engineering, recognition of the fact that *a professional engineer needs an education at university level* has only occurred very recently. When I graduated as an engineer in the early 'twenties, I doubt if more than three or four hundred engineers left our universities a year. In point of fact my first two responsible jobs were both with firms with foreign connections. Even just before the war the annual output of engineering graduates was in the region of a mere 500 a year.

Training for all the professions in this country is dominated by their professional bodies: the Royal Colleges in medicine, the Institutions in engineering. These are inevitably conservative influences. The engineering institutions were of course greatly influenced by the attitudes of the leaders of industry who largely formed their councils. They continued up to recent times to express their preferences for 'the practical man', trained by the same apprenticeship methods as the locomotive and machine-tool builders who had given us industrial supremacy a century before.

As a result some of our industries are only just beginning to emerge from the George Stephenson age in the training of their managers and technical staffs. The *White Paper on Scientific and Engineering Manpower* in 1959 showed that in the machine-tool industry only 1·3 per cent of its employees were qualified scientists or engineers. In the shipbuilding and marine engineering industry the figure was as low as 0·6 per cent. At that time British Railways, with over half-a-million employees and a modernization programme in hand, had about 1,400 scientifically or technically qualified staff. But even these figures do not tell the whole story. The definition of 'qualified' scientist or engineer adopted in these surveys includes many whose only qualification is membership of one of a number of professional bodies, some of which for many years did not even insist on examination as a condition of membership.[1]

---

[1] For instance, in the machine-tool industry a large number are members of the Institution of Production Engineers. Out of 870 new corporate members admitted by the Institution in 1959, *only* 100 were university graduates. Ninety per cent of the largest machine-tool firms in the country had, at that time, only *twenty-five* graduate engineers among them. Most of the qualified staffs in the shipbuilding industry are members of the Institute of Marine Engineers. Out of 630 new members admitted in 1959, only 40 were university graduates. Of the railway staffs in the same year, only just over 500 were university graduates In declining industries, such as textiles, the situation is, of course, much worse and the staffs in the university textile departments declaim bitterly at the lack of use made of them by the industry.

THE NARROWNESS OF THE EDUCATION of engineers is no doubt the reason for one of the characteristics of British industry which has been most harmful during a period when technological innovation has been becoming more and more essential for the maintenance of world markets. Consider the lack of scientists or engineers on the boards of directors. In a study made by Mr. Bosworth Monck in 1952 of the various branches of the engineering industry (where one would most expect to find them!) only 21·5 per cent of directors were found to be technically qualified, and of these only a small proportion would have been university graduates.

The lack of any system of technical education for industrial managers was already the subject of criticism in the last century. The campaign for Government support for it was led by Lyon Playfair, who had been one of the British jurors at the Paris Exhibition. It produced, at the end of the century, the establishment of a handful of university engineering departments and the founding of our system of technical colleges. But by that time the great Continental *Technische Hochschulen* and the American colleges for agriculture and the mechanical arts had already been in existence for many years. Even in the early 1920s when the National Certificate awards were introduced, it was still felt adequate that the majority of professional engineers in this country should be educated at *night school or, at best, on one day a week.*

Nearly eighty years after Lyon Playfair's campaign, the Percy Committee on Higher Technological Education had again to draw attention to the dangers arising to Britain's position as a leading industrial nation due to the shortage of scientists and technologists who could also administer and organize and develop. There was more parliamentary debate and two more reports by the Parliamentary and Scientific Committee. Twelve years later their main recommendation for the establishment of a number of Colleges of Technology (of 'University rank') began to be implemented.

IF TECHNOLOGICAL WEAKNESS in management is the cause of the backwardness of many branches of British industry, lack of training in the economics of business is probably just as important. Very few firms have any understanding of the methods of economic forecasting or of market analysis. Nor are their export salesmen trained in the intricacies of overseas trade. This has been particularly serious in recent times. Britain's overseas markets have been changing as other countries (previously her customers) developed their own industries and as competition from other highly industrialized countries in formerly British markets became more acute. Firms will *blindly* start up the manufacture of goods for which they have made *no survey* of sales possibilities either at home or abroad. This is so, even in supposedly modern industries (*e.g.* the manufacture of electrical goods), and has led to the proliferation of manufacturers of similar products (particularly in the domestic appliance field) so that there are more manufacturers of many articles in this country than in Continental countries or even in the United States. This leads to higher costs and, where prices are not protected by agreement, to closing down of production after a short period.

It is not only the small manufacturers who have failed to understand the need for more sophisticated methods of judging their future markets and planning their businesses. An outstanding example of the maintenance of an obsolete traditionalism until almost too late is to be found in what happened in Vickers.[1]

It was clear after World War II that Vickers could never again rely on the manufacture of battleships and heavy armaments. Armaments in the future would require 'more sophisticated' methods of research, design, and manufacture than those on which the company's reputation had been built; and the amount of work which they would provide in peace-time would hardly keep its vast resources occupied. Nevertheless it was *not until 1958* that a serious examination took place of the whole future of the company's policy! This led, for the first time, to the setting up of a 'Group Forward Development Department' to act as a technical and commercial intelligence service for the organization. Even a central research department had only been set up just the year before. Very few university graduates

[1] See J. D. Scott's excellent history of the company. (Weidenfeld & Nicolson, January, 1963.)

had been employed by the company up to the early 1950s when the new chairman of the company, Sir Ronald Weeks, set up for Vickers an elaborate education and training scheme which is today one of the most advanced in the country.

The following episode is characteristic of the prevailing attitude in a great many firms. I once asked the director of the machine-tool branch of a large company how many students his company had studying for the '*Diploma in Technology*' (which is generally obtained by students taking 'sandwich courses', alternating six months in college and six months with their firms). This award was at that time two years old, and its establishment had been the final outcome of the long debate on the Percy Report. He replied that he had never heard of it.

IF THE NUMBER of graduates with scientific, technological, or economic qualifications is small in many parts of British industry, the number of Arts graduates is certainly no larger. It is not surprising, therefore, that out of this limited pool of employees who have had any higher education the number to be found in management (except in a few progressive and mostly large companies) is very small indeed.[1] It is because of this lack of higher education, especially in subjects relevant to industrial or commercial activity, that British industrial management has been woefully behind its competitors.

[1] Figures quoted by David Granick, in his *The European Executive*, indicate that only between a quarter and a third of top managers in British industry are university graduates, although, as was to be expected with development of higher education since the war, the numbers are growing. Even more significant is the fact that only about 7 per cent of all top managers came from Oxford or Cambridge, which recruit, because of their prestige, the majority of the best brains in the country.

In France in large organizations, public and private, 40 per cent of the top executives were found to be élite graduates of the *École Polytechnique*, which provides a broad scientific education at the highest level. Many others would have come from one of the other *Écoles Supérieurs*, including the *École de Commerce* or the *École d'Administration* founded after the war. A number of these men now enter industry after a period in the Civil Service (a practice which is also growing in this country). In Germany the majority of business managers, if they do not have an engineering or scientific degree, have one in business-economics.

AFTER THE WAR a great deal was heard of the lack of 'management education' in this country. 'Management' became the
subject of study by several government committees, partly as
the result of the propaganda of a few enthusiasts and of the war-
time experience which had shown up the inadequacy of the
management of so many firms. The result of these studies was
the foundation in 1948, with the encouragement of Sir Stafford
Cripps, of the British Institute of Management (and the establishment of courses in technical colleges leading to National
Certificates in Management Studies). The Institute has never
acquired the influence nor undertaken the many educational
functions of the American Management Association, on which
it was partly modelled; its main activity has been the organizing
of conferences—generally at the 'tycoon' level. The National
Certificate courses have recently been abandoned and a new
'Diploma in Management Studies' established. This award,
too, has now come under severe criticism on account of the uncertainty of its subject content.

A number of universities have now started post-graduate
courses in industrial management of a more sophisticated kind,
including such fashionable subjects as 'operational research'
and 'linear programming'. But perhaps the most popular of the
post-war efforts in this field have been the courses for mature
students of the executive development type of which the most
famous is that at the Administrative Staff College at Henley.
It is difficult to ascertain the extent to which those who have
attended these courses or their organizations have benefited
from them; but in so far as they had not previously had any
formal higher education, the courses can hardly have compensated for this. They may well amount merely to an extension
of the amateur approach to business problems which is so
characteristic of British industry.

THE LACK OF educational background and the narrowness of
outlook of so many of the leaders of British industry is only a
reflection of more widespread social attitudes and of the relative
prestige accorded to different occupations. Until recent times
a career in industry would never have attracted those with the
best brains. For them a career as a university don or in the

Civil Service was the obvious choice. This gave us a highly intelligent body of public administrators, capable of logical thought and lucid expression, but without special knowledge. No doubt this was very suitable for an age when the business of government was to do as little as possible itself, but to ensure that the law was administered fairly as between all citizens. It was adequate for establishing the first welfare departments and administering the early social services. But can it be anything but inadequate to cope with the growing complexity of a technological society and welfare state in which government is more and more expected to take the lead in planning the economy?

After the Civil Service, as 'socially acceptable occupations' there came the older professions of medicine and the law; but banking and the various services of the City of London (at a time when it was the financial centre of the world) were also considered 'respectable for gentlemen'. It was the fact that in the early years of this century *a third* of this country's imports could be paid for by the invisible exports of shipping, insurance, overseas investment, commodity trading, etc., that prevented its true foreign trade position being understood until the modern era of balance of payments crises. What delayed the acceptance of the view that *only by the hard selling of technologically advanced goods in world markets could this country survive* was the nostalgia felt in conservative circles for the imperial days when the City's dominating influence in the financial world seemed to make this unnecessary. To some extent this attitude still remains. The brightest young Arts men from Oxford or Cambridge prefer to become bankers or stockbrokers or investment analysts, jobs for which they generally have no basic education or training, rather than go into industry. Those who read science prefer to remain 'pure' and to go in for research rather than sully themselves with the useful activities of the technologist.

AT A RECENT conference held by the Institute of Directors a market research consultant was explaining that women would be more likely to buy a perfume if it was attractively packed. Some of the audience reacted to this not very surprising information like old-time puritans. They objected that such forms of selling were dishonest and that the quality of the goods should be sufficient incentive for a potential purchaser. It would be very pleasant to live in a world where competitive selling was not necessary; it is certainly not the world in which this country has now to earn its living. The endless stories of the lackadaisical methods of British salesmen abroad seem to indicate that the news has not yet reached a large number of our managers.[1]

In AN AGE when industry needs not only its share of the best brains wherever they may be found, but also the uninhibited energies of those who work in it, the class division in our educational system is a handicap which it is surprising to find our industrial leaders trying to perpetuate. A few years ago the leaders of British industry raised a fund specifically to support the building of science laboratories in the 'public schools'. A large number of 'guinea-pig directors', often with titles—even if only that of M.P. (Conservative)—but without other qualifications than 'the right school', are to be found on the boards of hundreds of British companies.

It would be quite wrong to suggest that *all* British managements suffer from the faults of so many. There are outstanding exceptions; the truth is that British industry stands on the watershed between its past and its potential future. As more and more of the country's young men and women get the opportunity of a university education, and as younger, better-trained men come into responsible positions, industry may well acquire a higher prestige and become a much more professional affair. In that case we could well be on the way to a great industrial 'leap forward'.

But industry does not work in isolation from the rest of society; nor can it develop unaffected by social attitudes out-

[1] When in Italy the price for Scotch whisky was cut by 50 per cent through the activities of unauthorized importers—termed by the British Embassy in Rome as 'not exactly cricket, you know'—the total sales quadrupled. When normal procedures and prices were restored, sales of course dropped and British spokesmen expressed pleasure at the return to propriety: '*Whisky was entirely too cheap in Italy before this back-door trade, and we feel the product itself was therefore cheapened in the public eye. It lost something by being available to all. . . .*' (THE GUARDIAN, 23 March, 1963.)

side. The revolution needed in British management will not come unless there exists, in the country as a whole, *a real desire for economic expansion.* This involves an understanding that economic expansion is not just a policy of pure materialism. It is the essential basis for a liberal and humane society. Without it society turns sour, bitterness grows between social groups, and xenophobia and racial intolerance are bred. But economic expansion needs a willingness to accept changes. Among those changes, perhaps the most important will be a recognition of the *social* worth of those who work in industry— and a removal of the *class divisions* in our society which uphold an outdated hierarchy of occupational prestige.

Since the war, Communist influence in the trade unions has been steadily decreasing in Western Europe, steadily increasing in the United Kingdom. The significance of this fact is often exaggerated by those anxious to evade the real problems of our class-ridden society, and passed over in uneasy silence by others who fear being stigmatized as witch-hunters. The author, who belongs to neither of these categories, has recently completed a study of the subject.

'A Red Under Every Bed?'

Aidan Crawley

THE BRITISH PEOPLE have rejected Communism repeatedly and overwhelmingly ever since it emerged in 1917. No Communist has won a Parliamentary seat since 1951. There is not even a parish council they control; nor is there any trade union, co-operative society, or other institution with an open membership which has a Communist majority.

Abroad Communism has always had a certain intellectual appeal; in Britain this has never been the case. There are a few Communist dons at some of our university colleges and there are some Communist teachers in the employment of most of our educational authorities; they are a small minority. There is no flourishing school of Marxism in any of our universities. The best new recruits to the party are often the sons of old members or sympathizers. Thought is mainly imported.

Nor does the party have any wide emotional appeal. Its members are far from being a collection of zealots believing passionately in 'the brotherhood of man'. Most of the rank-and-file join the party not because of any belief, but through chance

94

or expediency. A scholarly study of the reasons why people become Communists, carried out by Princeton University, suggests that nine-tenths of the recruits to any Communist party in a capitalist country join for the most trivial reasons: sometimes they have been attracted to a girl who has taken them to a Communist dance; or they have had a row with their foreman or their boss. Women often join because a man 'speaks nicely', or because a meeting has been 'exciting'. The educational qualifications of Communists are, on average, low.

And because they often join on impulse, thousands of recruits leave the party during their first year. Estimates of the annual wastage among members of the British Communist Party vary as between a third and a fifth; in any case 'wastage' has been the subject of special lament at both the last two annual party conferences. Of the thirty-five-thousand-odd members, only between ten and fifteen thousand can have been in the party for as long as three years.

There ought, therefore, to be little difficulty in defeating the Communist campaign in Britain. It only needs a small proportion of the majority in any organization of which Communists are members to exercise their right to vote, and not a single Communist would hold a representative position either as a shop-steward, a trade union official, or anything else. Rejected politically and shorn of positions of power in industry, the party would soon disintegrate.

Yet the British Communist Party not only continues to exist, but shows remarkable resilience. Rocked to its foundations by the brutal suppression of the Hungarian revolt in 1956, it has since been assailed by a series of exposures culminating in the trial of the officials of the Electrical Trades Union, which would have broken any normal political organization. Nevertheless, today, the party is increasing its membership and extending its influence in various strata of British society. How is this to be explained?

APATHY ALONE is not a satisfactory answer. We are not apathetic where we believe that our vital interests are at stake. Even at by-elections, an 80 per cent vote is now common; and protest marches, letters to newspapers, opinion polls, television enquiries, reveal a greater alertness and interest in public affairs than has ever existed before. The truth is that although as a people we instinctively recoil from Communism, we do not want to study it or understand it. It remains a foreign disease whose symptoms we try either to ignore or to brush under the carpet.

This conceit is encouraged by an intellectual superficiality which either despises or condones Communism. The dilemma of the socialist intellectual is understandable. His hopes for the Russian revolution were so great and the idea of abandoning them so devastating that he naturally put off facing the matter as long as possible. But the point at which exculpation becomes complicity has long since been passed. Absolute power has corrupted the Russian revolution as quickly and completely as any other movement in history. The failure of some very influential socialist intellectuals to state this unequivocally, their attempts to excuse tyranny when exercised in an allegedly socialist cause, has not only weakened their own movement, but blurred the vital distinction between Communism and democratic socialism in the minds of some of their followers.

There is nothing mysterious about the Communist campaign in Britain. The resolutions adopted, and directives issued, at Communist international conferences in Moscow and at the headquarters of the World Federation of Trade Unions at Prague, are well publicized in both the Communist and capitalist press. The methods which the British Communist Party adopts to fulfil these directives are well authenticated. Particularly in the last few years, a mass of evidence has emerged from court cases and enquiries of one kind and another, to show how faithfully the party members follow the official doctrines and tactical precepts of Marxism-Leninism.

Small though they are in numbers, the hard core of British Communists—the officials of the 1,400 branches and 19 districts, the 42 members of the national executive and the 60-odd full-time officials of the party, the field workers in the trade unions, the professions, and in the Civil Service—are the least sentimental or starry-eyed group of people in this country. They are revolutionaries, and proud of it. Each of them has survived the shock, which comes to almost every Communist recruit, of discovering that democracy is exactly the opposite of what they had hitherto believed. For one reason or another they have all accepted the discipline of 'democratic centralism'. A bare handful at the top are thinkers; the rest are party workers dedicated to the capture and exercise of political power by peaceful or, if necessary, violent means. For although the idea of peaceful co-existence envisages the hope that victory over capitalism may be consummated without resort to a nuclear war, no Communist leader in any country has ever suggested that violence has become unacceptable. On the contrary, Chairman Khrushchev himself has emphasized that ultimate co-existence can only mean existence 'on Communist terms', and has reiterated the distinction between revolutionary and bourgeois violence. Mr. John Gollan, the General Secretary of the British Communist Party, is perfectly open about this. He hopes that the Communist millennium can be brought about peaceably, but he does not attempt to deny that if violence were necessary he would advocate it.

THERE IS NO DOUBT that under Mr. Gollan's leadership the British Communist Party is gaining ground. After Hitler's war the party suffered a series of reverses. In spite of the prestige enjoyed by our Russian allies, its hopes of reviving the pre-war 'popular front' with the Labour Party were dashed by the intransigence of men like Ernest Bevin and Clement Attlee. The failure of the Soviet leaders to honour the terms of the war-time agreements, the imposition of Communism on Eastern Europe by the Red Army, brought further disillusion. The war-time membership of 56,000 rapidly shrank. Then came Hungary. When Mr. Gollan succeeded Mr. Harry Pollitt as general secretary of the party (in 1959), its fortunes were almost at their lowest ebb. Divisions within the party hierarchy were so acute that many of the older members prophesied it would fall to pieces in his hands. But Mr. Gollan has confounded all his critics. Under his inspiration every aspect of the party's work has taken on a new vitality and is conducted with greater subtlety than before.

Mr. Gollan is a thorough-going Marxist-Leninist (he jibs at the word 'orthodox', saying that there is only one form of

Marxist-Leninism). His general strategy, laid down in successive Moscow conferences, is stated with neo-Churchillian brevity. It is to extend the Communist world-revolution by establishing the 'dictatorship of the proletariat' in Britain. Old-fashioned though the language sounds, Mr. Gollan endorses it enthusiastically and believes that he will succeed in his own lifetime. His tactics come straight from the textbooks.

According to these, it is the duty of the revolutionary leader to lull the society which he aims to overthrow into a state of false security. It is here that Mr. Gollan's superiority over his predecessor is most marked. After 1951, when the party lost its only representative in Parliament, it more or less abandoned any pretence of playing a constitutional role. Although the chances of winning seats at an election are perhaps even smaller today (in view of the rise in standards of living), Mr. Gollan has reversed all this. Determined to give the party a respectable appearance, he put a record number of candidates in the field for this year's municipal elections, and will fight several constituencies in the general election as well. At the same time he has carried out a nation-wide membership campaign, concentrating particularly on university students.

How successful he has been is shown not only in the membership figures but in the reports of this year's party conference. Almost without exception they conveyed a favourable impression. Even such experienced journalists as Mr. Peregrine Worsthorne of the *Sunday Telegraph*, a Conservative to his finger-tips, reported the mood of the delegates quite uncritically. Delighted by the wit and urbanity of the comrades, he gave the impression of a sensible and moderate party discussing reform rather more practically than its rivals, and nowhere even hinted that the Communist Party might be in any way 'different' from other parties.

Having succeeded so admirably in assuming the amiable disguise which is considered the essential preliminary to success for a Communist Party in a capitalist country, Mr. Gollan is carrying out his policy with less dissension and distraction than his predecessors. This policy has two well-established aims. First, to spread a measure of confusion and thereby undermine the morale of the working masses; secondly, to penetrate to positions of power, particularly in the trade unions and professions. Regarding the first, the party follows the simple but proven technique of playing upon selected emotions to make people doubt the values of their own society, at the same time painting a romantic picture of life under Communism.

Knowing the British weakness for fair play, propaganda begins by trying to induce a collective sense of guilt: the British Government is represented as an 'obstacle to peace' (because presumably it will not accept Soviet proposals for total disarmament without a system of guarantees). It is always the British and other colonial powers who are the 'ruthless oppressors of backward peoples', the 'brutal murderers' of Cypriots, Africans, or Arabs. And since the British do have a tender conscience, they are quick to develop a sense of sin often quite out of proportion to the facts, and ignorant of the terrors of the other side.

Next to guilt, fear is always easy to exploit. Communists have infiltrated the Campaign for Nuclear Disarmament and are trying to use it for their own ends. At one time it looked as if they had gone too far; several members of the Committee of 100 resigned and it seemed possible that the whole movement would disintegrate. But the success of this Easter's Aldermaston march seems to have given it a longer life.

In the third place, Mr. Gollan has a flair for exploiting the British feeling for the under-dog, and tries to create an image of the Communist movement as something purely humane and above party. Wherever there is a grievance—perhaps among tenants who have had their rents raised; among teachers or nurses who have received a smaller rise in pay than they asked for; in the ranks of the unemployed, or the skilled workers whose differential has been reduced—Communists come forward as their champions, urging the oppressed to stand up for their rights. Because their key men are so widely dispersed throughout society, they are usually able to do this with apparent spontaneity; only occasionally is it necessary to draft men in to take advantage of a special opportunity.

THE 'FRONT' ORGANIZATIONS by which Communists in all capitalist countries try to create a charitable image of their movement are so well known and transparent that one might expect them to have gone out of fashion. But the gullibility of some of our countrymen, at any rate, has not been exhausted. Under such simple disguises as 'teachers for Peace', 'artists for Peace', societies for Friendship, or committees for Culture, British Communists can still enrol the support of well-meaning compatriots, even though all these organizations have been publicly proscribed by the Labour Party.

It is difficult to gauge how widespread the effect of this kind of psychological warfare is. Probably a large majority of the British people is still sufficiently level-headed to resist this kind of propaganda. There can be no doubt, however, that the susceptible minority is large enough to help the party in its main task: the penetration of the trade unions and the Labour Party.

Since the conviction for fraud of the Communist officials of the Electrical Trades Union, there has been a certain ebb and flow in the pattern of trade union infiltration. Cleaned out of the headquarters of the E.T.U.[1] (they still control some of its branches), the Communists are making a dead set at the Amalgamated Engineering Union and have just won a signal success in getting their man elected to the vacancy on the national executive. Communists are losing control of the London division of the Painters' Union, but are increasing their hold in other branches of the building industry such as plumbers and woodworkers. In spite of being banned from holding offices in the national executive of the National Union of Bank Employees, they retain considerable influence in the middle ranks of this union. As a result of the changes introduced after Lord Radcliffe's first security enquiry, the Communists have suffered a setback in the Civil Service Clerical Association, which they dominated, but have increased their hold among teachers, draughtsmen, and scientific workers. Although banned from holding office in the Transport and General Workers' Union, they virtually control the Liaison Committee at the London Docks, which is resisting the scheme for the final

[1] An account of the High Court action which condemned the 'ballot-rigging' has been prepared by C. H. Rolph from the official transcript: *All Those in Favour? The E.T.U. Trial* (André Deutsch, 1962, 6s.)

'decasualization' of dock labour. Communist influence in the National Union of Railwaymen is increasing, and during the winter Communists made headway for the first time in the steel industry. Owing to redundancy they were able to foment a strike in a firm in Sheffield which had not known such an event for thirty years. Although there are fewer than two thousand Communists among the million-and-a-quarter members of the London Co-operative Society, they and their sympathizers have gained—and just retained—control of the management committee (and, incidentally, have brought the whole concern to the point of insolvency).

This penetration has more than the indirect exercise of power for its object; it aims not merely at control of the trade union movement, but at transforming it into a revolutionary force. This, to anyone who attends our sober trade union conferences, may seem the remotest of possibilities, but in some places it is happening. The reason why the Communists went to such lengths to keep control of the Electrical Trades Union was simply that it gave them an organization through which they could begin to train their followers in industrial action. This they did by announcing that any wild-cat strike called by any electrician anywhere would automatically receive the official approval of the executive, and through a special training college where electricians underwent a process of 'Marxist-Leninist indoctrination'. It is for the same reason that the British Communist Party is now concentrating on the Amalgamated Engineering Union and on the National Union of Miners. In each of these they have a fair chance of sooner or later winning control.

As a by-product of their penetration of the unions, the British Communist Party hopes eventually to dominate the whole Labour movement. Since the collapse of the 'Popular Front' in the 'thirties this too has seemed a remote possibility. But if, within the next two years, the Communists do gain control of the engineers' and miners' unions, and if the weight of the Transport and General Workers' Union should be thrown on their side, Communists may one day come close to commanding a majority of bloc votes in the Labour Party Conference.

A secondary but immediate purpose of penetrating the trade unions is to disorganize the British economy and thus to bring the 'inevitable collapse of the doomed capitalist system' nearer. When trade union leaders and industrialists point proudly to the large areas of British industry which are 'free from Communist interference', they miss the point. Communist penetration is not extensive but intensive; the party is concentrated deliberately upon the field of communications and upon three basic industries: mining, building, and engineering. It is doubtful whether it is yet in a position to bring the whole of any one industry to a standstill, but it has proved over and over again that it is able to cause serious dislocation.

THE MOST IMMEDIATE and serious effect of these Communist successes, however, is not the financial and trading losses incurred, but the worsening of British industrial relations. We may not be in danger of losing our constitutional liberties, but we are in danger of forfeiting our traditional tolerance and ability to co-operate with each other. The test of efficiency today is not so much 'the number of days lost in strikes'—these can often be made good fairly quickly—but the speed at which industry is able to modernize itself, accept new machinery and methods, and adapt itself to change. At the moment every major industrial country is adapting and expanding faster than we are. The reason is simply that the British people do not work harmoniously together. And however great the responsibility of management, one of the prime causes of this lack of co-operation is the 'militancy' everywhere encouraged by Communists. Moderation is always condemned by them, so that the impression may be created that only Communists have the courage to 'fight' for the workers' rights. It is this impression which is the real poison in our industrial relations. 'Militancy' is at the bottom of the general reluctance to accept new machinery, new methods of organization, or amalgamations within the unions. It makes employers afraid to grant concessions, and trade union leaders afraid to advocate compromise.

NEVERTHELESS, Communism in Britain is an ulcer in the body politic and not a malignant growth; it can be cured by physiotherapy rather than surgery. Can we any longer accept the complacent assurance that industry will 'set its own house in order'? We need legislation to ensure that consultation between management and workers is established throughout our industrial life; we must bring the questions of dismissal, compensation for redundancy, adequate unemployment pay, into a homogeneous system of industrial security. At the moment our attitude to these hazards is almost mediaeval, and it provides Communists with endless grievances to exploit.

We can reform and strengthen our trade unions by revising their rules and insisting that all ballots for whatever office are carried out by post, and are invalid unless at least 20 per cent of the trade unionists have voted. We can examine and reform all the antiquated safety and health regulations in industry which make 'go slow' and 'work to rule' legitimate means of bringing industry to a standstill; we can make it possible for the Crown to prosecute those who call strikes without notice. All these are positive reforms, necessary to establish security and encourage efficiency, and they would make it increasingly difficult for Communists to get a hearing or gain a following. But there is need for preventive action as well.

The best way of countering skilful propaganda is to forewarn its victims by keeping them properly informed. When so much is known, it is extraordinary how little about Communist activities is published. Newspaper editors, television and radio producers still hesitate to give any real and serious prominence to the work of the British Communist Party; yet they can scarcely pretend that it is 'of no interest' to their readers. Nor, I think, is the Government fulfilling its duty to keep the country informed.

Some extension of security is also needed. For example, is it sensible to allow Communists to occupy the positions of planning officers in local government where they inevitably acquire information vital to civil defence? If we are to preserve liberties we have to adapt their defence to the kind of attack to which they are subject. The way to stop irresponsible and ineffective 'witch-hunting' is to make abundantly clear the occupations which must be denied to Communists; and if necessary to extend to all public services the screening procedures established by the first Radcliffe enquiry. If this procedure had been in operation it is quite possible that Vassall would have been denied the opportunity of espionage.

Tolerance is the essence of democracy; but democracy is preserved by seeing that the limits placed upon tolerance are relevant to contemporary society. Freedom is not an absolute.

The Price of Obstinacy

Crises in the Trade Unions

John Cole

THE BRITISH TRADE UNIONS were built up in a different age to do a very different job, and as a result they suffer badly from the Maginot outlook. They also suffer from the fact that most criticism of them is produced by the wrong people for the wrong reasons and often along completely wrong lines. The besetting sin of the trade unions at present is not wildness, militancy, or Communism—which are symptoms rather than causes of their ailment—but an inbred conservatism that makes all change an anguishing process.

It is essential, however, to realize clearly that much of the pious talk about 'co-operation', 'common national objectives', and 'co-partnership' derives from an unrealistic kind of Erehwon thinking. If a trade union leader were to take too literally the advice that he should always put some supposed 'common national objective' above the interests of his members, he would not be separated by too great a distance from the Soviet union official who says that the State stands for the good of all its citizens, and that therefore no one need resist the manager of the State factory.

Any useful critique of free trade unions must be made against the background of an understanding that their ultimate responsibility is to their members, not to the State. The T.U.C. may figure in the public eye almost as a separate estate of the Realm, but it is worth remembering that unions are no more part of the State apparatus than is the Athenaeum or I.C.I. Whatever its pretensions, each of these is owned by shareholders or members, and exists to further their interests. This article is written on the assumption that genuine conflicts of interest exist between industry and its workers, and that a trade union's principal task is to act as advocate and defender of one of those interests.

This prelude is necessary, because it seems to me that trade unions in Britain have never had their proper place in popular —or perhaps one should say in popular middle-class—esteem. They have moved in the public imagination at one bound from being the under-dogs to being the tyrants. Their true role is neither of these, and until that role is understood and acknowledged, criticism only drives the unions back into the blind conservatism which now, unfortunately, seems part of their nature.

IF ONE HAD to nominate a single reason for this conservatism, it would be the fierce fight which unions had to make for recognition, and which some, in whole industries or individual companies, still have to make. Doctrinaire *laissez-faire* ideas have lasted a long time in British industry. A surprising number of people in influential positions still regard trade unions as an unwarranted interference with 'a man's right to run his business' and to employ his workers on the conditions that he thinks proper. This view is not often preached in the market place nowadays, but it is deeply held, and the message sometimes comes across to union officials. The knowledge that an employer, if he had the chance, would revert to the nineteenth-century practice of keeping the union organizer outside his gates is not conducive to a spirit of sweet reasonableness.

THE ATTITUDE OF FORD OF ENGLAND is an example worth considering. When the company established itself at Dagenham, it was bitterly anti-trade union, and it was not until after the war that recognition of the unions was forced on it. By that time, not only had a mood of antagonism and rancour settled firmly on the bleak Essex marshes where the factory lies, but the rudimentary union organization bore the seeds of the present chaos. Why do Ford have twenty-two unions operating in their works while Vauxhall have two? Principally, because

trade unionism at Dagenham began as an underground movement, and each union's organizers grabbed as many members
as they could in the hostile circumstances, without any regard
for the eventual shape of factory organization. Having fought
their way in against such odds, no union is now prepared to
withdraw from Dagenham voluntarily and so make way for
the sensible reorganization on the trade union side of the
National Joint Council that is so patently needed. No one is
even prepared to forgo his union's 'democratic right' to be
represented at all talks on the wages and conditions of its
workers. As a result, it is quite impossible to find a body to
negotiate with that is not hopelessly unwieldy and quite incapable of undertaking the radical reform in labour relations
that is needed.

The reaction of most sensible people when they hear a story
like this is to say that history should be forgotten, and that the
trade unions at Dagenham should bring themselves up to date.
But unfortunately the traditions of the past linger on into the
present on both sides. It came as a shock to some of us when a
company of the size and standing of Ford made an agreement
for its new factory at Halewood, near Liverpool, which was in
clear breach of its national agreement with the unions. The
company tried to give two unions exclusive negotiating rights
at Halewood in return for accepting wage rates which were
lower than those laid down in the Ford national agreement—
which says specifically that the wage rates negotiated under it
are to apply to *all* Ford plants in the United Kingdom.

That irregular agreement had to be abandoned, and a good
team of personnel officers on the Ford staff at Halewood is now
working to repair the initial damage done by the folly of those
who thought they had found a short-cut to labour peace. The
kind of thinking that lies behind this agreement explains, even
if it does not justify, the follies of Dagenham. Trade union
leadership there has been lamentably weak, to the point of non-
existence. Even after the Cameron inquiry a few years ago had
confirmed that the shop-stewards were completely out of control, no effort was made by the headquarters of the unions to
provide effective official leadership. The general secretaries of
the unions which have the largest membership at Dagenham

know that the union structure there is ruinously wasteful and unworkable, but they can see no hope of reforming it root and branch. So they have adopted a policy of hopeless and uninspired inaction. But it is worth remembering, when one has acknowledged all the ineptitude, even cowardice, of union leadership, and all the assiduous attention which the South Essex district of the Communist Party gives to this important industrial enterprise, that the original responsibility for the atmosphere in which Dagenham drags itself, slowly, wearily along, rests on the management.

THE FORD EXAMPLE is interesting, because it illustrates how bad traditions have developed in the unions. It was serious enough that most unions grew up in the nineteenth century against a background of hostility among employers and the community at large. It is worse that this atmosphere of hostility should be perpetuated in some parts of industry—shipbuilding is another example—today. The only effect this can have is to ingrain deeper the worst ways of thinking among trade unionists. As Bunyan's Pilgrim bent beneath his burden of sin, the British trade union movement is weighed down by a huge burden of tradition. This is to be found in its constitutions, its rules, its practices, in the jargon of its conferences and the hearts of many of its older members. It reflects nineteenth-century attitudes which may have been suitable for nineteenth-century conditions, but which are robbing trade union members today of the better life they could have.

WHAT IS MOST disturbing, of course, is the way in which resistance to change has built up during the post-war period of full employment, but again, it is not difficult to see the reasons for this. The unions have seen their members get improvements in wages and working conditions which would have been unthinkable in the lean years before the war. To ask the union leaders to undertake a major reform of their institutions now is like asking the English cricket captain to change his team after winning the Ashes. The time when the unions might have been amenable to outside advice that they should change was when they were doing badly. Needless to say, they could be doing much better now—and so, incidentally, could everyone else. Many union leaders who cut their teeth in the 'twenties and 'thirties have a deep feeling of separateness from society. In their most impressionable years in public life they saw widespread indifference towards the unemployment of millions of workmen. No one was offering advice on the reform of trade unionism then. It is a tragedy, but not altogether surprising, that they now fear the Greeks bearing gifts (and the Greeks are everyone outside the unions).

Yet the changes *must* be made if British industry and society are not to dig themselves so deep into their rut of inefficiency and quarrelsomeness that the country will meet the economic disaster that it has been promised for a long time. The difficulty is to know where to begin. Mr. George Woodcock, the general secretary of the T.U.C., has chosen to seek a definition of 'the objectives of modern trade unionism', in the hope that this will convince the unions of the need for internal reorganizations, to achieve these objectives. His initial task of convincing his own General Council is formidable enough. But it would be naïve to think that once this has been accomplished, everything else will flow smoothly on.

To CORRECT THIS ERRONEOUS impression, it is worth looking at the working of a single union in some detail. More than 180 unions are affiliated to the T.U.C., with a bewildering variety of traditions, shapes, sizes, constitutions, rules, electoral practices. All have to be catered for. The battle for change in each of the member unions would have to be conducted in a different way. When one adds to the confusion of structure the incalculable element of human personality, it is possible to see what a formidable task Mr. Woodcock has set himself. The leaders of individual unions, however good their intentions, have a frightening task too.

The Amalgamated Engineering Union is now the second largest in Britain. It has 1,063,694 members, and caters not only for skilled and semi-skilled workers in all kinds of engineering, motor manufacture, and shipbuilding, but also for maintenance men in most of the industries in the country. The A.E.U. has the constitution and rules of a nineteenth-century craft union, and is now doing the job of both a craft and general workers' union against a pattern of industry which is as different as can possibly be imagined from that in which it began.

The day-to-day business of the union is conducted by a president, a general secretary, and an executive council of seven members. The president and general secretary are elected by the votes of all members of the union. This, at least, is the theory. In practice, Sir William Carron, the president, did very well in the last election he fought to persuade 8 per cent of the members that the contest was important enough for them to vote either for him or his Communist opponent. Each member of the Executive Council represents an area of the country, and their ballots often show an even lower level of voting.

With this electoral apathy, the A.E.U.'s leadership may not be what the purist would call 'representative'. But on the whole it appears to reflect well, in its basic attitude, the views of the inactive mass of the members whose only participation in the union is the payment of their dues. At present, Sir William Carron has general support for his moderate policies from the general secretary and five of the seven members of the Executive Council. Of the two others, one—Mr. Claude Berridge—is a Communist, and the other, Mr. Hugh Scanlon, who was elected only recently, has long been an opponent of the leadership.

Each of the executive members, including the president and general secretary, is elected for an initial period of three years, and he subsequently must seek re-election every five years. The result is that a man who may have achieved a position of some eminence in the Labour movement, and whose way of life, together with that of his wife, has inevitably become middle class, faces right until his retirement at sixty-five the possibility that he will be swept from office. The cases in which men in their late fifties have had to pick up again the skills that they have not used for many years must have deterred many others from seeking office in the A.E.U.

BECAUSE OF THIS SYSTEM, and because of the perpetual Right-Left struggle in which the union is gripped, the leadership is oddly preoccupied. One member or other of the ruling group is always either just undergoing an election or within a year of an election on one side or the other. A tendency to trimming is therefore nearly always present. It was in evidence, for example, at the meeting of the National Committee this May, when the executive could not even unite in saying a hard word about bad shop-stewards. Executive members talk of the period when they are 'at ballot'—and it lasts for months—rather as a pregnant woman does of the last few months before her delivery: it is not a time for violent movement. However, at least the executive members are directly elected by those members who take the trouble to use their votes.[1]

By the very system of unnatural selection, the members of the National Committee are the keenest of the keen, and in the context of the A.E.U. this often means of extreme Left-wing opinions. The Committee usually contains about a dozen acknowledged Communists and a varying number of fellow-travellers. Add to this the fact that several of the Right-wing members are what the indulgent would call 'eccentric' (and the rest of us would regard as cranks) and the unenviable lot of the union's leadership may be seen. The results of having a Right-wing executive and a National Committee which takes occasional sweeps to the Left are even odder. The country witnessed with astonishment the performance of the A.E.U. during the Labour Party's defence controversy, when it simultaneously voted both ways. This was one of the attempts made by the executive to ignore the National Committee without actually breaking the rules. There are similar clashes on industrial policy. For years the A.E.U. leaders have been prevented from

[1] It is when one comes to examine the rest of the constitutional machinery created by the founding fathers and their successors that doubts arise about internal democracy in the A.E.U. The union is based on branches covering geographical areas, not on factories. Branch meetings are normally only attended by people who take a keen interest in the union's affairs, and this, as may be deduced from the size of the polls, is not a high proportion. Each branch elects two representatives to the district committee, which is responsible for supervising the working of local full-time officials and shop-stewards. The district committees in their turn elect two members each to the divisional committee, which supervises the divisional officials. The divisional committees, of which there are 26, each elect two men to serve on the National Committee. This meets annually for two weeks, and it is the nearest thing the A.E.U. has to a national delegate conference. It is a very odd assembly indeed.

making agreements for redundancy payments—because the National Committee had laid down a policy that the A.E.U. would fight all redundancies.

ANOTHER RESULT of the system is interminable delays in taking decisions. It is always difficult to know how far a machine is responsible for this, and how far the individual. The facts are these: During nearly every major dispute, and particularly the many unofficial strikes in which members of the A.E.U. are involved, the industrial correspondents troop down to its headquarters in Peckham on a Tuesday to hear what the executive has decided at its weekly meeting. They frequently find that some odd reason for delaying a decision is given—a report has not arrived from the divisional office; the executive member for that area was away, so the report did not come before the executive; or the procedure is to go 'round the board', and that member's turn was not reached; or there were not enough members in London to make 'a full board'. Meanwhile some huge company or industry grinds to a halt in an unofficial strike.

To the outsider, the way in which the moderate leaders of the A.E.U. deal with this is astonishing. Instead of attempting any kind of constitutional reform, they indulge in catch-as-catch-can wrestling under the ludicrous rules of the present constitution with the wilder elements on the national, divisional, and district committees. The A.E.U. is not so much a union as a perpetual tug-of-war. Employers often say in private that they find it the most difficult union of all to deal with—much worse than the Electrical Trades Union (either under its previous Communist leaders, or under the present executive which is zealous to show itself equal to its opponents in aggressiveness). In the A.E.U., officials at all levels are looking over their shoulders.

To SAY THAT THIS is the price of democracy is too simple. The A.E.U.'s constitution would only provide an adequate form of democracy for an organization in which almost 100 per cent of the members take an active part. It is always exposed to the danger of a *coup d'état* by a determined minority group. At present the only effective resistance to this seems to be a rearguard action by the Executive Council.

Why, then, do the leaders not seek constitutional reform?

The most honest answer is probably that the leaders of the A.E.U. are so overwhelmed by the day-to-day battle with their 'militants' that they can never raise their eyes to anything so ambitious as a campaign to arouse the lethargic mass of their members. Another institution imposed on them by the rulebook is the Final Appeal Court. To this, it seems, any member can appeal about almost anything. Since the election of the eleven members to this court also forms part of the perpetual Right-Left struggle within the union, and since about half of the present membership is opposed to Sir William Carron, his supporters claim that the court on occasion has strayed far beyond its quasi-judicial function. Some of its members are said to conceive of their duty as being not merely the enforcement of the rules, but the correction of the executive when it departs in policy from the paths of virtue (as seen by these members). The executive appears to have ignored the 'judgments' on occasion, and there are frequent rows about this also.

FROM THIS ACCOUNT, it will be seen that the obstacles to modernization are not trivial. Perhaps a Bevin could stump the country and win the right to reform the union. Until now the A.E.U. leaders have preferred the humbler method of trying to get their own supporters elected to national and local offices in the union and to the committees, in the hope that they will not be saddled with too many unpalatable decisions which they have to find a way round. But even this has its complications. A few years ago the Right was doing well in the elections for full-time office, but was left without strong personalities to fight Sir William's battles from the floor of the National Committee. The propaganda effect of Left-wing successes in the Committee, and no doubt, also, disgust at the manœuvres to which this drove the executive, produced recently a crop of election victories for candidates enjoying Communist support.

These problems of a single union seem bad enough, but when one looks at trade union organization on a wider scale, deficiencies, and the difficulty of putting them right, appear even more formidable. Currently, the most striking examples of weakness are the inability of the T.U.C. to participate in the making of an incomes policy, even if the Government could devise one in which the T.U.C. wanted to participate; and the adjacent follies of demarcation disputes and the poaching of members by one union from another. They are symptoms of an underlying rigidity of mind that lies at the root of all the problems.

THE SAD FACT is that the trade union movement, which ought to be the radical enemy of vested interest and privilege, has thrown up its own share of these obstacles to progress.

Individual unions have carved out their little spheres of influence, and bitterly oppose attempts, whether by larger unions, federations, or the T.U.C., to enter them. The visit of the T.U.C. Economic Committee to Sweden last year was, for many, an enlightening if disturbing experience. The Swedish unions are not perfect but many years ago they began to evolve their philosophy of trade union organization and purpose, and in working towards the goal they have not been at all respectful of *amour-propre*.

The direction in which the Swedish experiment on incomes points is the same as that in which all recent reports on inflation from international organizations like O.E.C.D. (the Organization for European Co-operation and Development) also point. It is to a centralization of trade union powers, both within the single union and ultimately in the T.U.C. To anyone who knows the British unions, the chances of centralization on this scale in the foreseeable future seem poor.

Briefly the system is based on a central agreement made by S.A.F. (the employers' confederation) and *Landsorganisationen i Sverige* (the Swedish T.U.C.) about how much wage increase, on average, the national economy can afford. This bargain is reached only after the fullest consultation between economists employed respectively by the Government, the employers' confederation, and the trade unions; and it represents an agreed 'guiding light'—a very different piece of illumination from those with which the British Treasury has tried forcibly, but unsuccessfully, to dazzle the British labour market in the past two years.

The British unions have deliberately kept the T.U.C. weak,

and it is in the wages field that they are particularly jealous of their own powers. Indeed, the relationship between unions is very much one of 'competitive co-existence'. Can one conceive of their allowing the T.U.C. General Council to reach a central bargain, and then bargain separately to provide special increases for industries which have fallen behind or which are particularly short of labour? On past experience, the answer must be 'no'. It can even be argued that in the present state of society, the unions are entitled to use 'leapfrogging' as a tactical weapon. Mr. Cousins' famous dictum—'So long as there is a free-for-all, we are part of the "all" '—is widely accepted in the unions. But the suspicion lingers in one's mind, and in the minds of most intelligent and honest trade union leaders, that even in a more perfect society the unions would still resist change.

MR. WOODCOCK's greatest contribution to trade union thought is a simple but important one: 'Horses jump best when they are put at fences. . . .' During the whole of the wages controversies of the past two years, he has privately been warning the Government that they are failing to put the unions under pressure to examine themselves. It is probably true that the most influential trade union leaders now accept the truism that total increases in personal incomes which exceed the increase in national production are self-defeating. But with a membership which takes singularly little interest in economic theory, even as it affects their daily lives, it is difficult for these leaders to do anything about it while the present national mood persists.

It seems just conceivable now, however, that either this Government or a Labour one will put the unions to the test. The last Budget was unique among those presented since 1951 in that it did not run flagrantly counter to what the unions regard as 'social justice'. The Government has also realized, belatedly, the connection between wage pressures and the imbalance of supply and demand of labour by region and by skill. The measures to promote industrial development in regions of high unemployment, and the training boards for each industry which are foreshadowed in the White Paper on Training, should go some way towards alleviating social injustices, and lessen some of the more unnecessary economic pressures that affect wages.

The economists still have a blind spot on the subject of profits, as far as they affect trade union thinking. The first report of the National Incomes Commission is merely the latest of many documents in which the quantitative insignificance of profits, compared to labour costs, has blinded the authors to the quite different psychological relationship between profits and wages in trade unionist minds. When the T.U.C. eventually comes to produce its own philosophy, it may have great difficulty in deciding whether it is more interested in the size of the cake or in the method of slicing it. Opinion on this at present is very confused, and some of the most powerful men in the T.U.C. are in disagreement about it. In the meantime, any Government which hopes to bring the unions to agreement on an incomes policy will have to regard the 'fair' distribution of the fruits of industry—and how many questions that phrase begs!—as an essential preliminary.

To anyone who thought that this preoccupation with profits only affected the Left-wing of the trade unions, the presidential speech of Sir William Carron at this year's A.E.U. conference must have come as surprise. He made it clear that the most aggravating factor in wage claims was the annoyance of trade unionists with people who get 'vast sums of money' without contributing to economic progress. Some economists work on the assumption that because the consumer extravagances of the rich are economically trivial, they can be ignored. They would do well to note the anger that these produced in even such a sober trade unionist as Sir William, and to remember that industrial relations lean as heavily on psychology as on economics.

BUT WHEN OTHERS have done all the necessary preparation of the soil, will the trade unions be able to produce the crop? One of the most interesting struggles if Labour comes to power will be that for the soul of the unions. If the unions' own Government were to take over the country—for the first time under relatively normal conditions—and if it were to give them the social and economic policies they have craved for so long, then there would be no further opportunity of bilking the question. The men in the unions who claim that they are socialists would then have to stand up and be counted—or, alternatively, admit once and for all that British trade unionism is by its very nature freebooting.

In both examples that I have discussed above, the reformers —Sir William Carron in the A.E.U., Mr. George Woodcock at the T.U.C.—have shied away from too direct an approach to their problems. Each in his different way is a man with vast experience, skilled in the manipulation of committees and in the ways of men. But the outside observer must sometimes wonder if they are not too close to their own difficulties. The tendency in the trade union movement is to accept the vested interests which protect the most outmoded practices and systems of organization as laws of the universe, which must gradually be bent or circumvented by the reformer. To a radical, some attempt at root-and-branch change must always appear more attractive.

In organizations dedicated to the principle of democratic control, this can mean only one thing: the leaders of the individual unions and of the T.U.C. would have to begin the long and weary task of converting the members from *apathy* to *intelligent participation*. There is no substitute in a democracy for an educated electorate. The unions are perhaps beginning to realize this now, but it is a slow awakening. This year, the British Employers' Confederation and the T.U.C. have reached an agreement to promote co-operation in the training of shop-stewards in their duties. Employers will be encouraged to release their men on full pay to attend courses, and in return will be allowed a say in the curricula.

This is something; but when one compares the limited kind of training in the basic functions of a shop-steward to be expected in most of these courses, with trade union education in Sweden, the contrast is frightening. One of the first factors in his success that Mr. Arne Geijer, president of L.O. in Sweden, mentioned to me was the existence in every trade union branch of two, three, or more men or women who 'really understand and accept' what their leaders in Stockholm are trying to do for their benefit when they agree to restraint in wages. The Swedish unions give large numbers of their members courses (often residential ones) in economics and the way in which their labour market system works. Since this education is no doubt based on the assumption that the system is good, it is possible to stigmatize it as 'propaganda'. Certainly this must be the most elaborate effort, outside the Communist countries, to propagate a theory of trade unionism.

Some of the most intelligent of the T.U.C. leaders who went to Sweden to study wage-bargaining at first believed that 'trade union education' lay outside their field. To their credit, they allowed Mr. Geijer to convince them that they were wrong. Some have grasped the theory that to be able to follow right policies, they must have their own enlightened followers at branch level, to whom they will be able to appeal when the going is sticky. British trade unionism is suffering from a dearth of such informed opinion in the branches. A union leader must be painfully aware that beyond the shell of activists—some of whom are badly informed or totally out of sympathy with the policies of their leaders—there lies a vast company of the indifferent and the ignorant. It is because they find the thought of changing this too daunting that reform tends to follow the serpentine rather than the radical route.

APART FROM INCOMES POLICY, and the vast task of internal re-thinking and education that goes with it, the other great current problem of union management flows from the competition between unions.

The T.U.C. has tried to reduce the worst consequences of this through its Bridlington Agreement, which forbids 'poaching' of members. It sometimes seems that the letter rather than the spirit of this Agreement is observed. Certainly when unions operating in the same field are changing their level of contributions, they keep a very careful watch on each other; one must assume that they believe that if they charge more than their rivals, the forces of the market will operate, whatever the Bridlington Agreement may say. This is one of the great handicaps of trade union finance, and it explains why unions often have not enough money to sustain decent educational or research services, or even to pay their officers reasonable salaries.

There was an enlightening and depressing example of trade union conservatism in this field a few months ago. When the unions in the railways industry were contemplating a strike against the Beeching Plan, the engineering unions—which were concerned because they have members in the railway workshops—appeared to speak with two voices simultaneously. While the National Union of Railwaymen (the majority organization in the industry) was advocating a three-day strike, some engineering union leaders appeared to be saying, on the one hand, that there should be no strike, and on the other hand, that if there were a strike, it should last a week at least. This seemed an odd amalgam of moderation and militancy. A persistent reporter found the explanation: some engineering unions are forbidden by their rules to pay strike benefit in stoppages *lasting less than a week*. So when the railways had a one-day strike in the autumn of 1962 (over workshop closures), their members had got no money from their unions, while the N.U.R. men received strike pay. Some leaders, apparently, would have preferred the unions to hold a longer strike than they considered really necessary—and the country, incidentally, to suffer a long strike—instead of tackling the problem at its roots.

THE COMPLEMENTARY ISSUE is 'demarcation'. This probably gets more attention from distant observers of the industrial scene than any other aspect of trade unionism, and again *the ignorance* of the critics has often only served to consolidate the unions in their more foolish ways.

It is important to understand the basis of demarcation before attempting to criticize it. It is significant that some of the madder manifestations of the demarcation-conscious mind have occurred in shipbuilding and construction, two industries where work is still of a casual nature, and where even skilled workers tend to suffer unemployment. In another case, printing, there are more complex reasons, including an unenlightened self-interest which believes in keeping the number of skilled men available down and the level of earnings up by the ruthless control of entry into the trade.

The basic cause of demarcation disputes is insecurity—either a fear of losing a job, or at least a fear that earnings will fall sharply if the work is shared with other groups of workers. Undoubtedly the Government is on the right lines in its belated discovery that the proper approach to many such problems is from the apparently 'wrong end'—to make redundancy less fearsome, and so encourage men and unions to seek the more positive benefits of higher productivity, rather than the negative safeguards of restrictive practices.

But the suspicion remains in one's mind that demarcation is so deeply ingrained in British trade unionism that it will not be rooted out even in the unlikely event of a new Government's industrial millennium. Mr. Ted Hill (general secretary of the Boilermakers' Society) will not even acknowledge that the phrase 'restrictive practice' is a valid one. He has coined some magnificent circumlocutions like 'the traditional practices of our craft' to cover the same ground. The depressing fact is that the 'hole-boring' disputes which reach the headlines in the newspapers are only the top of the iceberg. The real concern should be over *strikes which never take place*—because some board of directors, frightened by a long and expensive quarrel with the unions in another company, funks the decision to install a new machine or adopt a new process. Mr. Hill may not believe in the theory of the deterrent in defence policy, but it is working all too well in British industry—and in the process is causing us to fall far behind our competitors in many important fields.

THE INITIAL responsibility, of course, lies with management, because no board of directors which misses a chance to make a really major improvement in efficiency by the introduction of new methods is fit to hold office. But however enlightened managements became, the problem of archaic union structure would remain. Any experienced observer could write his own blueprint for reform. The best would probably be based on 'industrial unionism', which would allow some sort of permanent relationship to be built up between a single union and a single employers' association; it would have the additional advantage that the continuing quarrels over demarcation could at least be dealt with inside a single union.[1]

[1] How angry one gets with the simple-minded people who think that once the boilermakers and shipwrights are in the same union 'all sorrow and parting will be done away!' This is another product of ignorance, since there have actually been demarcation rows between existing sections of the boilermakers' membership.

It is when one comes to consider how 'industrial unionism' will be achieved that difficulties again arise. The N.U.R. is dedicated to this principle, but it has shown no sign at all of a willingness to hand over its members on the buses (which were once owned by the old railway companies) or those in the railway docks, to the majority unions in passenger or port transport —where, of course, they logically belong. Why should it, when the T.U.C. has been unable so far to bring unions to any coherent philosophy of trade unionism?

THE 'PERSONAL INTEREST' enters into the argument at every level. A delegate at one union conference this year, talking of amalgamation, said that many union officers preferred to be 'admirals on a barge rather than duty officers on a liner'. The gibe is just, but it does not apply only to the general secretaries of unions which are overdue for a take-over bid from a larger and more efficient organization. Minor officials and conference delegates also enjoy the power and the privileges which they have built up over the years. It sometimes takes a keen trade unionist a long time to break into the circus of delegations, conferences, and negotiating sessions, with all the excitement and feeling of influence, not to speak of the opportunities to travel and the novelty of hotel living that go with them. It is only human that a man who stands to lose these perquisites through reform or amalgamation fights as hard to save them as does a company chairman facing occupational extinction in a take-over bid.

'Human', but perverse. The unpleasant truth is that the trade union movement, though the repository of much idealism and old-fashioned decency, also suffers from the human failings of selfishness, lethargy, and simple cowardice. The unions, built up as protectors of the weak in a society which treated them harshly, have found it difficult to adjust themselves to positions of power. It can be argued (and rightly) that the power is nothing like as great or as positive as is often suggested. The unions' selfishness must be seen against the selfishness of a society which refuses to change the environment in which they operate. No union is an island, and we need not expect to see a crusading trade union movement, valiant for change in industry, eager for labour mobility, bursting for new ideas, until British society as a whole has found new and radical economic planning, housing, education, and general social policies.

BUT NONE OF THIS is adequate excuse for the skilled tradesman who can never see any merit in wage increases that are confined to the men on a much lower wage than his own. It is no excuse for men who would rather see work go abroad than relax one of their demarcation rules, or their 'principles' of apprenticeship entry. It is no excuse for cynical declarations of sympathy with old-age pensioners combined with a blind refusal to help bring about price-stability—the pensioners' only hope of a life free from fear. British trade unionism, for all its many virtues, is shot through and through with a selfishness that at its best is myopic, and at its worst wilfully cruel to others.

Perhaps, however, the lethargy is worse than the selfishness, for the former is often a symptom of the sin of despair. I hope no one who has read this article will think that the way of the reformer of trade unionism will be easy. But it has now become fatally common for sensible men at the top of their unions to be so overcome by their internal difficulties that they use the obstinacy of external factors—the Government, employers, international trade, almost everything but the weather—as excuses for inaction.

Behind the lethargy there sometimes lies cowardice. There is a whole book to be written by a psychologist prepared to devote years of study to the unions. A good starting point for him might be a statement from a 'militant' delegate at a union conference recently that shop-stewards would never learn their jobs from 'correspondence courses', but from the 'struggle with the employer on the shop floor'. It may be said that this is only a pale reflection of the speaker's Marxist training, but the truth is that this reverence for 'struggle' goes much deeper in British trade unionism than the Communist Party has ever penetrated. The movement found its character and personality in the great dock, coal, and railway strikes of the late nineteenth and early twentieth centuries. It was hardened by adversity during the Depression. From it has developed a half-understood psychology of trade unionism which, for want of a better description, appears to regard as 'masculine'—and therefore good—unions whose members are engaged, or are likely to be engaged, in 'struggle' with their employers, the Government, or society. It is all a bit like the British Legion.

For this reason, the T.U.C. will almost certainly be dominated by the great manual workers' unions long after they have been outnumbered by the clerks, civil servants, variety artists, scientific workers, and the rest. It is for this reason that only the press uses 'militant' sometimes as a convenient (and legally safer) synonym for Communist, whereas many Right-wing union leaders assure their conferences that they are as 'militant' as the next man. It is for this reason, indeed, that only a handful of honest men will allow themselves to be described as 'Right-wing' at all. The basic principle of union psychology remains: '*Left-wing good, Right-wing bad.*' It is for this reason that union leaders who know better sit silent and afraid to speak out against the misuse of the strike weapon; even when they have to witness the kind of demonstration that Tillett and Bevin, Will Thorne and Annie Besant used for serious purposes, degraded to a caricature, and used to add five minutes to a tea-break or to persecute some religious zealot who refuses to conform.

BRITISH TRADE UNIONISM will never be right until it is given the climate in which to reform itself.

Class hatred or aversion is not the exclusive preserve of the Marxist; and the stupid antagonism of the English middle classes to the decent operation of trade unions, in the present as well as the past, bears a heavy responsibility for their waywardness.

But when all the reservations have been made, the reform of the unions still awaits men so single-minded in purpose, so fervent in their belief in a new society, that they can persuade their unions to help create it.

Islanders (I) . . .

THE WHOLE KINGDOM *is in strange disorder. The men seemed directed by a low sordid interest alone; they seemed mere machines. It was proper to speak to them in the tones of anger, and sometimes it was even necessary to use blows, to excite them to their duty. How different these from the common people of England, whom a blow might induce to return the affront sevenfold. . . .*

The enthusiasm of liberty an Englishman feels is never so strong as when presented by such prospects as these. I must own, in all my indigence, it is one of my comforts (perhaps indeed, it is my only boast), that I am of that happy country.

OLIVER GOLDSMITH

Spain, 1795

OTHER PLACES *attract the eye of a traveller, but Coruna takes his attention by the nose. My head, still giddy from the motion of the ship, is confused by the multiplicity of novel objects . . . the dress of the people . . . the projecting roofs and balconies of the houses . . . the filth of the streets, so strange and so disgusting to an Englishman; but what is most strange, is to hear a language which conveys to me only the melancholy reflection, that I am in a land of strangers.*

ROBERT SOUTHEY

Netherlands, 1815

THE CHURCH BELLS *were very loud, frequent and troublesome—this an-noyance alone would have told us that we were in a Catholic country.*

ROBERT SOUTHEY

Milan, 1818

THE PEOPLE HERE, *though inoffensive enough, seem both in body and soul a miserable race. The men are hardly men; they look like a tribe of stupid and shrivelled slaves, and I do not think that I have seen a gleam of intelligence in the countenance of man since I passed the Alps.*

SHELLEY

France & Italy, 1824

THERE IS A *wonderful keeping in our prejudices; we reason as consistently as absurdly upon the confined notions we have taken up. We put the good, wholesome, hearty, respectable qualities into one heap and call it English, and the bad, unwholesome, frivolous, and contemptible ones into another heap, and call it French; and whatever does not answer to this pretended sample, we reject as spurious and partial evidence. Our coxcomb conceit stands over the different races of mankind, like a smart sergeant of a regiment, and drills them into a pitiful uniformity, we ourselves being picked out as the* élite du corps, *and the rest of the world forming the forlorn hope of humanity. The French have no idea that there is anything in England but roast-beef and plum-pudding, and a number of round, red faces, growing fat and stupid upon such kind of fare; while our traditional notion of the French is that of* soupe-maigre *and wooden shoes, and a set of scare-crow figures corresponding to them. All classes of society and differences of character are by this unfair process consolidated into a sturdy, surly English yeoman on the one side of the Channel, or are boiled down and evaporate into a shivering, chattering* valet-de-chambre, *or miserable half-starved peasant on the other.*

WILLIAM HAZLITT

Syracuse, 1833

IN ENGLAND *we have no idea what a Sicilian flea is.*

JOHN HENRY NEWMAN

Rome, 1840

A GREAT FUSS *about Pope officiating in the Sistine Chapel—Advent Sunday. Got into a crowd, and made myself very uncomfortable for nothing; no music worth hearing, a little mummery with Pope and dirty cardinals. Outside and west façade of St. Peter's certainly very fine: the inside would make a nice ballroom, but is good for nothing else.*

JOHN RUSKIN

Athens, 1844

I SWEAR SOLEMNLY *that I would rather have two hundred a year in Fleet Street, than be King of the Greeks, with Basileus written before my name round their beggarly coin. The shabbiness of this place actually beats Ireland, and that is a strong word.*

W. M. THACKERAY

New York, 1861

SPEAKING OF NEW YORK *as a traveller I have two faults to find with it. In the first place there is nothing to see; and in the second place there is no mode of getting about to see anything.*

ANTHONY TROLLOPE

Turin, 1865

I HAVE MORE *and more come to papa's way of feeling about the Italians. The Piedmontese is the only virile element—he is like a country Frenchman—but he is a small leaven to leaven the whole lump. And the whole lump want backbone, serious energy, and power of honest work to a degree that makes one impatient. I am tempted to take the professors I see in the schools by the collar, and hold them down to their work for five or six hours a day—so angry do I get at their shirking and inefficiency.*

MATTHEW ARNOLD

Italy, 1923

ITALY *is so tender—like cooked macaroni—yards and yards of soft tenderness, ravelled round everything.*

D. H. LAWRENCE

Lausanne, 1927

LORD CURZON *paused at the doorway of his apartment and surveyed it. 'How ghastly!' he sighed. He walked towards the window, pulled aside the yellow cretonne curtain, and gazed across to the lights of Evian. 'How positively ghastly!' he repeated.*

HAROLD NICOLSON

... *Mainlanders (I)*

1592

LONDON *is a very populous city, so that one can scarcely pass along the streets, on account of the throng. They care little for foreigners but scoff and laugh at them. . . . As mentioned before, this kingdom is an island and encompassed on every side by water. Many witches are found there, who frequently do much mischief by means of hail and tempest.*

JACOB RATHGEB

1695

THE CRUELTY *of the English is not that they do the things themselves but that they allow them to be done.*

DE MURALT

1726

ENGLAND IS *a country where men think freely and nobly, without the restraint of any servile fear. If I followed my inclination, I would settle here with the sole idea of learning how to think.*

I must confess that one of the things I very much wonder at is that they should never have once thought to imitate Louis XIV in his munificence with regard to the arts and sciences...

VOLTAIRE

1763

THE FOREIGNERS *arriving on English soil must be resigned to face unpleasantness. The customs' examination was meticulous, annoying, indiscreet and even impertinent.*

The Englishman, fortified by the rights which the law confers upon him, and only allowing himself to do what the laws do not forbid, is brusque, inexorable, and rude.

CASANOVA

1782

IT IS NOT AT ALL *uncommon to see in Parliament a member lying stretched out on one of the benches, while others are debating. Some crack nuts, others eat oranges, or whatever else is in season. There is no end to their going in and out; and as often as any one wishes to go out, he places himself before the Speaker, and makes him his bow, as if, like a schoolboy, he asked his tutor's permission.*

PASTOR MORITZ

1787

ENGLAND *is the country where, on the one hand the rights of the individual are most carefully safeguarded, and on the other class distinctions are most respected. . . .*

BENJAMIN CONSTANT

1791

AN ENGLISHMAN *will, during the severest weather, rather shiver at the side of a chimney, which consumes a deal of coals, produces clouds of ashes, and blackens the room, than make use of the better sort of stoves, or ovens, which we use in our country: for his ancestors styled a fire a sort of company; they spoiled their eyes by looking thoughtfully at it; and he must do the same.*

FREDERICK WENDEBORN

I LOATHE *this country. Invitations without cordiality, curiosity without interest, enormous receptions but no conversation, and what I find more painful than boredom is that people of all parties are equally hostile to us and France. All this makes my stay here unendurable.* . . .

BENJAMIN CONSTANT

SEND A *philosopher to London, but not a poet. Send a philosopher here and place him at a corner of Cheapside; he will learn here more than from all the books of the last Leipzig Fair.* . . .

But do not send a poet to London. The bleak seriousness of everything, the colossal uniformity, the machine-like movement, the peevishness of even joy—this over-driven London oppresses the fancy and tears the heart.

HEINRICH HEINE

I ONCE *went to Manchester with a bourgeois, and spoke to him of the bad, unwholesome method of building, the frightful condition of the working-people's quarters, and asserted that I had never seen so ill-built a city. The man listened quietly to the end, and said at the corner where we parted: 'And yet there is a great deal of money made here; good morning, sir.'*

FRIEDRICH ENGELS

ANYONE *who knows how to live alone, has nothing to fear from the dullness of London. The life here, like the air, is bad for the weak, for the frail, for those who seek support outside themselves, who look for kindness, sympathy, attention; the moral lungs must here be as strong as the physical, which have to rid themselves of the sulphuric acid in the smoky fog. The masses are saved by the struggle for daily bread, the commercial classes by their tireless quest for riches and all by the anxious fuss of business; but highly strung, romantic temperaments, fond of companionship, of intellectual sloth, and emotional idleness are here bored to death and fall into despair.* . . .

I read the newspapers, stare in taverns at the unknown race and stand on the bridges across the Thames.

You sit and you look and it grows quieter and more peaceful in your heart. And so through all this I came to love this dreadful ant-heap.

ALEXANDER HERZEN

SUNDAY IN LONDON *in the rain; the shops are shut, the streets almost deserted; the aspect is that of an immense and well-ordered cemetery. The few passers-by under their umbrellas, in the desert of squares and streets, have the look of uneasy spirits who have risen from their graves; it is appalling.*

TAINE

—continued on page 180

PART II

Island and Mainland

I AM very ready to excuse the roughness of a people who live in so fine a country, who cultivate a soil that yields them plenty of all necessaries for human life, who besides all these conveniences find themselves surrounded by the sea, which is a fence to secure them from other nations. . . . 'Tis a natural enough thing for people who have so good a share, to despise all the rest of mankind.

SAMUEL SORBIERE
(*Voyage to England*, 1663)

I REMEMBER being much amused last year, when landing at Calais, at the answer made by an old traveller to a novice who was making his first voyage. 'What a dreadful smell!' said the uninitiated stranger, enveloping his nose in his pocket handkerchief. 'It is the smell of the continent, sir,' replied the man of experience. And so it was.

MRS. FRANCES TROLLOPE (1835)

Commonwealth, Common Market, Common Sense

Hugh Seton-Watson

THE PROSPECTS for international politics in 1963 are more obscure than they have been in any year since the end of World War II. Both the Atlantic Alliance and the Soviet Bloc are weakened by schism. The passions of African nationalism are growing fiercer as independence moves southwards. The Caribbean and the Himalayas remain danger zones. Economists talk darkly of approaching slumps. The prospects for Britain within this uncertain world are particularly bleak. Humiliation at Nassau was followed by exclusion from Europe. Both white and black nationalists in Southern Rhodesia utter dire threats if their mutually irreconcilable demands are not met. It seems indeed certain that Britain will incur the contempt of the former and the enmity of the latter. It is some consolation to find that there are nations, notably Italy and Japan, which still think the friendship of Britain worth seeking. But in the world as a whole British influence does not stand high. The probability of a change of government within a year does not make things easier.

This is surely a time for thinking about our position in the world, how we got where we are, and how we can get out of it. Anyone who writes on these subjects from outside the government machine must be aware that he lacks up-to-date detailed information, and—still more important—that he lacks the experience possessed by the senior officials who conduct policy, of years spent in taking (or refraining from taking) practical decisions. Yet the outsider's view has its importance, for good or ill. Public opinion influences vote-dependent politicians, and through them the officials who carry out their orders. Public opinion is largely formed by the ideas, prejudices, and illusions of outside writers.

In 1945 Britain was both a world Power and a Great Power. Huge forces under arms, on land, at sea, and in the air, held not only the whole British Empire but also large territories of enemy Powers. An important additional factor in Britain's real strength at that time was the prestige derived from its war record. Britain was the only nation that remained at war from September, 1939, to August, 1945. British refusal to surrender, between the fall of France and the American landing in North Africa, deprived Hitler of victory. This remains true, although it is equally true that Russian sacrifices were greater than British, and that the Russian army made a greater contribution to the final Allied victory than the British. Without British resistance, Hitler would have crushed Russia, and nobody can say what would have happened in and to America. In this sense Britain was the main victor of the war. This the Allies knew in 1945, even though the Russians never admitted it.

Morally and materially Britain in 1945 was a Great Power: in 1963 she is neither. Soon after 1945 British military strength was demobilized. In the nuclear and missile age which has followed, it has become clear that only Powers with gigantic economic resources can remain in the top class, and there are only two of these in the world today. It is true that Britain and France can have some nuclear weapons today, and it may be that Egypt or Ecuador can have some tomorrow. But to maintain all the expenses of weapons research and development, to explore all the avenues of the missile age and to meet all the new types of threat which arise, is more than any but the two monster Powers can face. It will be a long time before China can enter this class. An integrated Western Europe of 300,000,000 skilled persons could compete, and Britain might have competed if she had kept her empire. But there is no integrated Western Europe, and the British Empire has disappeared.

Britain gave up her empire because the British political élite had ceased to believe that it could or should be maintained.

Indian independence was a proud triumph of the British radical tradition, in which liberals and socialists had played their part. This was what the British Left had fought for, at least since the beginning of the twentieth century. As for the opposite tradition, imperial paternalism, its spokesmen were forced to admit that its time was passing. It could not be denied that British political principles, which the British had brought to India, required that power must be handed to the Indian people when its political feelings had found effective expression, nor that in 1947 popular demand for independence was real. Two great facts obliged the British rulers of India to abdicate, even though they vainly sought a slower pace in order to save their subjects from massacre: (1) the political ferment in India, which was bound in time to affect Britain's most prized creation, the Indian army, and (2) the massive indifference of the vast majority of the British public, who wanted to settle down to peace and a higher standard of living in Britain and could not care less what happened to an empire created by and for 'them'. Those who cared, the *frères ennemis* who passionately pursued their contradictory aims—to give India her freedom, as the radicals saw it, to protect the people of India from the party demagogues, as it appeared to the paternalists—were a minority. The bitterness of Attlee's victory is that it was made possible by the support of voters who cared little for his ideals.

But the radicals and the paternalists, though numerically a small minority, included most of the political class in Britain. Their emotions mattered, their frayed nerves needed comfort. This was provided by the myth of the Commonwealth.

COMMONWEALTH was the word which came into general use between the world wars to describe the association between Britain and the old Dominions—Canada, Australia, New Zealand, and South Africa.[1] These four countries were independent, yet were associated with Britain by ties closer than

[1] No better name than 'old Dominions' can be found to describe them. One is inclined to think of them as 'Anglo-Saxon', until one remembers the French Canadians and Afrikaners; or as nations of 'European stock', until one remembers the varied races of South Africa, not to mention the Maoris, Red Indians, and Australian aborigines.

those between the most friendly foreign countries. In the case of the Australians, New Zealanders, and the majority of Canadians there was personal kinship, affecting hundreds of thousands separated by the oceans, and a far-reaching similarity of political and cultural outlook. These bonds remained strong in spite of the development of very different societies in very different physical environments. In the case of South Africa, the same considerations applied to a minority of the European population, while the magic of the names of Botha and Smuts for long persuaded many in both countries that the imponderable factors of Commonwealth fraternity extended to some extent even to the vanquished of the Boer War.

The old Commonwealth was a reality, even if there clung to it at times distasteful fumes of after-dinner rhetoric. In 1947 it was decided to extend the concept of Commonwealth to include India and Pakistan, and later still the various other new States that emerged from the disappearing empire. The Commonwealth formula indeed played an important part in the solution of Mountbatten's problems in 1947. Everybody was delighted by the extension of the Commonwealth idea. Indians and Pakistanis found themselves treated as friends. In Britain, the imperial paternalists could feel that much of what was best in the imperial tradition had been saved, indeed that at some rarefied spiritual level the old empire was still in existence; while the radicals, proud of their democratic achievement, could feel that the empire had been replaced by an association of morally elevated and like-minded nations. As the leading nation in this unique family, Britain remained, it was felt by Right and Left alike, a Great Power of a unique type. As such, they argued, she remained only a short distance behind the two monster Powers. As a nation with world-wide interests, she remained far above any European nation, and so her leaders—not always politely—rebuffed the appeal from Europeans that they should play a leading part in the creation of a new Western Europe. Many British politicians felt that West European politicians had a parochial view of the world as a whole, and failed to notice that they themselves had a parochial view of the continent of Europe. The fact that the leading figures of the new Europe were Catholic conservatives did not endear them to the post-war Labour Party.[1]

AS THE YEARS PASSED, the Commonwealth idea became more mythical, but it did not lose its appeal. From the Korean War onwards, Indian foreign policy diverged sharply from British, while the unsolved Kashmir problem ensured continuing hostility between two Commonwealth members. However, relations between British and Indians remained agreeable, and the moralizing rhetoric of Nehru (the outstanding exponent in mid-twentieth century of the English Victorian-governess tradition) awoke frequent echoes in British hearts. The first African recruit to the Commonwealth, Ghana, also aroused high hopes. But its foreign policy soon diverged no less from British than had Indian. Though a small State, Ghana became an important political factor, as the centre of a Pan-African policy which was increasingly adopted by the new nationalist movements in other parts of the continent, and which saw in the European communities of Kenya, the Rhodesias, and South Africa its chief enemies. In 1961 the Asian and African members of the Commonwealth were able to ensure that conditions were put to South Africa for entry into the Commonwealth in its new status as a Republic, which it was bound to refuse.

THE COMMONWEALTH idea played a valuable part in smoothing for the political class in Britain the painful period of the

---

[1] In May, 1950, the French Foreign Minister, Robert Schuman, put forward his Plan for a coal and steel community, and invited the British Government to take part. It refused.

In 1954, when the European Defence Community was running into difficulties in France, it was hoped that Britain might save it by joining, thereby removing the fear held by many Frenchmen that the E.D.C. would be dominated by the Germans. The British Government made no move, and E.D.C. was rejected by the French Chamber.

It is true that the British Government then took the lead in providing a solution for the problem of German rearmament through the West European Union. But when the next step towards European unity was taken, in the economic field, at the Messina Conference in June, 1955, the British, once more invited, once more refused. In 1957, after the Six had signed the Treaty of Rome, negotiations began with the British about a Free Trade Area, but these broke down owing to French opposition in November, 1958.

dissolution of empire. The claim that the manner of the ending of the British Empire has been more elegant than that of other modern empires may or may not be justified. It certainly imposed less immediate suffering on the people of Britain. Half a million people perished when Hindus, Moslems, and Sikhs massacred each other, but there were no British casualties. Most victims of Mau Mau were other Africans, of EOKA Greeks or Turks, of the Malayan guerrillas Chinese or Malay. If there is a blood-bath in Kenya or Southern Rhodesia, the white victims will be the local settlers. The British have suffered little, but this has not prevented them from showering advice and abuse on those they left behind, especially on those of their own stock. When the legions were withdrawn from the British Isles to Rome, it is not recorded that Roman politicians denounced as reactionaries the remaining Anglo-Romans for not handing over political power to the Welsh or to the Saxon invaders.

In the other empires that have fallen in the twentieth century, the metropolitan nations suffered more. The Ottoman Turks, whose empire lasted twice as long as the British Raj in India,[1] fought many savage wars against their rebellious Balkan subjects. The Habsburg Monarchy collapsed after defeat in a war waged partly against the kinsmen of some of its disaffected subjects, but in which few of the latter took up arms against it.[2] The hatreds aroused by the conflicting nationalist passions of the Monarchy's last days grew fiercer under the Successor States and exploded in the age of Hitler. Bohemian and Styrian Germans became Nazis, and proved themselves by massacring Czechs and Slovenes, while Hungarians massacred Serbs, and Croats and Serbs and Moslems massacred each other. The dissolution of the French Empire cost thousands of French lives, even if Vietnamese and Moslem Algerians suffered still more.

[1] The Ottoman Empire in Europe lasted approximately from 1389 to 1913, the British Raj from 1757 to 1947. The rule of the Habsburgs, outside Austria proper and Bohemia, lasted a little longer than the British Raj—approximately from 1699 to 1918.

[2] The total number of Czech, South Slav, and Roumanian volunteers, deserting from the Austrian army in the first World War, amounted to some tens of thousands.

SUCH HORRORS were spared the British, but not their former colonial subjects. And the end is not yet. It would be rash to prophesy that Nigeria will not have suffered the horrors of Balkan nationalist strife before as many years have passed as separated the fall of the Monarchy from the defeat of the Third Reich. On the contrary, the African nations have been quick off the mark when it comes to the creation of dictatorships and the picking of frontier quarrels with neighbours.

But at least, it may be objected, our former subjects hold us in affection because we let them go so graciously? Surely in this at least we have done better than other empires?

It may be so, but it is too soon to be sure. Kindness does not always win love, nor harshness hatred. Austria produced a large proportion of the most bestial Nazis, yet there is little hatred of Austria among the people of Eastern Europe. Neither the continued popularity of Frenchmen as individuals in North Africa and Indo-China nor the unpopularity of Dutchmen in Indonesia seems closely related to the actual record of their governments. Certainly British people enjoy friendship and respect in many parts of Asia and Africa. But excessive desire to please, willingness to admit that Africans (or Asians) are always right, seems, at least in personal relationships, to create contempt rather than affection.

It would perhaps be prudent to conclude that, though the British record both of empire and of de-colonization gives ground for pride, it is premature to assume the existence of some esoteric Commonwealth virtue that guarantees a moral superiority of the British over other empires. The end of empire is essentially a similar process wherever it occurs. The predicament of an ex-imperial nation is always painful, and we might endure ours with more dignity if we would show a little more understanding and compassion for our predecessors and our contemporaries in this experience.

THE COMMONWEALTH in 1963 is a network of personal and institutional relationships which defies any simple description. Thousands of families are united by ties of affection, some of which go back for several generations. Hundreds of business firms, large and small, are accustomed to work with each other in different parts of the Commonwealth. Then there are the links between universities, and the uniform qualifications in the professions. There is a similar vocabulary in politics, at least at the highest level, and a similarity of bureaucratic structure. As Mr. Patrick Gordon-Walker showed in his recent book, in the new States of the Commonwealth there are 'opposite numbers' to most British institutions and officials.

All these things are of value, and they both should and can be maintained. They are of course far more marked in the three remaining old Dominions than in the new States. These three are also bound to Britain by military alliances; their foreign policies are nowhere in serious conflict with that of Britain (even if there are inevitable disagreements from time to time); and they are governed on democratic principles which derive from the same sources as our own. This is not true of the new States. Ghana has a dictatorship of the modern one-party demagogic type which is well on its way towards full-blooded totalitarianism. In Nigeria freedom is clearly in danger.[1] Pakistan has a military dictatorship. Whatever happens in Southern Rhodesia, it is unlikely to be democracy.

In foreign policy, too, there is no unity. Pakistan belongs to the C.E.N.T.O. and S.E.A.T.O. treaty systems, though its devotion has been visibly diminishing since the outbreak of the Indian-Chinese conflict. Malaya has a treaty with Britain. The other new States prefer 'non-alignment', a rather pompous phrase for the obvious and natural policy of the pursuit of their own national interests in their own part of the world. In the case of India, this policy was for many years accompanied by a steady

[1] One of the most melancholy aspects of the Commonwealth relationship was revealed by the case of Chief Enahoro. This leading Nigerian was, under existing law, deprived of the right of political asylum to which he would have been entitled if he had been a citizen of any foreign country, because he is a citizen of a State member of the Commonwealth. Here the Commonwealth seems to resemble nothing so much as Mr. Khrushchev's *sozdruzhestvo*, or commonwealth of 'socialist nations', which of course deny political asylum to persons who have offended against the political principles of a fellow-member. The British Government has made things still worse by dragging in the irrelevant question of the quality of justice in the Nigerian law-courts —which there is no reason at all to doubt. It has thus succeeded in antago-nizing all those concerned, depriving Chief Enahoro of his liberty, and insulting Nigerian public opinion.

flow of self-righteous moralization from Nehru, and the adoption, in words though not usually in deeds, of a double standard which favoured the Communist Powers at the expense of the West. In Africa, 'non-alignment' is in some though not all cases accompanied by an active policy of Pan-African expansion.

THE CHAMPIONS of the 'Commonwealth ideology' in Britain have all too often failed to distinguish between polite relationships and political reality. This mistake the French have avoided. Though French policy in Indo-China and Algeria took a tragic course, in tropical Africa the French were at least as successful as the British at peaceful de-colonization. In West and Central Africa the French enjoy essentially the same type of goodwill and the same complex of personal and business relationship as the British in the new States of the Commonwealth. But the French, while not underestimating the political value of this goodwill and these relationships, have not deluded themselves that they provide the basis for the security of France. This security they have sought in their own immediate neighbourhood, in Europe.

Was it reasonable for British politicians in 1947 to think that Britain, as the centre of the Commonwealth, could remain a world Power, only a little behind the two giants? As the years went by, with the development of military technology and the revelation of the political disunity and fragility of the Commonwealth, it might have been expected that British governments would have reconsidered the basis of policy, and would have paid more attention to Europe. This did not happen. Labour leaders distrusted European leaders who were not socialists. Conservative governments lacked this particular prejudice, but they showed no more general understanding. Eden clung to the illusion that Britain could still play a leading part in the Middle East, and this led him to the Port Said fiasco of 1956. While the European Economic Community was being formed in the late 1950s the British attitude was indifferent or hostile. For this, and for a long list of earlier grievances, General de Gaulle took his revenge at the beginning of this year.

BRITAIN in 1963 is *not* the centre of a great empire, or of a great world-wide community of high-minded nations of all colours looking to her for moral leadership. To eyes unclouded by the haze of after-dinner rhetoric, the shape of Britain appears quite clear, in more modest dimensions. Britain is an island inhabited by 50,000,000 highly skilled and potentially efficient people—a powerful compact State but not a monster Power. It also has three further characteristics which distinguish it from other States of similar population and potential strength.

1. It possesses, scattered across the globe, a number of minor colonial possessions, to whose inhabitants it has obligations, and a smaller number of military bases. The bases are questionable assets, and some may be serious liabilities. One wonders, for example, whether the real military advantages, either to Britain or to the whole Atlantic Alliance, from the retention of Aden outweigh the hostile feelings aroused in all Arab nationalists from Iraq to the Maghreb.

2. It has its imponderable relations of kinship and friendship with Canada, Australia, and New Zealand. Despite mutual irritation, which was increased during the negotiations with the Common Market, these are a real and valuable asset. It is a great pity that they have been to some extent devalued by rhetoric about the Commonwealth. Increasingly empty talk about the unity of a wider Commonwealth, held together by nothing more than an agreeable sense of membership of the same club, has diverted attention from the unity of the real Commonwealth of four kindred nations. The argument that this unity must not be stressed because it might offend Asians and Africans is grotesque, and unworthy of a self-respecting people. If the Africans have the right to Pan-African solidarity, have we not the right to solidarity with our kinsmen across the ocean—and with Europe too?

3. The third special characteristic is one noted by Bismarck nearly a hundred years ago—that the people of the British Isles and the United States speak the same language.

This island state, this medium Power with its imponderable links with the old Dominions, must have a policy towards four parts of the world—the United States, Western Europe, the Soviet bloc, and the underdeveloped societies.[1]

Britain is allied to the United States and Western Europe, but more than this, Britain belongs to the community of Anglo-Saxon civilization of which the United States and the three old Dominions are the other members. Britain belongs to Europe, not only in the obvious geographical sense but also because for two thousand years her history has been part of the history of Europe. The security of the island State is based on its links with Western Europe and North America.

The Soviet bloc is the source of danger. It threatens Europe directly, though at present the threat is not very acute. It threatens also other positions, control of which would increase the pressure on Europe, and would open the way to further expansion and further pressure. Persia and Turkey are the most obvious examples.

Finally, the underdeveloped countries[1] are the area of opportunity for the future. Here it is perhaps worth setting out future possibilities in an inverted order of desirability, while recognizing that the desirable and the possible do not always coincide. From the point of view of British interests, the worst that can happen to an underdeveloped society is that it should be conquered by the Soviet army or be taken over by Communists completely subservient to the Soviet Union. More tolerable is that it be ruled by some totalitarian régime, Communist or Nationalist, which is independent of the Soviet bloc. More desirable is some humane and modernizing dictatorship. Best of all is a democratic régime. In the economic field, too, a wide range of situations may occur, reaching from chaos and starvation through varying degrees of inequality and corruption to a

[1] This ungainly phrase is still the least unsatisfactory description that can cover the large number of societies concerned. They are to be found in Asia, Africa, and Latin America. Their inhabitants have white, brown, yellow, black, and red skins. Some have comparatively democratic governments, some almost totalitarian. Some are allied to the West, most are 'non-aligned'. The category should strictly include the Communist countries in Asia, including China. But it will be clear that what is said here is not for the most part applicable to them. On the other hand, it clearly excludes countries, such as Australia, whose *resources* are still less than fully developed but whose *societies* are highly advanced and even sophisticated.

progressive economy offering a decent minimum living standard to all its citizens. The ability of British or other Westerners to influence the economy or the politics of such societies is limited but real.

LET ME BRIEFLY consider in turn these three aspects of Britain's tasks in foreign policy—the opportunity in the under-developed societies, the menace from the Soviet bloc, and the base of security in North America and Western Europe.

Britain may possess a larger number of persons who have experience and understanding of underdeveloped societies, and a larger body of useful knowledge on which even the inexperi-enced can draw, than any other Western country. But the underdeveloped societies are a world problem, and a Western problem, not just a British problem. There is rather widespread British belief that the British do this sort of thing best, a kind of proprietary interest in the underdeveloped, which antagonizes both the receiving nations and the other Western nations. There is also, especially among part of the British Left, a curious sur-vival from the Woodrow Wilsonian era, a belief that small new nations are more virtuous than other nations simply because they are small and new. This belief easily merges with the Victorian-governess complex, the assumption of British moral superiority. We hear a lot about the duty of Britain 'to give a moral lead to the nations of the world'.

In recent years a mirage has appeared of a happy brotherhood of the virtuous British and the virtuous new nations, free from the guilt of militarism and aggressive alliances, teaching peace to the sinful practitioners of power politics. This mirage appeared to be dissolving after the Chinese attack on its most eminent follower. But it would be unwise to assume that the climatic conditions which led to its formation have ceased to exist.

The truth is that Britain can play a great part in helping the underdeveloped societies, and can thereby benefit both their economies and its own, both their internal stability and world peace. But practical tasks are more important than moralizing dreams, and Britain is not the only Western nation that can contribute. The French effort in this field, both before and since de Gaulle, has been bigger than the British.

AGREEMENT WITH the Soviet Union is, of course, as desirable as ever, but the prospects do not seem to be improving very fast in any of the three most important, and inter-related, issues—arms control, the underdeveloped societies, and a European settlement. Discussions about disarmament produce only oceans of useless words. Co-operation between the Soviet Union and the West in aid to the underdeveloped, as a common task in the interests of world peace, is unhappily still no more than a dream. Soviet words and actions—from *Pravda* to the specialized academic journals on Asia and Africa, from diplomacy at the United Nations to subversion in Vietnam—point clearly to Soviet determination to 'support national liberation movements' and 'intensify the class struggle' in all these countries; in short, to exploit every crisis in Asia, Africa, or Latin America for their political warfare against the West. It is true that they lay less stress on violence, and are less inclined to brinkmanship, than the Chinese, who accuse them of cowardice and of ideological error in this field. But between implacable hostility pursued by relatively mild means and co-operation there is a vast distance.

Agreement with the Soviet Union in Europe depends, of course, on some agreed solution of 'the German problem'. Here two ideas are at present being publicly discussed in the West. One is the plan attributed to President de Gaulle, that the Soviet Union should allow Germany to be reunited in freedom in return for the removal of all American forces from Europe. The other is the proposal, favoured by a section of the British Labour Party, that the West should recognize the Soviet zonal régime as an independent German State, in return for guarantees for the security of West Berlin, and that this should perhaps be followed by agreements on de-nuclearized zones in Central Europe. There are arguments for and against these proposals on their merits. Neither seems at all likely to be achieved.

IF THE SOVIET GOVERNMENT would consent to de Gaulle's proposal, this would be a tremendous success for France and Germany, and—it must be admitted—for all Europe. But if one thing has become clear in eighteen years of Soviet policy in

Germany, it is that Moscow is not prepared to abandon the Communist régime in Germany,[1] which is the Soviet blue-print for the whole of Germany, and ultimately for the whole of Western Europe, including Britain. Withdrawal of American forces from Europe would not be so valuable a gain as to induce the Soviet leaders to change their mind. A complete dissolution of N.A.T.O., with a formal repudiation by France and Germany of the American alliance, might be a sufficient price, for in this case it might be argued that the temporary loss of Communist East Germany would soon be compensated by the conquest and Communization of all Western Europe. But even in his wildest moments President de Gaulle is unlikely to abandon all alliance with the United States, and if he so wished, the Germans would certainly not follow him.

The second proposal is also unlikely to succeed, owing to the almost invincible aversion of all Germans—socialists as well as followers of Adenauer and Erhard—to recognition of the D.D.R. as a German State. This is a matter on which individual British or Americans may legitimately hold various opinions. For my part, I admit to sympathy with the German point of view. This colonial régime, created by Russian military power and ruled by a Russian colonial governor, is not a German State. It has far less right to be regarded as a State than had Tshombe's Katanga. There is no comparison with the other East European States. These do at least include almost all members of their nations, and there is no other Czech State but Czechoslovakia, no other Bulgarian State but Bulgaria, and so on.[2] Apart from this, it is difficult to see what guarantee for the

[1] The famous Soviet proposals of 1952 are not an exception. If they are closely examined, it is clear that they never envisaged freedom for the people of East Germany to get rid of the Ulbricht régime. They were designed to bring about a coalition Government, similar to that set up in Czechoslovakia in 1945. The intention was that the Communist base in the eastern zone should be preserved, within a confederal German State.

The only moment when it seems *conceivable* that Moscow did think of abandoning Ulbricht was in the months after Stalin's death when Beria was in the ascendancy. But there is far too little evidence to enable us to assert that such a plan *was* then taken seriously in Moscow. On balance, it still seems improbable.

[2] There are, of course, still large minorities in Eastern Europe (Hungarians in four neighbouring countries, Roumanians in the Soviet Union, etc.). But

security of West Berlin could be given, in return for recognition of Ulbricht's *pashalik*, that would be more—or less—effective than the present state of affairs. In short, it is unlikely that any West German Government would consent to such an agreement, and unlikely that the United States could act against West German wishes. And without United States consent there is nothing that Britain could do. Britain cannot provide any solution to the West Berlin problem independent of her allies, even if some British Government were prepared to ignore its obligations of honour to the people of Berlin. A unilateral British recognition of the Ulbricht régime would be of no value to the Soviet Government, which would not be willing to pay any price for it.

THIS BRINGS us, in conclusion, to the home base, to Britain's relations with North America and Western Europe. Here the first and essential fact is that Britain cannot separate herself from either. An Atlantic Community is desirable for the Americans and Europeans, but vital for the British. General de Gaulle's remarks about *les anglo-saxons* have a core of truth; yet it need not follow from this that Britain would only enter a European community in order to act as an 'American Trojan Horse'. Certainly the views expressed by some British newspapers, and some of the arguments used by Conservative politicians to justify entry into the Common Market, could reasonably be interpreted, even by persons less suspicious than the French President, in this sense. The whole public attitude of Britain since 1945 to efforts for European unity was bound to create resentment beyond the Channel. In fact, it is pleasantly surprising to find that so many Dutchmen, Italians, Germans, and even Frenchmen still do want to have Britain in Europe. Devotion to the Commonwealth myth at the expense of the European and Commonwealth realities, and condescending comparisons of Britain's world-wide obligations with European 'parochialism' inevitably offended many Europeans who in 1945 had been Britain's firm friends. All too often the impression

none of these *irridentas*, not even Transylvania for the Hungarians, are of the same order of magnitude as, for the Germans, the line which cuts their country in two.

was created that the British were using their 'special relation-ship' with America to play off America and Europe against each other instead of bringing them together. This may have been an unjust suspicion. Yet the fact remains that in 1963 we are far from the Atlantic Community which is the only guaran-tee of British security. And it is unwise to put all the blame for this on the Americans or the Europeans.

ATLANTIC COMMUNITY must remain the aim. But Britain is and has always been part of Europe, and cannot live without Europe nor Europe without it. Europe's freedom and Europe's civilization owe as much, at least in the last two thousand years, to England and Scotland and Ireland as to France. The people of these islands, especially the young people who are growing up without any consciousness of empire, have still plenty to con-tribute to Europe. That the British have plenty to learn from Europe is also true.

De Gaulle's refusal decided nothing. The road back from empire still leads to Europe. There are other forces in Europe besides de Gaulle and Adenauer, and it is at least probable that in the next years their political influence will grow. Britain will have other opportunities to enter Europe, and the Europeans will have new chances to build an Atlantic Community.

But before the new time for decision comes, we must hope that the heads of British politicians will be cleared of the hang-over of 'Empire' and the dreams of 'Moral Leadership'.

The Logic of Survival

John Mander

IN AUGUST, 1954, the French Assembly rejected the concept
of a European army. The chief motive for this rejection was
France's lingering dread of any rearmament of Germany, and
her lack of confidence that she could—without British assistance, which seemed unlikely to be forthcoming—hold her own
in a reviving Europe. In November, 1958, on General de
Gaulle's instructions, Britain's negotiations with the European
Economic Community over a free trade area were broken off.
France had decided that Britain's presence was no longer
necessary to her interests in the new Europe.

What had occurred between those two dates? General de
Gaulle, I submit, is only part of the explanation. Despite
Algeria, despite political chaos, the revival of French self-
confidence—and particularly of economic self-confidence—had
begun before de Gaulle's return to power. Between those two
dates, it would seem, French self-confidence had grown as fast
as British confidence had declined. De Gaulle's rejection of us in
November, 1958, was the first of a chain of humiliations: the
failure of Mr. Macmillan's Summit policy; the failure of a
second bid to negotiate with Europe; the Skybolt fiasco and
Nassau. Personally, I believe that Mr. Macmillan's new
approach to Europe was as courageous as his attempt to mediate
between East and West was unfortunate. But all these policies,
whether right or wrong, have met with humiliating ill-success.
These policies were typical of—and rooted in—Britain's
attitudes to the world since 1945. What underlay these attitudes? How did British self-confidence come to be sapped after
the middle 'fifties? Why has Europe, so deeply humiliated

147

between 1939 and 1945, apparently fared better than Britain in the post-war world?

I suggest three main reasons. The first has to do with the differing effect of de-colonialization on Britain and on Europe. It is customary to say that Britain's record is better than that of her neighbours. In one sense, this is indubitably true. Nevertheless, I believe Britain to have suffered more from de-colonialization in the long run than her fellow-colonialists on the Continent. Britain has severed her ties with empire more decorously, but in exchanging the fact of empire for the fantasy of commonwealth she has seriously impaired her sense of reality. Europe's sense of reality on the other hand—sadly diminished during the inter-war period—has been sharpened by the traumatic events of the past generation. Continental Europeans have experienced not only violent loss of empire, but violent conquest by foreign armies, and the prospect of violent revolution within their own frontiers.

AT FIRST SIGHT, these terrible experiences of war and revolution would seem poor soil for the growth of political self-confidence. Indeed, that was the view President Truman took when he launched the Marshall Plan in 1947: Continental Europe seemed virtually on the point of collapse. This was also the view taken by the Labour Government when it held Britain aloof from Europe after 1945. It is clear now that it was a mistaken view, for whose conceit we have paid dearly. But if Europe's slow recovery of self-confidence—given generous American assistance—was predictable, the parallel phenomenon of Britain's slow loss of self-confidence was not. It is the seesaw effect that needs to be explained. Certainly, there were material advantages in being the loser in war (and we should remember that all the countries of the Common Market had been 'defeated Powers' between 1939 and 1945). Factories had to be re-equipped, and once re-equipped, they were often more efficient than the obsolescent plants on which British firms had to rely.

There was a similar law of obsolescence in the psychological and social fields. As British socialists, we used to claim that 1945 had brought about 'a social revolution'. But we ought to admit that Europe's desperate need to re-equip, replenish, and restore a broken economy blew away more cobwebs than Labour's abortive 'social revolution'. Europeans were prepared to put up with worse conditions, to work longer hours, to expect less immediate reward; they did not feel that the world owed them a living. Britain's tragedy was that she had it 'too good'—in 1945, not in 1959. Our role was that of old-man-down-on-his-luck; Europe's role that of young-man-on-the-make. The former role may be more entertaining; the latter is more rewarding, for at least it has beginner's luck. The former presents a loser's face to the world, once things cease to go his way; he puts on a good show, but is not really confident; to redeem his luck, mysteriously lost, he is tempted to gamble. That was the cruel portrait of Britain John Osborne painted in *The Entertainer*.

WAS IT a fair portrait? Had John Bull become Mr. Osborne's Entertainer, whose jokes nobody laughed at, whose advice nobody needed? After Suez, it began to seem plausible. Not since the Boer War had Britain been so publicly humiliated, and made the butt of men with black skins, yellow skins, brown skins, and even white skins. It was a traumatic event. But what was our reaction? Was Suez Britain's moment of truth, the moment when her post-war weakness was brought home to her, compelling a new realism in her outlook? Or did the shock of Suez cause the national organism to contract into its shell, to withdraw from foreign contact, to cultivate its nostalgia and sentimentality? Perhaps we are still too close to the event; certainly the reaction was not a simple one. On the Right, it appears to have been twofold. On the one hand, in the name of realism, conscription was abolished and priority given to Britain's independent deterrent. On the other, the public was encouraged to forget its troubles: 'It's *great* Britain again,' we were told, and 'you've never had it so good'. At the time, the new realism in defence was widely welcomed. Soothing syrup was not quite the tonic for a bruised and bewildered nation. But at least it prevented us from nursing our resentment and brooding over the past.

On the face of it, the reaction of the Left was very different: at a deeper level, very similar. The Sandys White Paper of 1957, which abolished conscription and adopted a policy of massive retaliation, gave rise to the Campaign for Nuclear Disarmament. It was fashionable when the movement began (and it is again fashionable now) to make light of its political significance. I do not agree. The Nuclear Disarmament movement seems to me the most spontaneous, virile, and sincere Britain has seen since the 'thirties—and last Easter's demonstration does not suggest any slackening of enthusiasm. Those who saw only bearded weirdies and political beatniks on the road to Aldermaston missed the point badly. That was the cap of the iceberg. Among the new Left-wing generation after Hungary and Suez it was rare to find firm opponents of C.N.D. The strength of unilateralism was that those who were not for it did not care to speak against it.

It was only when the movement won a majority at Scarborough, and challenged the authority of the Labour leadership, that the late Hugh Gaitskell fought back. Frustrated on the political plane, the Committee of 100 urged the movement into illegal, if non-violent, agitation. It would be a mistake to measure the influence of C.N.D by a party-political yardstick; like the Peace Ballot of the 'thirties, its impact was out of all proportion to its strength. Baldwin, in the 1935 general election, thought it prudent to take into account the popular pacifism of which the Peace Ballot was an expression. I believe Mr. Macmillan acted in much the same way when he went to Moscow.

UNILATERALISM was never easy to pin down, for it was always intellectually ambiguous. The essence of the movement might be described as 'nuclear pacifism': the arguments which traditional 'absolute pacifism' applies to warfare in general were applied to nuclear warfare alone. The intellectual weakness of this position is evident. How is moral pacifism divisible? Where is the line of legitimate destruction to be drawn: at 1,000, at 100,000 at 100,000,000? Absolute pacifism would seem intellectually sounder; and many unilateralists were in fact absolute pacifists. Most people, not themselves pacifists, are careful to say that they 'respect' the pacifist position. I would be more sure of this if I knew what it involved. The argument seems to me valid only so long as the pacifist himself respects his position. An honest pacifist ought to admit that, in refusing to fight against Hitler, he made Hitler's victory more likely. This may sound harsh, but the absolute pacifist has made his decision; he has preferred the voice of his conscience to every other obligation. Does not the logic of this demand an abstention from politics? The absolute pacifist can advocate non-violence for himself. Does he have the moral right to advocate non-violence for his countrymen—knowing, if he is honest, what the consequences must be? Perhaps he has. Personally I respect the pacifist who admits he has not.

And this has some bearing on the matter of nuclear pacifism. It is certainly possible to respect the nuclear pacifist as a private individual. I am less ready to respect him as a political demonstrator shouting 'No war over Berlin' or 'Hands off Cuba'. Here, he is recommending to his fellow-countrymen a policy whose assumptions they do not share, and which he himself does not openly declare. For he has already made his choice: *any* course of events is preferable to the use by his country of nuclear weapons. But this is something with which the majority of his fellow-countrymen almost certainly do not agree. They are not prepared to pull out of Berlin because 'the alternative is nuclear war'. They are acting on assumptions different from the nuclear pacifist.

In practice, both nuclear and absolute pacifists take a weaker line altogether: they argue that the threat is not really there. I confess that in this case I do not find it easy to 'respect' the pacifist position.

Thus, how much of the supposed 'liberalization' of Communism we hear about today reflects just such wishful thinking? In any case, it is clear that the logic of absolute pacifism resembles that of nuclear pacifism. The nuclear pacifist recommends to his fellow-citizens policies based on assumptions which he does not openly disclose. Thus the consistent nuclear pacifist cannot advocate a non-nuclear policy for Britain and yet rely on American nuclear protection; he ought to be prepared to advocate total surrender as preferable to nuclear war. Again, the argument is a harsh one. But the nuclear pacifist, like the absolute pacifist, ought in honesty to admit its logic—even if it implies (as for the absolute pacifist) an abstention from politics. In fact, nuclear pacifists are seldom so consistent, and in evading the argument they are often led to a highly immoral conclusion. They find themselves arguing that Americans may handle weapons which would pollute the hands of mere Britons. The alternative is to abandon—unilaterally, if you will—the moral logic of the argument. Nuclear weapons, then, are not bad in themselves: it is British possession of them that is bad. British control of nuclear weapons is bad, not in any absolute sense, but for practical political reasons. This, of course, is a perfectly reasonable proposition (though not, I happen to believe, a correct one). That Britain should abandon her independent deterrent is now widely accepted. For unilateralists, however, this has two equally undesirable implications. They must give up, on the one hand, the nuclear pacificism which was the moral force of their movement. On the other hand they must accept, as staunch anti-Americans, a greater degree of dependence on the United States than Britain has hitherto known.

No wonder unilateralism has tended to exalt emotion above reason! But to point to its fallacies is not to dismiss C.N.D. politically. It remains, I repeat, by far the most significant new political movement Britain has produced since the war. Even in terms of practical politics it has left a far deeper mark than is usually admitted. Ten, twelve, fifteen years ago, few voices were raised against the manufacture of atomic weapons by Britain. Labour, whose post-war Government had initiated the process, was no less committed than the Conservatives. Today the greater part of public opinion seems to reject the independent deterrent as an expensive and dangerous chimaera. (The Government's own position is ambiguous: Britain's future deterrent is to be both 'fully independent' and 'fully integrated'.) It is a remarkable shift of opinion. True, the technical difficulties were not understood ten years back but would such a *volte-face* have come about without five years of C.N.D. agitation? Is it wrong to assert that the public, alerted to the significance of nuclear war, has taken the same escape-route as C.N.D. itself?

FOR IT IS, surely, an escape. Whether or not Britain owns an independent deterrent, she is a member of an alliance which relies on nuclear weapons. Politically it is far from irrelevant,

I believe, whether Britain does or does not have an independent deterrent; morally it *is* irrelevant. Britain participates in the nuclear equation by being a member of the Western alliance. I do not myself think that the distinction between absolute and nuclear pacifism is valid: it is all or nothing. But one certainly cannot salve one's conscience by relinquishing the burden of guilt and decision to another member of the alliance. There is, of course, one obvious solution: let Britain have no part in such an alliance. And, not surprisingly, from the beginnings of C.N.D. neutralist voices began to be heard. By the 1960 Scarborough Labour Conference, political neutralism was explicit: a country committed to unilateralism could no longer be a member of N.A.T.O. Soon, nuclear disarmers would be demonstrating against the Common Market as a 'Cold War grouping,' and in favour of British neutrality in the Cuban conflict. Here, evidently, a more straightforward escape from the moral dilemma was being attempted. Britain must not only renounce her own nuclear weapons, she must renounce complicity in the balance of power depending on such weapons. A neutral, non-nuclear Britain, it was argued, had nothing to lose but the chains of N.A.T.O. membership. In compensation, the moral leadership of the non-nuclear, non-aligned world would be hers for the taking. Once more, Britain could take up the White Man's Burden.

Up to a point the argument is logical enough. If the moral case against the bomb is accepted, Britain has no alternative but to go neutral (although many 'neutral' states would have nuclear weapons of their own if they could afford them. Britain might be unique in not wanting them. Nor does neutrality necessarily imply a non-nuclear status: the opposite, as the debate in Sweden and Switzerland has shown, might be the case.) Of course, the moral case against the bomb is one thing, the political and strategic arguments against a British deterrent another. The two arguments have become confused in the popular mind: Britain's renunciation of nuclear weapons, instead of being a confession of technical defeat, is presented as a virtuous act. Nuclear capability is to become the exclusive responsibility of the United States. Although certain other factors—resentment at American and European 'usurpation' of Britain's lost world power—have contributed to the neutralist

trend in British public opinion, the 'moral' argument is
emotionally important.

EARLIER, I said that the reactions to Suez on the Left and on
the Right were more similar than surface appearance suggested.
I said also that C.N.D., despite its superficial political weakness,
was really the cap of an iceberg. Let me now combine the two
hypotheses: the post-Suez isolationism of the far Right and of
the far Left were the two caps of the same iceberg. Both types
of isolationism had, after all, a great deal in common. Both
were strongly anti-American—though not for the same reason.
Both were anti-European; the Left because Europe was
'reactionary', the Right because Europe was a rival. Both were
pro-Commonwealth: the Right because of the white dominions,
the Left because of the Commonwealth's neutralist non-white
majority. On some issues, certainly, the two were opposed: the
U.N., the independent deterrent. On other issues, the two were in
unexpected harmony. *Tribune* shared the pro-Russian, anti-
German line of the Beaverbrook press during the Berlin crisis.
(Indeed, they shared the same contributors.) Mr. Michael Foot
and Lord Sandwich adopted the same pro-Commonwealth,
anti-Europe platform during the debate over Britain's entry to
the Common Market. From both extremes of British politics,
demands for British neutrality in the Cold War began to be
heard.

What would a neutral Britain be like? There is more than one
type of neutrality; and the type of neutrality desired by Right
and Left is significantly different. There is a Swedish, an
Austrian, an Indian neutrality. There is a 'strong' and a 'weak'
neutrality. A 'strong' neutrality is willing to defend itself against
all comers; that was America's neutrality until 1917, and again
between 1919 and 1941. Its post-war equivalent was the
troisième force; in a different form, this is now the official policy
of Gaullist France. A 'strong' neutrality requires the strongest
available weapons: it requires the hydrogen bomb. With this
weapon, the smallest nation-state can hope to assert its sovereignty and at the same time observe an armed neutrality in any
conflict that arises. This is the Gaullist conception, and it was
also the conception implicit in much British Right-wing

thinking after Suez. It was not, of course, Khrushchev's threat to bombard Britain with rockets that broke Britain at Suez: it was diplomatic isolation and American political pressure. Even those who disagreed with Suez strongly (as I did), had to recognize that Britain had lost her freedom of action in certain important respects. The independent deterrent was not designed to 'duplicate' American efforts: it was intended to restore Britain's freedom of action. Perhaps the project was technically misconceived, but the decision to build the deterrent was a *political* decision. Indeed, even under the Attlee Government, the independent deterrent contained an anti-American component. If America could be fully trusted, why was a British deterrent necessary? It was this assumption that British and American policy might not always agree which prompted the Attlee Government to go ahead with the bomb. That was not in itself an unreasonable assumption: indeed, the more anti-American you are, the more plausible it must seem. Certainly, Britain showed little sign of 'neutralist' leanings at the time; the desire for independence implied in the decision was 'strong' rather than 'weak'. It was nourished by the suspicion that America might one day pull out of Europe, and Britain have to defend Europe against Communist aggression. Ironically, that is precisely the position of de Gaulle's France today.

IF THE RIGHT was tempted after Suez by the 'strong' neutralism implicit in a British independent deterrent, the Left wore its neutralism with a difference. Britain should contract out of the Cold War and adopt the non-aligned, non-nuclear, neutralist posture of the coloured Commonwealth. The motive was, originally, 'negative'. Only by leaving the Western alliance could Britain ensure her survival.

The original motive was to salve British skins and consciences. But unilateralism soon offered a strong positive inducement for Britain to go neutral: she would thereby shake off the moral opprobrium of alignment with either of the Cold War blocs. With Nehri's India, she would become the leader of the non-aligned world.

In this conception, chauvinism and neutralism were curiously blended. By adding her strength to that of the non-aligned nations, Britain would, it was argued, proportionally weaken the forces making for world war. The lesson the Right learned from Suez was that Britain's aims had been frustrated by the combination of the two nuclear super-powers. The Left saw in the frustration of Britain's Suez adventure a moral victory for 'world opinion'. Suitably strengthened, this same world opinion might be mobilized against other acts of aggression, whether Communist or Western; in the end, the Cold War must be snuffed out for lack of fuel. It was an altruistic conception; indeed, suspiciously so. Behind it lurked a frame of mind not at all dissimilar from that on the Right: here would be a new role for Britain in the world—a role that would enhance her prestige as association with America or with Europe could not. For the anti-European, anti-American Left it was the ideal solution.

CLEARLY, IT IS A CONCEPTION well calculated to appeal to a people with a diminished sense of power and a large reserve of moral idealism. It explains the fact, which puzzles the outsider, that British enthusiasm for the Commonwealth has steadily grown as its actual power has decreased. It explains, in particular, why this enthusiasm is now the property of the Left rather than of the Right, for it is to the Left that the altruistic, internationalist aspect of the Commonwealth appeals. But the chauvinistic aspect is there too: *Tribune* and Beaverbrook now speak of the Commonwealth in the same tone. It is this aspect that is evident to the outsider, as the dispatches of the foreign correspondents in London attest.

TO THE OUTSIDER, it is obvious that the British are constructing a surrogate, a fantasy empire to console for the loss of the real one. In no European country are the ex-colonialists so obsessed with their colonial past. Italians, Frenchmen, Dutchmen do not continually boast of their colonial achievements. Perhaps that is because they have 'less to boast of'—the retort is on the tip of almost every Englishman's tongue. But the retort is unfair. The French have a great deal to their credit: despite the horrors of Vietnam and Algeria, the constructive aspects of France's economic and cultural policies (in Black Africa and elsewhere) have been at least as successful as Britain's, and to-day France gives *more* assistance to underdeveloped nations than Britain. It is argued that Britain's concern with her Empire's successor-states expresses a higher sense of responsibility, and there is some truth in this (though less, as the French example shows, than is often assumed). But the *fact* of Britain's continuing obsession with the theme, in contrast to the rest of Europe, is not open to question.

Both in its extreme neutralist form, and as a general sentiment, the new obsession is significant. It seems to be a product of those 'withdrawal symptoms', that isolationism and that growing alienation from power-politics, that have come to shape public thinking on foreign policy. Of course, to say we exaggerate the Commonwealth's role in world affairs is not to say it has no role at all. Properly limited and defined, the Commonwealth can do some of the things its enthusiasts say it can. It can forge links between distant peoples, bridge distinctions of creed and colour, keep alive traditions of equity and political justice. But these are not political links in the strict sense; the links between the N.A.T.O. nations, for example, are much stronger. An act of war against these islands does not commit India, Australia, or Nigeria to come to our defence. It does commit Holland, Germany, or the United States to do so. The ties between Commonwealth countries are ties of custom, sentiment, and convenience, and they vary in strength from country to country; they are often no stronger than the ties that normally exist between independent states. The line between membership and non-membership is itself vague and arbitrary.

This is not set down in contempt of the Commonwealth. But I submit that all arguments about what Britain might do if she 'led' the Commonwealth rest on a false premiss. The Commonwealth is not that kind of political organization; indeed, it is not a political organization at all. The moment Britain attempted to 'lead' it, her Commonwealth would vanish into thin air.

IF THIS CONCLUSION is correct, it is as damaging to the neutralism of the Left as to the neo-imperialism of the Right. If the opposition of the coloured Commonwealth to neo-imperialist policies can be assumed, wouldn't its unwillingness to accept

Britain as the leader of a non-nuclear, non-aligned club be quite as strong? Britain is still, and will remain for many years, a colonial Power. In Central and Southern Africa, she is approaching the most difficult years of her colonial history—at a moment when the process of de-colonialization is complete in the case of every European Power except Portugal. On the Persian Gulf, Britain has important interests, whose ultimate sanction is armed force. The future of Malaysia is unsettled. Even were Britain to shed all her dependencies, she would remain 'neo-colonialist' in the eyes of Afro-Asians. It is not only the past they remember, for they insist that Britain's interests, like those of France and Germany, are those of an advanced European industrial Power. Nor are they mistaken. The strongest argument against Britain joining a non-nuclear, non-aligned club is that she would be blackballed by its present members.

There is a further difficulty. Britain is said to lack a 'national purpose'. The Left sees a national purpose for Britain in giving the new nations the benefit of her advice and experience, and it is a noble if contradictory aim. It is true that the new nations look to us for guidance. But that means Britain herself must be strong and self-confident; and how can she seek guidance from those who seek it from her?

Few poetic commands have been as fiercely ridiculed as Kipling's 'take up the White Man's Burden'. Today, it takes a different form. As the guilty conscience of white Europe, the White Man's Burden is still with us, and nowhere more so than in Britain. I do not dispute that we should bear this burden; I dispute only that, as former imperialists, we can relieve ourselves of it by creeping into other men's skins.

THE ILLUSIONS OF the Right are more straightforward, and therefore more vulnerable, than those of the Left. It is no accident that, during the Common Market-Commonwealth debates of 1961-2, the realists about the Commonwealth were to be found on the Right, the sentimentalists on the Left. The reversal of position was remarkable, but not surprising. The Right has its own sentimentalities, but it does not lack a sense of power, and its decisive argument was that Europe's power was rising and that of the Commonwealth declining. General de Gaulle's rebuff in no way affects the truth of this perception. Indeed, the rising power of Europe constitutes a further argument against British neutralism. A neutral Britain will obviously not be acceptable to the Common Market—less so than Sweden, Austria, and Switzerland, who can plead mitigating circumstances. America, the largest foreign investor in Britain, would quickly divert the mainstream of her investment to Common Market Europe. In matters that concern Europe's security and political future Britain would no longer be consulted. Nor, having abandoned the Western alliance, could Britain expect American support in those parts of the world where it is still vital to her. This, too, would have serious political and economic consequences. It is hardly necessary to stress the effects on British home politics: mass unemployment, a declining standard of living, a permanent sense of insecurity and inferiority, all could give rise to something far more frightening than the malaise of the past decade.

Fortunately, it is a vision unlikely to be realized. But the neutralist tendencies are there. Few people would go all the way with the neutralism of the C.N.D.; many would assent to the crypto-neutralist sentiment implied in the wish that 'Britain ought to mediate between Russia and America'. The sentiment is crypto-neutralist for this reason. One cannot claim to have a 'special relationship' with America and also claim to be the impartial judge of her actions; the role of 'honest broker' is not open to the country that would be America's staunchest ally. This is not to say that Britain should not criticize America. But we ought to recognize the hidden neutralism in the general thesis, for if it is not apparent to us, it is certainly apparent to our friends; it is also apparent to our enemies. I believe it lies behind that attitude to the Cold War which has come to seem specifically British.

On the Continent, the tendencies towards neutralism—in the 'weak' not the 'strong' sense—have been dramatically reversed. And if Britain and Europe have exchanged roles, the explanation must lie in the different political experience of Britain and Europe since 1940. Europe had to learn by tragic violence certain lessons which, however unpleasant at the time, were to prove salutary in the long run. By violence, Europeans learnt what foreign conquest and occupation by a totalitarian enemy implies. By violence, Europeans learnt what Communism means in practice. By violence, Europeans learnt what it means to lose an empire. Needless to say, this is not set down in praise of violence. But I believe Germany and France, Italy, Belgium, and Holland, learnt lessons which Britain, in her very gentleness, failed to learn. They learnt not only that the loss of empire is an irreversible and agonizing process, but that it necessitates a total national reorientation. Nostalgia for empire, powerful in Britain, has vanished from the European consciousness. In the end, the painless loss of our Empire has hurt us more. That it should be so is cruelly ironic. Our post-war record in liberating our dependent territories was better than that of our neighbours. What our eulogists say of the benefits Britain's ex-colonies have reaped from their experience with Britain is all true. What they fail to mention is the damage the gentle passing of empire has done to the spirit of our own islands.

A Cure for Westminster

John Grigg (formerly Lord Altrincham)

> 'A SEVERE though not unfriendly critic
> of our institutions said that "the cure for
> admiring the House of Lords was to go
> and look at it.". . .'
> WALTER BAGEHOT

APPROACH the Palace of Westminster from the Underground Station in Bridge Street. The tunnel of lavatorial white tiles suddenly gives way to a sham-Gothic cloister. An iron grille divides the real world from the world of make-believe. The London Undergound, like British democracy, is a creature of the modern age: Parliament is a creature of the Middle Ages.

During the night of May 10th, 1941, the Commons Chamber was destroyed by enemy action. In December, 1943, a Select Committee was appointed to consider plans for rebuilding. At Coventry, where they had a similar problem, a cathedral of contemporary design was brought into being alongside the Gothic ruins. At Westminster, most significantly, the new Chamber (completed in 1950) was 'as like the old Chamber in all its features as was compatible with modern ideas of ventilation and acoustics'. Moreover,

acoustic considerations were not allowed to weigh too heavily against the force of aesthetics and tradition. The ceiling, for instance, was . . . sloping, though it was known that a ceiling of this shape reflected the sound waves . . .[1]

[1] Eric Taylor, *The House of Commons at Work* (Penguin).

In England, the mediaeval structure of government and law has never been repudiated. On the contrary, it has been lovingly maintained, while the economic character of the nation has been altered beyond recognition. Parliament's victory over the King in the seventeenth century was not a real revolution, nor was it really a victory for Parliament. It was the triumph of a co-alition of private economic interests, whose leaders appealed to mediaeval precedents (Magna Carta, etc.). Executive power passed from the King to an oligarchy, but the function of Parliament did not essentially change. More recently, executive power has become concentrated in the hands of the Prime Minister—a feudal monarch writ large—while Parliament has been losing whatever vestiges of independence it may have had under the Grand Whiggery and during the Victorian period. Universal suffrage has strengthened the executive *without* making it democratic.

It is a gross mistake to assume that democracy is a natural development of what we call Parliamentary government. The opposite is true: the idea of popular sovereignty is in conflict with the traditional English theory and practice of the Constitution. The people here are not sovereign: they are neither meant to be sovereign nor do they feel themselves to be sovereign. They are *subjects*. The Crown is sovereign and the Crown is the Government. Every four or five years the people are given a chance to change the Government, but the system lives on. British politics have more in common with the Wars of the Roses than with the principles vaguely but potently set forth in the Gettysburg Address.

Well before Lincoln's day de Tocqueville had seen the point—had appreciated the crucial difference between the British and American political traditions.

All the British colonies . . . from their beginning, seemed destined to witness the growth, not of the aristocratic liberty of their mother-country, but of that freedom of the middle and lower orders of which the history of the world had as yet furnished no complete example.[1]

[1] Alexis de Tocqueville, *Democracy in America*, Vol. 1, Chapter 2.

Within the last century the 'lower orders' in Britain have achieved a relative degree of economic freedom and the semblance of political freedom; but they have not acquired the habits of democracy. They have become, like the 'middle orders' before them, either active or passive adherents of a political system which is aristocratic in form—though not, alas, in fact. As a country, we are making the worst of both worlds: we have lost the virtues of 'aristocratic liberty' without gaining the virtues of democratic liberty.

FROM THE VERY FIRST, Parliament's role was ambiguous. It came into being partly as an accessory to, and partly as a brake upon, the power of government. An intermittent assembly of leading taxpayers, it was able to establish a limited measure of control in return for services rendered. The ambiguity remains. Parliament meets the old demand that there should be 'no taxation without representation', but for the rest it is little more than a tool of the governing party and of its boss, the Prime Minister. As an outlet for grievances it has the advantage that Ministers of the Crown have to belong to it and are answerable to it. On the other hand, its members are subject to party discipline. Now that the same man is Joint Chairman of the Tory Party and Leader of the House of Commons the relationship of Parliament to the political machine is brutally emphasized.

During the present century the machine has enormously increased its power. The mass franchise has given British general elections, which are held at longish intervals, the character of plebiscites, while the so-called 'electoral mandate' has turned M.P.s into little more than delegates, pledged to support their party through thick and thin. Deviation from the official Government or Opposition line is largely confined to private (and ostensibly secret) party meetings. Debates of the House of Commons as such have become empty charades, and the result of almost any vote when the Whips are on is a foregone conclusion. The 'two Houses' of our Parliament are now, in reality, not the Commons and the Lords, but the Parliamentary Labour Party and the 1922 Committee—both meeting *in camera*.

Meanwhile the public sector has been vastly widened by the

advent of the Welfare State and by the extension of public ownership. The responsibilities of modern Government are such that a Minister is now a hard-pressed, full-time public servant, who would anyway tend to be cut off from Parliamentary work by the exigencies of his departmental work. He is all the more decisively cut off, however, during those long periods of the year when Parliament is in recess. Whitehall works a full day and a full year: Westminster is operational for only part of the day and part of the year. In 1900 the House of Commons sat for 113 days. In 1961–62, despite a stupendous increase in the range and bulk of the nation's public business, it sat for less than fifty days more, a mere 160 days—among which, moreover, Fridays cannot be regarded as Parliamentary days, even in the normal inadequate sense.

WHAT IS A NORMAL Parliamentary day? Apart from committees, the Commons do not meet in the mornings, from Monday to Thursday inclusive. They meet at 2.30 p.m. and sit until 10.30 p.m. or later. On Friday they meet at 11 a.m. and rise (the few of them who are there) at 4.30 p.m. Nothing more perfectly illustrates the futility and out-of-dateness of the present system than the hours which the Commons keep on their normal working days. They sit late, because they will not meet early and because they will not sit for more days in the year. They preserve a time-table which, while they are in session, is disruptive of family life and of ordinary civilized social intercourse, and they do this in order to make quite sure that membership of Parliament remains a part-time occupation.

The amateur status of M.P.s is upheld through a sort of unholy alliance between the bosses and the rank-and-file. The bosses do not want a more active and professional Parliament, because they are afraid that it would undermine their authority and make life more difficult for them. They want to be the only professionals in the game, so that they can dominate it without effort. The rank-and-file have mixed motives, but it is fair to conclude that a majority of them are well content to supplement their meagre Parliamentary pay with what they are able to earn outside Parliament, thanks to the ample spare time available to them, and thanks also (in many cases) to the kudos of being M.P.s.[1] They do not want to become professional politicians, because to do so would mean curtailing their outside activities; and so they easily convince themselves that their involvement in other tasks does not impair, but on the contrary enhances, their value as legislators. Of course there are some who would do more strictly political work if they were paid more and were given the necessary facilities. There are also, it must be admitted, a few who devote all their energies to politics because they are not fit for any other kind of gainful employment. The average M.P., however, is a man of above-average ability, who could be serving the nation better if his mind were concentrated upon the affairs of State, but who is not prepared to face the necessity for such concentration as the *sine qua non* of better pay and conditions.

Let me define here some of the attributes of a 'professional politician', because the term has unfortunately acquired a pejorative usage. Politics, like teaching, is mid-way between a science and an art. Those who practise it need not be experts in any particular field, but they need to have a good grounding of knowledge and a general inquisitiveness. They also need to have the gift of synthesis and at least a glimmering of imagination. Finally, they must be capable of absorbing and communicating ideas. With this basic equipment they should be able to probe the machinations of Government; to ensure its honesty and efficiency; to form intelligent opinions on the present and future needs of society; to promote legislation which the Government is willing to accept, but which it might never of its own accord introduce; to do much of the work which is now farmed out to Royal Commissions and committees of inquiry;[2] to read, write, and think—and at the same time, of course, look after their constituents (though not to the extent of becoming local welfare officers). The work of M.P.s will be further considered in relation to the modern role of Parliament itself: meanwhile it should be obvious that the functions which I have outlined are

[1] See Andrew Roth, *The Business Background of Members of Parliament* (Parliamentary Profile Services Ltd.).

[2] For the unhealthy proliferation of these, itself a comment on the supine state of Parliament, see Sir Alan Herbert's essay in the volume *Radical Reaction* (published by Hutchinson's for the Institute of Economic Affairs).

incompatible with the present amateurish and part-time approach to national politics.

I HAVE SUGGESTED that our Parliamentary system is still recognizably mediæval in some of its essential features, and of course the most striking, if not the most important, of its mediaeval features is the House of Lords. A second Chamber whose membership is still largely recruited by the process of inheritance, and which still retains a limited power to frustrate the intentions of the elected Chamber, is, on any view, a startling anachronism. Those who defend the Lords' residual veto on legislation argue that it is a safeguard against a revolutionary Government acting in defiance of public opinion. The Lords are assumed to be more independent and less partisan than the Commons—an assumption which seems to have little basis in fact. In support of the hereditary principle it is argued that the Second Chamber would be less independent, and would also lack the refreshing influence of youth, if its membership were confined to life peers and peers of first creation. Again, there is no evidence that hereditary peers are less amenable than other peers to party discipline; nor is there any reason to accept as final the statement that youth can find its way into a second Chamber only through the accident of birth. (More will be said later about the composition of a properly reformed House of Lords).

Since 1945 (or, to be more exact, since 1940, which is the truly climacteric date in modern British history) the country has undergone huge changes. Society has been transformed, and the State has played a major part in the transformation. During the same period, however, Parliament has remained almost literally static—as it were, fossilized. The university and business franchises have been abolished; the House of Lords 'veto' (on non-money Bills) has been reduced from two years to one year; the principle of life peerage has been extended, and women—the only notable change—have been brought into the House of Lords. *That is all.* No wonder the drastic reform of Parliament now seems to many of us an urgent national priority. No wonder a group of Tory M.P.s has produced a pamphlet entitled *Change or Decay*. No wonder a prominent

Cabinet Minister, whose love of Parliament seems to outweigh the natural instincts of a party boss, has asked 'whether the so-called "Westminster model" is really doing its job, whether our present apparatus is really adequate to the strains which are being put upon it'.[1]

The gravity of the problem is now recognized by all who bother to think and who are not enervated by the fatal British disease of complacency. But what is the solution?

WE MUST CONSIDER first what we are aiming at. The form of government which we profess to want (and which many believe we already have) is Parliamentary democracy. But neither our political institutions themselves, nor the spirit which informs them, can at present be described as 'democratic'. We have therefore somehow to adapt our Parliamentary system in accordance with the idea of popular sovereignty. If the institutions are made more democratic, the spirit will gradually change.

Whatever happens, we must not throw away the benefits of strong and stable government, for which we have long been justly envied. At the same time we cannot be happy with the prevailing trend towards almost unfettered Prime Ministerial rule, which is tantamount to Presidential rule without the American safeguards of a separate independent legislature and deeply entrenched States rights, and without the French device of a referendum on any national issue of overriding importance. The people of Britain have to be brought more often and more effectively into the political process, both directly (through elections) and indirectly (through their representatives in Parliament). It goes without saying that the people cannot actually govern, nor can Parliament actually govern. But it is surely quite evident, too, that unless the people are more closely associated with the process of government we shall not be a democracy in any meaningful sense; and that unless Parliament is much more closely associated, we shall not be a Parliamentary democracy.

The role of Parliament is, first of all, to *represent* the nation.

[1] Lord Hailsham, speaking at Wigan, April 5th, 1963.

This seemingly trite requirement is, in fact, beset with difficulty, because an ideally representative Parliament would almost certainly lead to the stultification of government. Our present system of voting is by no means calculated to mirror the electorate with exactitude, but it has been found serviceable in producing clear-cut results and in securing a fair approximation to majority rule. All the same, there have been occasions (the last was in 1951) when the party with a clear majority of votes did *not* win a majority of seats. Without adopting an entirely new system it should be possible to reduce the risk of such a flagrant misrepresentation of the popular will.

But a far more important step would be to shorten the statutory life of a Parliament, so that general elections would be held at more frequent intervals. Three years is surely long enough for any man or group of men to be entrusted with the vast resources of a modern government, without coming back to the people for a renewal of their mandate. Our present statutory term of five years dates from before the first World War, when conditions were very different. There is a strong case, too, for a fixed election date: the convention whereby the Prime Minister of the day can choose his own moment to ask the Sovereign for a Dissolution is hardly fair to the Opposition.

ANOTHER DESIRABLE CHANGE, in the interests of making Parliament more representative, is that younger people should be brought on to the Register. The mystic age of 21 reflects the upper-class cycle of education (public school, followed by university): it has no relevance to the life of most citizens, who leave school and start work in their mid-teens. It is true, of course, that many teenagers would be ignorant and irresponsible voters; but this is equally true of a great many adult voters, and it is inevitably true that some people, as they advance in years, begin to lose their mental faculties—without, however, losing their right to vote. Democracy must be based upon the right of *all* citizens to vote, or it is a sham. Literacy or 'responsibility' tests are the favourite resource of anti-democrats who want a respectable excuse for protecting their own special interests. Who, then, is to be regarded as a fully fledged citizen? If 16 is thought to be too young, no reasonable person could object to 18 as the qualifying age for a vote in modern Britain.

BUT IT IS NOT ENOUGH for Parliament to be representative: it must also be of high quality and it must help to set the pace in a dynamic community. *An elected Chamber of part-time amateurs and a second Chamber still rooted in the hereditary principle will simply not do.*

I have already said something of the characteristics required in a professional politician. They are characteristics which have enabled, for instance, an Aneurin Bevan to be a good Minister of Health without being a doctor, or an Iain Macleod to be a good Colonial Secretary without being previously acquainted with the Colonies. Not every M.P. can have what it takes to be a top Minister, but all should possess, in some degree, the qualities which constitute political professionalism. In many cases it will be helpful to have served in some other line of business, and there are a few professions or occupations (journalism is an obvious example) which may overlap the work of a professional politician. But no work must be undertaken or retained which is likely to distract M.P.s from their overriding duty to serve the State in Parliament.

If they are to do it properly, they must clearly be on the job—like Ministers—for most of the year. The Palace of Westminster must not, for months at a time, be an echoing vault—visited by forlorn groups of tourists while M.P.s ply other trades. Except at the major festivals it must be a hive of ceaseless activity. It is wrong, however, that important Parliamentary business should be transacted after normal working hours. Debates and divisions after the time when civilized men and women go home for an evening meal are an abomination. Midnight argument conducted by people who have been working during the day is unlikely to be balanced or fruitful. A man who works on night-shift in a factory has been sleeping during the day; but M.P.s cannot afford to be out of circulation during the daylight hours. The obvious solution is that the Parliamentary day should start earlier and end earlier.

Westminster must not, however, become a prison for M.P.s,

while Parliament is at work. Though it is against the public interest that they should be engaged in *non-political* activities outside Parliament, it is very much in accordance with the public interest that they should 'get around' and not be tied to a particular building. The most vexatious restraint upon their freedom of movement is the obligation to vote in divisions—a function which for most M.P.s, in any vote contested by the main parties, is purely mechanical. It is hard to see why, on a party vote, every M.P. should not be assumed to vote with his party unless he gives express notice to the contrary before the 'division'. The tellers would thus take note, not of votes recorded for or against the motion—there would be no mass parade through the lobbies—but of any votes recorded against the respective party lines. Every absentee would be counted as having voted with his party. It may be objected that this procedure would deprive M.P.s of the only inducement which they now have to turn up at the House of Commons, but this objection is ridiculous. Most debates in the Chamber are now ill-attended, but while they are going on there are likely to be many M.P.s more or less usefully employed in some other part of the building. There is no virtue in summoning all M.P.s to vote at the end of a debate which most of them have not attended. It would surely be more sensible and less hypocritical to change voting procedure to take full account of the exigencies of modern party government.

SUBJECT TO THE electoral mandate, the Government of the day must both govern and legislate with the assurance of steady support in Parliament. Debates on Government Bills, which now take up so much Parliamentary time, are therefore bound to be unrealistic, *qua* debates. The Third Reading of such Bills is an almost total waste of time, because the main confrontation of the parties has already occurred on Second Reading. Moreover, the usual legislative process—Bills passing through all their stages in one House, then through all their stages in the other, after which further amendments have to be considered before the Royal Assent is given—is agonizingly slow without necessarily producing the best result. The traditional rivalry between the two Houses, and the separation of powers which marks their relationship, is an archaic survival. Co-operation, not conflict, should now be the dominant theme.

THIS PRESUPPOSES a fundamental reform of the Lords. Briefly, the second Chamber has to become exclusively what it is already in part—a reservoir of experts. The hereditary element must disappear and with it what remains of the suspensory veto. The Lords would thus consist of first creations (who might or might not be 'life peers': the transmission of a title is relatively innocuous so long as it does not carry with it the right to apply for a writ of summons to Parliament), and also, for the sake of greater flexibility, of men and women who might not wish to bear a title at all, or who might be appointed to serve in Parliament for a limited period of time—say, for the duration of one Parliament. Some excellent people might decline to serve if they had to adopt the nominal style of nobility: a nation of snobs cannot fail to have its quota of inverted snobs. A Chamber still called the 'House of Lords', but containing a fair sprinkling of Misters, would be a typical British anomaly: even the traditionalists might welcome it on that ground. Appointment for a limited period would facilitate the recruitment of younger members. Nobody could seriously doubt that there are people in their thirties and forties who would have much to contribute to Parliament in an expert, advisory capacity; but the Crown might hesitate to nominate them if they were all going to have the right to sit there—and to draw attendance allowances—for life. (Schemes for composing the second Chamber through either direct or indirect election need not detain us: the House of Commons would never tolerate a rival elected body.)

Evidently, a House of Lords reformed on the lines suggested would command a measure of public confidence which would offset the loss of outright political power. The supposed safeguard against party dictatorship in the Commons—a fantasy at the best of times—would anyway be largely superfluous in the context of triennial Parliaments, which would guarantee a more frequent popular check upon the Executive. Membership of the Lords would remain (as it is now) unlimited in number, and the members would, unlike M.P.s, be of their very nature part-timers, attending intermittently when their own subjects were under discussion, and not dependent upon their Parliamentary allowances for a living. Parliament would thus consist of professional politicians in the Commons, who would wield the power, and of part-time experts in the Lords, who would have influence without power—unless they happened also to be Ministers. (It is right that a Prime Minister should be free to appoint some people to his Government who can be technically members of Parliament without having to stand for the Commons.) The primacy of the elected House would thus be established once and for all; at the same time Parliament would be equipped with its own ready-made corps of experts, who would be able to assist in its work without diluting its democratic character.

For the purposes of legislation the reformed House of Lords could be of immense value, especially if the present legislative procedure were changed. Would it not be possible for Government and other Bills to be introduced simultaneously in both Houses, and for the committee stage to be held, quite often, in joint session, with the Lords submitting opinions and amendments, but not actually voting? The benefit of expert advice would thus be available to M.P.s while they were debating clauses in committee. This procedure would not be used whenever either House objected to it, but its use on suitable occasions would help to speed up, and at the same time to improve, legislation. In some quarters the view is held that legislation, like litigation, is inherently vicious and that every obstacle should be put in its way. But another, and probably saner, view is that many laws which ought to be passed are now not passed —or not even introduced—because Parliament functions so slowly and clumsily as a legislative machine. 'Year by year,' said Lord Hailsham in the speech already quoted, 'I have seen legislation delayed or, worse still, left to die uncompleted, for want of Parliamentary time.' Extension of the Parliamentary time-table would go far towards remedying the situation; but there is reason to believe that more streamlined procedure will also be necessary, if the legislative tasks of Parliament are to be adequately discharged.

One conspicuous advantage would be the provision of more time for Private Members' Bills. There is, of course, a limit to what can be achieved in the way of legislation not initiated by the Government (which has to bear the practical responsibility for any laws which are passed). But there are unquestionably many projects of legislation which the Government may tacitly approve, while preferring not to introduce them itself. There are also projects which the Government of the day may not approve, but which ought nevertheless to be introduced and debated. Parliament has a duty not only to reflect but also to educate public opinion, and the Private Member's Bill is one method whereby matters of importance, which may be too tricky or controversial for inclusion in a party programme, could be dealt with at Westminster.

LAW-MAKING must always, however, be in the main a prerogative of Government. The vital function of Parliament is not to legislate, but rather to *investigate*. It is here that the amateurishness of the present set-up has been most disastrous in its effects. Because Parliament is a *roi fainéant*, the probing and researching tasks which it ought to perform have been distributed to 'laymen', invited by the Government to sit on Royal Commissions and Committees of Inquiry. The bulk of this work could be done, and should be done, by working parties drawn from the two Houses of Parliament. Groups of Parliamentarians should also be sent more often on missions abroad, to report on trade prospects or to advise the Government on aspects of foreign policy. In the last century Richard Cobden negotiated a whole commercial treaty with France—as a back-bencher.

The case for Parliamentary Standing Committees on the American model—covering major fields of policy and enjoying a quasi-autonomous status—deserves to be carefully examined (though I have not the space to examine it here). The authors of *Change or Decay* suggest the formation of Standing Economic Committees, which could 'play a very useful part if the parties were to select back-bench Members with the best industrial or technical experience to serve on them and co-opt industrialists, economists, scientists, and other experts to advise them'. Question Time, uniquely valuable as it is in many respects, is no substitute for the more searching inquisition to which Ministers could be subjected by a well-briefed Standing Committee, with the power to question official witnesses on oath.

WHEN—BUT ONLY WHEN—Parliament has become the great political workshop of the nation, it will be right that M.P.s should be paid more than their present salary and peers more than their present attendance allowance; and that both should be given the facilities for research, office work, and travel, to which they would then be entitled. Their remuneration and amenities should never be quite on the lavish scale accorded to American Congressmen. Our politicians should be encouraged to do their job properly: they should not be encouraged to 'live it up'. Nor should they be given—except in old age, or after long service—security against the vicissitudes of public life. The sort of people who stand for election to the House of Commons must be the sort who either have done, or could have done, other work, and who could at any time find alternative employment if rejected by the voters. They must not be spivish types who are in politics *faute de mieux*. But while they are at Westminster they must concentrate on the nation's business: the calling of a professional politician must come to be regarded as an honourable calling.

INDEED, it is vital that Parliament should not merely do well, but should be *seen* to do well. This means, in practical terms, that it must be televised. Parliament is now out of touch with the public, not only because its methods of work are antiquated, but also because they are conducted behind a screen of mystery—not *on* the little screen which is the unrivalled medium of mass communication in our age. The Leader of the House of Commons (Mr. Macleod) has come out in favour of televising Parliament —though his personal view does not commit the Government. The Labour Party seems to be distinctly conservative on this issue (as on a variety of others). The argument that the intimacy of Parliamentary discussion would be destroyed by television, and that M.P.s would start playing to the gallery instead of reasoning earnestly among themselves, must be dismissed as either silly or hypocritical. Parliamentary proceedings are already held in public: there is a public gallery and there is a press gallery, to which M.P.s are more likely to play than to the handful of individuals who bother to sit in the Chamber.

'Press intrusion' was resisted in the past: now it is the intrusion of the TV cameras. And the underlying motive is the same: M.P.s do not want their cosy club to be broken into, as it were, by strangers. They are afraid—and with good reason— that their time-honoured mumbo-jumbo, their silly time-consuming ritual, their wordy speeches, their lackadaisical habits, would all be threatened by the ever-watchful eye of the public, whose servants and representatives they are. The arrival of the TV camera at Westminster would be as momentous an event as the adoption of universal suffrage.

When Parliament is fit to investigate thoroughly the work of the Executive, and when the public is free to watch, day by day, the work of Parliament, we shall have come nearer to reconciling our ancient aristocratic machinery of government with the spirit of modern democracy.

The French Paradox

A Note from Paris

AT THE time of writing—summer, 1963—France is the fore-most power in Western Europe. Yet within the last ten years, she has been slowly bleeding herself white through the Algerian War; her Parliamentary system, unworkable and discredited, has been giving her less and less effective government; her people have contained the biggest Communist Party this side of the Curtain. All this came on top of a series of blows to her military honour, from Vichy through Oran and Syria to Dien Bien Phu.

Pride, visionary and injured, is the main thread in her leader's policy. The form this has assumed, aided by good luck and good timing, was foreshadowed in de Gaulle's memoirs. It has been achieved by the patience and the formidable will of an individual in whom consistency and deviousness are so mixed that, as Raymond Aron said, adults find him difficult to understand.

He would not have been able to achieve his purpose so swiftly since 1958 but for a paradox. The disorganization of French Parliamentary institutions during the 1950s meant that the country had to be directed from a level below the Ministers, if it were not to collapse. It was run, more or less effectively, by civil servants, until de Gaulle harnessed their strength and talents to his own ends. A cadre of high functionaries, often young and ambitious, receiving only discontinuous direction from a political roundabout of Coalitions and Ministers, seized the chance—which indeed was thrust upon them—to put into effect a novel throng of ideas and plans. Sometimes these were conflicting, but their range was fascinating, extending from a supra-national Europe to new patterns for Afrique Noire.

These ideas, in an abstract form, had been worked out in places like the Inspectorate of Finances or in the *École Nationale d'Administration*. They could be translated into practice with less than the usual political frustration, when the men who had thought them out were given actual responsibility in the exercise of power. It was not easily achieved; it required intelligence of an original kind, a grasp of detail which could only come from hard 'homework' in exploring all round a subject, and in testing ideas ahead by endless discussion.

These top French civil servants are a new breed. They are often astonishingly young. Class consciousness has been largely replaced by a sort of caste consciousness based on their educational success and their privileges of power. One could describe their type by a composite picture; they dress well but restrainedly; they speak well and with exact emphasis; gesticulations and excitement are gone; they can be maddeningly self-assured about their opinions; above all they play it 'cool'. Is one being too British to suggest that their ideal appears to be something like the aloof imperial tradition of the I.C.S. at the turn of the century, but brought up to date with this scientific age?

Their framework, upon which de Gaulle has successfully revived France's economy, is not dictatorial, although powers of compulsion exist. Take for instance their economic planning: their Four Year Plans are evolved in outline in the *Commissariat au Plan*. (Incidentally this body is quite small, not much larger than our own N.E.D.C. and tiny compared with the Planning Ministries in Russia.) The outline Plan is then divided into a wide range of industrial sectors, and for each sector there are committees composed of representatives of Government, Employers, and Labour. They have to agree among themselves whether they can or cannot fulfil the target set in the outline Plan—which means assessing in broad terms input and output of material, capital investment, prices, and wages. If they decide that the target is wrong, they go back to the Commissariat to argue for an alteration (which, because it would affect other sectors, is not easily achieved but is possible). This is planning by consent, rather than by 'monolithic' methods of compulsion.

But the French Government has some powerful weapons of inducement to conformity, even something near coercion in its tight control of investment funds.

Are there any pointers for Britain in this? Our Parliamentary system did not suffer the paralysing crises of the Fourth Republic; the social structure and political climate of our two countries are basically different. Nevertheless the methods by which the spectacular economic recovery of France was achieved deserve careful study by all who have Britain's own recovery at heart.[1]

[1] The author of this note is a British executive of an international company.

Islanders (II) . . .

Brussels, 1815

BRUSSELS *has been too much modern-ized, too much Frenchified in all respects. As a specimen of the lep-rous filthiness with which the French have infected these countries, I saw some toys in a shop window represent-ing men with their loins ungirt, in the attitude of the* Deus Cacaturi-ens, *each with a piece of yellow metal, like a sham coin, inserted behind. The persons who exhibit such things as these for sale deserve the pillory or the whipping post.*

ROBERT SOUTHEY

Jerusalem, 1833

AS IN THE ARMY *of the Crusaders, the word Jerusalem! was repeated from mouth to mouth; but we, who consider ourselves civilized and super-ior beings, repressed our emotions; we were above showing that we partici-pated in the feelings of our barbarous companions. As for myself, I would have got off my horse and walked barefooted towards the gate, as some did, if I had dared; but I was in fear of being laughed at for my absurdity, and therefore sat fast in my saddle. At last I blew my nose and I rode on slowly towards the Bethlehem gate. . .*

HON. ROBERT CURZON

Albania, 1834

'LET THAT *fowl alone, you scoun-drel!' said I in good English. 'Put it down, will you? if you don't I'll . . . !'*

The man, surprised at this address in an unknown tongue, put down the fowl, and looked up with wonder at the explosion of ire which his actions had called forth. 'That is right,' said I, 'my good fellow, it is too good for such a dirty brute as you.'

HON. ROBERT CURZON

Philadelphia, 1853

EVERYBODY *prospers. There are scarce any poor. For thousands of years more there is room and food, and work for whoever comes. In travelling in Europe our confounded English pride only fortifies itself, and we feel that we are better than 'those foreigners' but it's worth while com-ing here that we may think small beer of ourselves afterwards.*

W. M. THACKERAY

Rome, 1854

IF I HAD *to write a book about Rome what on earth could I say? I might as well be at Jericho or Islington.*

W. M. THACKERAY

Amsterdam, 1859

A SMALL TASTE *of Holland is sufficient, one place is so exactly like another. . . . The climate is detest-able. When the sun shines, the exhalations from the canals make an atmosphere which is the closest and most unwholesome I ever breathed, and when the sun does not shine, the weather is raw, gray, and cold. The general impression Holland, curious* as it is, makes on me, is one of mortal ennui.

MATTHEW ARNOLD

Toulouse, 1864

IT IS *not by its playgrounds and means of recreation that a French lyceum, as compared with the half-dozen great English public schools, shines. The boys are taken out to walk, as the boys at Winchester used to be taken out to hills; but at the end of the French schoolboy's walk there are no hills on which he is turned loose. The court in which he takes his recreation is somewhat more agreeable and spacious than we English are apt to imagine a* court *to be; but it is a poor place indeed—poor in itself and poor in its resources—compared with the* playing-fields *of Eton, or the* meads *of Winchester, or the* close *of Rugby.*

MATTHEW ARNOLD

Prussia, 1871

THE ONLY *Prussian I ever knew who was an agreeable man was Bismarck. All others with whom I have been thrown—and I have lived for years in Germany—were proud as Scotchmen, cold as New Englanders, and touchy as only Prussians can be. I once had a friend among them. His*

name *was Buckenbrock. Inadvertently I called him Butterbrod. We have never spoken since.*

HENRY LABOUCHERE

Norway, 1899

THEY ARE *the kindest people in Europe but they frighten me to death.*

SIR EDMUND GOSSE

Germany, 1929

THE GERMANS *are most curious. As a bourgeois crowd, they are so monstrously ugly. My God, how ugly they can be! and it's because they never live direct from their spontaneous feeling; except in the matter of eating and drinking. God help us.*

D. H. LAWRENCE

Persia, 1951

NO, PERSIA WASN'T *all depressing. Beautiful Ispahan and Shiraz. Wicked, pompous, oily British. Nervous, cunning, corrupt, and delightful Persian bloody bastards. Opium no good. Persian vodka made of beetroot, like stimulating sockjuice, very enjoyable. Beer full of glycerine and pips. Women veiled, or unveiled ugly, or beautiful and entirely inaccessible, or hungry. The lovely camels who sit on their necks and smile. I shan't go there again.*

DYLAN THOMAS

The quotations included in 'Islanders and Mainlanders' have been excerpted, respectively, from those two excellent compilations, *The Englishman Abroad* by Hugh and Pauline Massingham (Phoenix, 1962) and *Strange Island* by Francesca M. Wilson (Longmans, 1955).

... *Mainlanders (II)*

THE ENGLISHMAN *has no great inclination to go to work and opens not his shop even in summertime, till after seven in the morning. This makes manufactures dear, and renders the natives angry with the French people; for our tradesmen are usually more industrious, and as they are more handy at their work, folks go the willinger to buy of them, and they can sell cheaper than the English, who would have as much for the little they do as the others, and the loss of their time made up to them that way. Such, together with their voracious and lazy temper, is the reason why the Dutch always undersell the English. . . .*

SAMUEL SORBIERE

1695

THE BEAUTY OF ENGLISH WOMEN *does not touch me much; they are all fair and of delicate complexion but nothing animates their pretty faces. The greatest fault I find with them is that they do not take care of their teeth. When they give themselves up to passion they are easily carried away. Most men prefer wine and gaming to women, in this they are the more to blame as women are much better than the wine in England. But usually when they look for pretty women they do not want to owe the favours they have from them to delicate attentions; lazy even in love they ask only for easy pleasure.*

DE MURALT

1727

THE BODIES *and clothes of the dead belong to the executioner; relatives must, if they wish for them, buy them from him, and unclaimed bodies are sold to surgeons to be dissected. You see most amusing scenes between the people who do not like the bodies to be cut up and the messengers the surgeons have sent for the bodies; blows are given and returned before they can be got away, and sometimes in the turmoil the bodies are quickly removed and buried. Again, the populace often come to blows as to who will carry the bought corpses to the parents who are waiting in coaches and cabs to receive them, for the carriers are well paid for their trouble. All these scenes are most diverting, the noise and confusion is unbelievable, and can be witnessed from a sort of amphitheatre erected for spectators near the gibbet.*

DE SAUSSURE

1784

THE WEATHER *was always bad. What a terrible climate! Several Englishmen told us that it does not rain here more than in France. In vain did I assert that I had never seen such horrible weather repeated day after day, that sometimes it was warm in France. They replied that there had never been such a summer in England and that we should have a better autumn. A fine consolation! Meanwhile we have had a fire nearly the whole summer and England* consumed as much coal in August as France consumes wood in October. . . .

DE LA ROCHEFOUCAULD

1790

LONDON HOUSES *are built with an underground part in which there is usually the kitchen, the cellar, and some very dark rooms for male and female servants and the poor. In Paris poverty climbs up to the clouds, to the garret, here it goes underground; in Paris you carry the poor on your head and here you stamp on them with your feet.*

NICOLAI KARAMZIN

1847

AN ENGLISHMAN, *while he eats and drinks no more, or not much more than another man, labours three times as many hours in the course of a year as another European; or, his life as a workman is three lives. He works fast. Everything in England is at a quick pace. They have reinforced their own productivity, by the creation of that marvellous machinery which differentiates this age from any other age.*

RALPH WALDO EMERSON

1862

WHOEVER *has been to London has been at least once to the Haymarket. It is the district where in certain streets at night prostitutes gather in their thousands. The street is festooned by gas jets in a way of which at home we have no conception. At every step there are superb cafés all*

gilt and glass. You meet your friends there—and you take refuge there.

I remember going into a dance-hall; there was music and dancing —the place was packed. The décor was magnificent but the English are sad even when they are amusing themselves; they dance with a serious almost sulky air and execute their steps as though it were a duty.

DOSTOEVSKY

1902

ONE SUNDAY *I went with Lenin and Krupskaya to a London church where a social-democratic meeting alternated with hymn-singing. A compositor who had returned from Australia stood up and talked about the social revolution. Thereupon everyone got up and sang 'Almighty God, make it that there will be no more kings nor rich people'. I could not believe my eyes or ears.*

TROTSKY

1923

AND THAT IS *the strangest thing: the London streets are just a gully through which life flows to get home; in the streets people do not live, stare, talk, stand, or sit; they merely rush through the streets.*

The poetry of the English home exists at the expense of the English street which is devoid of poetry. And here no revolutionary throngs will ever march through the streets, because these streets are too long. And also too dull.

KAREL CAPEK

183

PART III

Towards a New Society?

THE AUTHORS in this last part are mainly concerned with those imponderables which influence a culture's climate and mood. Cyril Connolly is off on a Palinurian excursion into the past; Marcus Cunliffe studies an allegorical temperature chart; Dr. McGlashan reflects on Struthonian attitudes to sex; Elizabeth Young and John Vaizey are concerned with the original sin from which all our afflictions derive: an antiquated and class-ridden educational system. Lastly, we get a glimpse of the hesitantly emerging contours of a new élite, strikingly different from its predecessors.

This Gale-swept Chip

Cyril Connolly

I THOUGHT OF WRITING a piece about the joylessness of
English life but what right has one to say that other lives are
joyless? Such essays always include a comparison between the
sober pub and the cheerful café but many cafés are not cheerful
and the atrocious English climate is no more suited to them
than the Dutch or Flemish; it is more surprising that there are
no cafés in Australia or America, perhaps evidence that the
consumption of spirits is still a masculine activity best performed
standing up. I soon decided that I really knew very little about
my fellow-countrymen, in fact that all my life I had avoided
them in bulk—which in itself is something very English: the
ethic of overcrowdedness—otherwise known as respect for
privacy. Perhaps the highest praise one can give a country is
that it is possible to spend nearly sixty years in it from birth
without ever really feeling one belongs. No one has ever said to
me: 'Remember you're British!' Sometimes I think the England
I know now is like a parent that has had a first stroke. Gentle,
understanding, walking on eggshells, gazing with the unspoken
resignation of those who have received their boarding cards—
can this be the ferocious figure who tried to bend us to his
will? 'I simply won't have it. . . .' I think of the England of the
'thirties in that way, an autocrat at the last gasp, Chamberlain
in office, the City rattling its moneybags, the Establishment like
a group of poker-faced prefects who know there is going to be
a beating.

It is not much of a distinction to be able to claim to have
lived through the decline of a great empire, a decline which
has been so imperceptible that despite two wars one is hardly

conscious of it. It is even hard to say what has declined. Power and wealth were vested in such a small minority that most people had no idea of their extent. The assumption that Britain ruled the world, supported by her navy and strong sense of principle, and that this was for the best, was already threatened by the gains of American heavy industry in the 1900s—and Shaw was with us as soon as we learned to read—like the lesson of the *Titanic*. I try to cudgel forth significant reminiscences. The 'Hydro' at Limpley Stoke about 1910. An enormously fat man, an Indian rajah who weighed twenty stone, is a guest, I suppose taking a slimming cure as one day I would do myself; he wears a blazer and so is 'all right'—on the other hand he is an Indian and I am aware of a baffling mixture of tolerance, even affection, yet a slight contempt in my parents' attitude. No, he simply won't do. Cricket, hot summers, county matches, score-cards trampled in the grass, the smell of 'gaspers', then the Coronation, a houseboat on the river, a cousin, in immaculate white flannels, punting girl-cousins down our backwater deliberately falls in; what a dare-devil! He was killed at Gallipoli four years later. Gold sovereigns, scent of river water and sweetbriar . . . Hythe. Another hot summer: August, 1914. Liège, Namur, impregnable fortresses—I rush to bring in *The War Illustrated* and study the photographs. My copy of the *Evening News* (August 5th, 1914) is open before me.

Brussels, Wednesday

A stubborn battle has been fought on the outskirts of Liège, where 80,000 Germans attempted to force their advance across Belgium and were engaged by the garrisoned troops of the Liège militia.

After a fierce encounter they so harried the German troops on the right that they were forced to retire.

Brussels, Wednesday

A hundred thousand Germans are marching on Liège where an attack is expected.

At this very moment the Empire is on the brink of the greatest war in the history of the world. In this crisis your

Country calls on all her young unmarried men to rally round
the Flag and enlist in the ranks of her Army. If every patriotic
young man answers her call, England and her Empire will
emerge stronger and more united than ever. If you are
unmarried and between 18 and 30 years old . . .

The war drags on. My preparatory school is in the thick of it.
Old boys appear in khaki, some are killed, others write letters
from all over the Empire which are read out to a chosen few—
Orwell, Cecil Beaton, myself, to make us more 'responsible'. To
some of our families the Empire is no further than the Home
Farm. Rivett Carnacs have always been in India and are
mentioned in Kipling. Right across the atlas islands have been
dipped in red like sheep. From Cairo to the Cape is red all the
way: except for a streaky bit, the Anglo-Egyptian Sudan (a bad
business). 'Here's a letter from Tom Swindon-Didcot, in charge
of the whole of Donagoo-Tonka—"I often think of St. Wulfric's
and wish I was back there. Today I had to go out into the deep
jungle after a wounded Impetigo. Holed out in one and the
boys made a great feast on my return." He'll end up as a
colonial governor! Here's one from Jock Malteezers (the Master
of Malteezers). "Just moved in to splendid new billets at ——
not a hundred miles from the old dump at ——. The men are in
fine fettle and we all played stump cricket by Verey light. Do
you ever hear from old Tom Didcot? I bet he wishes he was in
it. I often wonder when I will get down to St. Wulfric's"—
He'll have the regiment if he doesn't decide to go back to his
broad acres. Character, responsibility, modesty, consideration,
and like all great men, of course, astonishingly simple.' (Killed
in action.)

The war is over. The coaches reassemble at Lords and the
rump of the Whig oligarchy recline on them eating their
lobster and strawberries, watching the performances of R.
Aird and G. O. Allen. Agitators are abroad; one old Etonian is
an active Communist, another strolls past the benches of
spectators in a lounge suit.

'Tell me what you did in the Great Strike, Daddy?'

Daddy was a special constable. He wore an armlet and
carried a truncheon and nearly arrested an American for taking

photos of a milk-float in Hyde Park. Ten years later (typical) he was with the Reds in Barcelona.

AT THIS POINT I have to stop. I am overcome by a wave of boredom. The particular soul-destroying boredom of English life through the 'twenties and 'thirties—the sludge of being. Logan Pearsall Smith, the naturalized American writer whose secretary I became, used to speak of his Anglophobia and treat it as a disease. He would recommend a visit to Paddington when it came on. What produced it? Sundays, of course—the intolerable depression (melancholy is too fine a word) of London Sundays. And the mixture of complacent philistinism, smug superiority, and latent cruelty in the English character. Land of the cat and the hangman, of military punishments, of badger-baiting and homosexual hounding, of savage prosecutions of banned books, land of co-respondent and bottled sauces, of sinister officiousness.

'Excuse me, your collar is turned up, your briefcase is open, your shoelace is undone.'

Coming back from abroad one saw the seamy side, the endless rows of little red houses with slate roofs, the terrible meal on boat or train, the immigration officials who could turn so very unpleasant if one didn't belong, the huge grey newspapers with their pages and pages of sport and their snide gossip columns (so rare on the Continent) and their preoccupation with money, murder, divorce. Sometimes I think that in England divorce is the right true end, that out of this thistle marriage we pluck the flower divorce. The bride and bridegroom should attend their simple wedding with only their solicitors and detectives to get off to a good start on the cruelty case. Divorces on the contrary would be celebrated with great pomp, with friends and relations of bride, groom, and co-respondents administering ritual cuts while at the reception the guests congratulate and claim back their wedding presents.

One of the radical changes since the war and partly due perhaps to our decline as a great Power is a loss of arrogance. We are less cruel and less smug than we used to be and certainly more tolerant. This is a sign that we are declining in the right way. I think, too, we are genuinely less philistine. The England

I knew in the 'twenties and 'thirties possessed an extremely cultivated minority, devoted to such things as silver of the Britannia Standard, walnut furniture, herbaceous borders, Jane Austen quizzes, *The Times* crossword puzzle, *A Shropshire Lad*, and *The Diary of a Nobody*. I remember one of those magnates who was doing some kind of propaganda work in France in 1939 telling me that he proposed to cheer them up by explaining to them that there were in fact quite a few '*jardins à la française*' in England with parterres and trellis, and that it had been by no means a one-way traffic in the '*jardin anglais*'. Another tycoon, met on the boat within twenty-four hours of war being declared, still believed it would not take place because the quality of German steel as revealed in their Shannon work was so inferior. With the philistinism went in fact an extraordinary complacent obtuseness in political judgment; never have so many people believed what they wanted to believe, nor has what they wanted to believe been the instrument of handing so many more over to destruction.

This can be said of other countries but the philistinism, if one did not happen to subscribe to the values of the cultivated minority, was something all-pervading, transcending all barriers of class or creed. Everybody hated *Ulysses* or Lawrence's paintings, everyone disliked modern art except perhaps Sickert or Eliot's poetry. Stravinsky was constantly belittled. Everyone despised a writer unless he made a lot of money and I don't know which would have been the greater blow to the home, for a son to throw up his job to try to paint or a daughter to marry a painter.

A permanently philistine monarchy such as we have enjoyed from James II onwards has certainly contributed greatly to the prestige of the philistine, and this philistinism has also helped to enshrine the monarchy in the hearts of the people. It is difficult to say what the effect of a dynasty of creative artists would have been; perhaps it is better to be governed by people who enjoy racing, cricket, golf, and tennis rather than by lovers of action painting or fine prose; there is less ignominy in being cold-shouldered and one's envy has less to bite on. There are now several members of the Royal Family who care for the Arts but I can think of hardly any in the Government. Under a republic it might be much much worse for then philistines would be in power without the enduring moral qualities plus the charm and warmth and blend of pageantry with common sense which have made the present Royal Family so beloved.[1] But philistinism is still endemic; it is not so rampant in the middle class for they have taken a rather severe beating. They have lost their servants and their assumption of being always right; one hears fewer of those screechingly assured Harrods voices. But try to start up an unsubsidized little magazine or get a book of poems published and we would not find life much easier than did Orwell or Dylan Thomas or Lawrence or Gissing or Wyndham Lewis.

It is clear that the needs of education now absorb a far greater number of writers as teachers than in the 'twenties or 'thirties, often to the detriment of their talent, and that the new entertainment industries like television bring success quicker. But the problem remains. Most of us have no ear and no visual sense, no patience, no education in the art of appreciation, no spiritual longing, no desires that are not satisfied by the Light Programme; we have the worst taste in the world, the ugliest streets, the gloomiest interiors, the most desecrated countryside. I have known hundreds of writers as I approach the last frontier of middle age; most of them have led penurious lives and been lucky to end up in a cottage or a poky flat; those who have achieved success or who have been spared poverty through a private income have all been warped by the east wind of incomprehension. Some are clowns, some are drunks, some are culture diffusionists, some manage to wink across their wife's dinner table, others are literary journalists or American lecturers. Perhaps 60 per cent of the waste and failure is inevitable but the other 40 per cent I am sure is the result of the English conditioning, the poor audience, the shrunken reading public, the weary critics, the worldly publishers, the deep native indifference of the man in the street or the woman in the home, the endless grinding cancer of the income tax, a torture unknown to dying Keats and tortured Baudelaire. The two worst blights on English life are high taxation (and over-legislation) and the English climate when each season succeeds the other like a prisoner being re-arrested as he leaves the gaol.

[1] Cf. *infra*, p. 198.

It should therefore be the right of every Briton to spend at least two months a year outside of it and this is again where high taxation frustrates him. We should all be entitled to at least 2,000 hours of sunshine. Unfortunately there are still some favoured climates with light as well as warmth and with little or no taxation but it is always impossible to earn one's living in them. The State is determined that the artist shall have no possessions.

ONE OF THE MOST depressing factors in the 'twenties and 'thirties was the destruction of the countryside because it revealed not only the indifference of the many to their heritage but also the acquisitiveness of the few, of speculative builders, estate agents, landlords. I do not see any end to this for now the great greed and cupidity of the English people (which has always been more apparent to their neighbours than to themselves) has been turned inwards and the passionate desire to get rich, the worship of status and the property millionaire have dominated the post-war world. It is quite difficult to find people who are not constantly enumerating sums of money.

LET US END UP, however, with some of the good things.

England remains a truly civilized country, a country where civilization spreads up and down and permeates everyone; it is a country where people are more intelligent than they seem, not less, and as in all civilized countries there is a highly developed sense of humour. Again, as has often been said, it is a kindly and decent country. This fact becomes more and more important when cruelty and torture and informing and bullying are so rife in the world, when police are so brutal and race-hatred so relentless. Whatever we believe in we know that happiness depends on freedom from fear, and here our record is better than anyone's.

Then again England is a country which has hitherto triumphed over its geographical insignificance. This gale-swept chip off the old Europe has a greater density of artefacts than anywhere except parts of Italy, Germany, Holland, and France. If we take a few square miles on the ordinance survey we will find a trace of Roman or Saxon culture, at least one lovely mediaeval church and a Tudor manor or farmhouse, perhaps a cathedral or a Palladian country house, certainly some late Georgian ones, a town with a fine square, unspoilt villages, a folly, a mill, woods with some original bird and animal life, a squire, a rector or two, retired Anglo-Indians, experts on various extraordinary subjects, some good books, china, pictures even, a variety of antique dealers (far more common than publicans), bird-watchers, dog-lovers, a large garden worth a visit, a local museum, a Buddhist, and a witch. This enormously rich texture is quite unlike anything to be found in, for example, the greater part of Ireland, a country which has not been able to live beyond its ecological income. Even if all our houses possess television aerials the inhabitants will not necessarily be rendered less sympathetic by their enforced acquaintance with world affairs.

Television is, I suppose, the greatest single factor for change in people's lives and probably has done much to undermine English puritanism. As a literary critic much of my work has lain among the banned or the nearly banned, and I view the new liberty with bewilderment. What is England going to be like when everyone has read the *Kama Sutra*, the *Tropic of Cancer*, *Lady Chatterley*, and *The Naked Lunch*? A Bali in goose-flesh? It should prove quite extraordinarily interesting, for I find it impossible to conceive an England without sexual inhibitions, without its lavatory jokes and lust murders, its virgins and sadists of all ages and sexes, its squeamishness and evasions. I dread the greed of publishers—so anxious are they to coin money in the name of liberty that they will surely overreach themselves and bring down fire from Whitehall on all our heads. What will happen when the Englishman steps out from his niche in the Freudian textbook? Sometimes I wonder if London is not becoming like Berlin in the 'twenties and will invite the same retribution.

> *It was not taught by the State,*
> *nor willed by the Powers above;*
> *it broke like a river in spate—*
> *when the English learned how to make love.*

ONCE AGAIN I cast back to the 'twenties. It is summer as usual, in a long, low, first-floor sitting-room in a converted farmhouse near the sea; the window is open, moths are drawn through it to the lamp; outside it is still light enough to see the green cornfield and beyond the cornfield the Solent and across the Solent the Isle of Wight. It tapers off beyond the aerials into the three gently undulating hills above Freshwater, contours of unearthly promise and repose. The wireless is playing—not the B.B.C. of the 'thirties when everything led up to the Midnight News, always more sinister, but the B.B.C. of the late 'twenties, the golden voice of David Tennant, the soothing syrup of Christopher Stone—but what I am listening to are those desultory snatches of Debussy or Delius which were used to fill in gaps—harpsichord or piano solos which grip the memory and drift out to sea to form part of my apprehension of the magical landscape; magical, I see now, like the poem of Li Po I was reading—with hope.

> Blue water . . . a clear moon . . .
> In the moonlight the white herons are flying.
> Listen! Do you hear the girls who gather water-chestnuts?
> They are going home in the night, singing.

The Comforts of the Sick-bay

Marcus Cunliffe

I HAPPEN to be in hospital just now, more preoccupied with my own condition than with the Condition of England and not easily able to separate the two. I am drowsy, passive, self-absorbed, and a bit panicky. After only a few days, so suggest-ible is mankind, I feel ill simply because I am surrounded by illness. My irritations become petty (why *will* they put so much sugar in the tea? why is the newspaper boy so slow to arrive each morning? why, when the papers finally reach me, are they so repetitious and insubstantial—can I be reading yesterday's by mistake? does it make any difference?). My satisfactions seem equally small and shrivelled. (Selfish relief that other men in the ward are so much sicker than I. Even, perhaps, a little ugly worm of pleasure in the disappearance of the yellow motionless effigy of a man who lay in the side-ward next to me. In the dim red glow of the night-lamp, I saw a sad woman seated next to him, gazing at the wall. Hours later I awoke to hear whisperings, a clump of rubber-soled shoes, the rattle of a trolley. Next morning the bed was empty, the effigy removed. The day nurses, polite but non-committal, admit that he probably died in the night, being incurable.)

The hospital is old, dingy, and inconvenient, though the atmosphere is friendly. Ceilings are absurdly high, as if built for a bygone race of giants. The walls have been wiped clean of the pervasive grime as high as 1963 can reach. Above, tiny patches of tinsel are stuck on with tape—remnants of last year's Christmas decorations.

All day the ward has reverberated with the Royal Wedding, relayed from the television set. Hour upon hour of it: bagpipe noises, fanfares, crowd sounds, anthems, clerical chanting,

Dimbleby in full unction. The nurses flock in to watch the high moments of the ceremony: still, they are girls, and fond of weddings. One of them jokes about the Queen Mother's terrible hats. Some of the patients lie in bed, ill or bored, heads turned away from the set. Others crouch near in armchairs. It is hard to tell how the spectacle affects them—or indeed how *any* spectacle would affect them in our indrawn mood. In the lavatory extension which is called the sluice I stand beside another man. In shabby communal ignominy we urinate into specimen bottles. What does he think of the Wedding? He grunts, a little suspicious. 'Oh, it's all right.' I say that I find it overdone. He agrees, readily and almost vehemently. 'Taxpayers' money,' he mutters.

Evening. I sit in bed and try to write. No use: the Wedding is on again. 'What's this?' a nurse asks, coming on night-duty. 'I stayed up till two o'clock today to watch it.'

'This is the Wedding,' says an old man in a tartan dressing-gown. 'It's still on. Been going on all day.'

'No,' another patient tells him. 'This is a recap. It's just a film. The real Wedding was this morning.'

'It's still going on,' says the stubborn old man.

The nurse laughs pleasantly.

'Oo,' she says, 'we shall have it for the next week.'

Now the Archbishop of Canterbury is intoning. 'Togeth-ah . . . Togeth-ah . . .' I dislike his voice and try to shut him out by clapping the radio headphones over my ears. There is a choice of two programmes. In fact more: on one channel two concerts are being relayed simultaneously—Rachmaninoff and something from Wales. The other channel has a lugubrious football commentary. One of the Manchester teams, near the end of a bad season, is losing yet again. The commentator cannot disguise his partisanship or his exasperation.

'Oh, what's the *matter* with them? Why don't they use their brains? They're playing *backward* again, instead of *forward*! They'll never get a goal that road.'

PARABLES? I wonder lazily what we are all like, whether the world outside is more of the same: whether we British are all in some sense incurable. I wonder about symptoms, diagnosis, palliatives.

Perhaps there are clues in the phenomenon of the Wedding,

and our ward's attentive apathy. For me, the bits I watched were somewhat farcical: they touched me not at all. The cutting from one scene to another, as the processions converged on the Abbey, was a slow-motion parody of an old Western melodrama. (*Meanwhile, back at the ranch* changed to *Meanwhile, back at Kensington Palace*.) The days and days of meticulous rehearsal, the whole well-managed affair recalled in burlesque minuscule older, grander occasions—the planning for Normandy, or Home Fleet exercises. Indeed the convoy of Rolls-Royces, photographed head-on, advancing at a crawl into the TV cameras, fat and foreshortened, is a parody of those old news-reels of the Fleet steaming in line ahead, invincibly broad and numerous. It is all shrunken, telegenic, a little silly and pathetic: for the tourists.[1]

I am free of that England of pomp and circumstance, in company with the millions of others who yawn at *God Save the Queen* or giggle at *That Was the Week*. We are liberated from a carapace, an official, gentlemanly, deferential England which for millions of us never really made sense. There was an English 'identity', an English 'image', to use jargon-words of this decade, that were peculiarly out of focus for the elementary-school millions. In one such school, thirty years ago on Tyneside, I remember having to learn Rudyard Kipling's 'Glory of the Garden':

> *Our England is a garden that is full of stately views*
> *Of borders, beds and shrubberies, of lawns and avenues.*

Our England? Pit-villages, housing-estates, shaggy moorland? I had never seen a great house, at least not in occupation. The nearest thing was Seaton Delaval, an empty and reputedly haunted shell of a house in the middle of a coalfield. I had never seen thatched cottages, and probably doubted their existence. Later, of course, I did discover surviving and even flourishing patches of the England that Kipling celebrated, and all that went with them: gentrified and countrified people, Oxford colleges, Sandhurst, London clubs. To some extent I imitated them and accepted their styles.

GOING TO AMERICA as a student, after the war, was for me both a shock and partial emancipation. At first I was touchy,

[1] Cf. *supra*, p. 192.

easily affronted, and a little supercilious. I accepted the Yale college-plan as an inevitable but rather ridiculous tribute to Oxbridge. I was amused by Anglophiles and bruised by Anglophobes. One evening with aggressively liberal Americans I found myself denying, with anger but without success, that I was 'stuffy' or 'snobbish'. They mimicked my accent, they charged me with imperialism, anti-Zionism, and a dozen other grave offences. Soon however I seemed to escape such incrimination: to escape the whole prim, cloying, too-familiar, class-and-status-obsessed English atmosphere. I became perhaps too uncritically pro-American. The ease of movement and utterance, the largeness and openness, and also the restlessness, the uncertainty, the blur as to what exactly America 'meant': these stirred the imagination, evoking affection and sympathy. They seemed part of a warmer, clumsier, more important context than the English one. In the United States, I thought, vices and virtues alike were on the heroic scale.

I realized how far I had gone native when after about six months I was introduced to a visiting English celebrity. At home I would no doubt have been impressed and intimidated by his aplomb, his elegance, his idiosyncrasy; and it must be admitted that he had this effect upon most of the Americans who met him. But to me suddenly he was a stage Englishman, a caricature, and moreover a semi-fraudulent one. His manners appeared as mannerisms. His accent struck me as unbearably affected, and distorted; every vowel was squeezed out of shape. Since then the Queen's English has never sounded right to me. No doubt my view was distorted also: American ideology, the ideology of homespunness which produces its own caricatures, had me in thrall. Certainly there are American defects, including domestic forms of snobbery. Yet the word hardly applies to the United States, in the sense it holds for me, a sense with a peculiarly English connotation. In America the viler and more violent aspects of snobbery become something else—open and defiant bigotry. Snobbery in the English sense has no proper hold there. The essence of snobbery is that it is a minor, non-violent, second-rate, and above all hermetic vice. It is a game within the closed circle which everyone not only may but must play. It is cosy, indirect, inhibiting, malicious. The art is to put oneself at ease by making someone else uneasy: to be one-up by making someone else one-down. The real intent of the old school tie is to remind others that they have no right to wear it, though ostensibly it is a badge of good fellowship. Willy-nilly, the snobbish society makes us connoisseurs of these shades of privilege. Reading about Vassall, I pounce with cruel enlightenment upon the disclosure that this debonair creature went to Monmouth Grammar School, and left at sixteen. What an apprenticeship, one reflects if one is English, he must have served in concealing that stigma before he moved on to wider evasions.

OF COURSE I WAS NOT ALONE in reacting critically to English weaknesses, nor was a trip to America an essential aid to detachment. There has been a long and vigorous tradition of dissent. Much of the appeal of the Labour Party was built upon the indignations of class-consciousness. In the last ten years a whole literature of disaffiliation has sprung up. When its history comes to be written, a place will surely be accorded to Nigel Dennis's brilliantly sardonic novel *Cards of Identity*, which supplied keys to the satirical analysis of our society years before the sport became universal. What interests me, though, is that the sport *has* become universal, and that the results may be more enervating than invigorating. There has been a marked and rapid decline in English power and prestige. But the process has been outpaced by our readiness to proclaim that this is so. Liberation has been accompanied by almost total deflation. The carapace has come off but the flesh underneath is soft and shapeless. Other peoples presented before our eyes the ungainly comedy of their struggles to define and assume national identities: we were snug. Now the painful comedy preoccupies us, when we thought such matters were long settled, with a certain amount of assistance from Providence in the early stages. Who are we, what are we, what do we mean to be like? Our answers at present are sorry ones.

AND SO I FIND MYSELF generalizing from the narcissistic circumstances of the hospital ward. One recalls Auden's description of England as this country where no one is ever quite well.

In hospital, and perhaps in England too, we are unwell and become further debilitated by inactivity. We are a little ashamed of ourselves and feel a little dishonoured. But most of our pride has gone, along with indignation: the higher altitudes of snobbery are a mere pageant, a charade, and the lower ones have correspondingly lost their edge. We are tired, companionable, sorry for ourselves. We sleep during the day but not so soundly at night. Past and future cease to concern us urgently. Economic issues have receded: we do not know whether we are rich or poor. The world outside is a spectacle on television, a sports commentary. We do not react violently, in enthusiasm or in disapproval. Our strongest hope is that no more harm may befall us; our longing for peace is in large part a wish to be left in peace. We do not expect our teams to win. We read about our statesmen on the gossip pages, and take for granted that they will act as we do in the ward, from day to day, without foresight or nobility. We are good-humouredly pessimistic. Life has been a bit unfair, though things could have been worse. We have been struck down by something congenital, or something in the air. Our life is in other hands. Things are done for us and to us, not by us.

I am not saying that England has altogether stopped being snobbish; or that no one is interested any longer in Royal Weddings or other symbols of what used to be called the British Way and Purpose. I do not maintain that nothing is done with skill, success, and devotion any more (what of the doctors and nurses in the analogy?); or that our entire society, at all levels, is plaintive, nervous, bewildered. Yet the analogy is disquietingly relevant. 'Our' England is more truly ours than a generation ago, yet we are disappointed rather than gratified. Something has collapsed, or we think it has. We have lost, or mislaid, our sense of direction. Nationally we are in a mild state of shock. We are like those Victorian females who under stress would take to their beds or couches and rest there for indefinite periods, the victims of unspecified ailments whose supposed severity attested to the sufferers' fineness of sensibility. In other words, our chief trouble is not disease but hypochondria. We follow an inverted Coué system, according to which every day, in every way, things are getting worse and worse.

THE SYMPTOMS are widespread and not confined to any one class. As a nation we do not take ourselves seriously: we are either mournful or frivolous. Even our Blimps seem to parody themselves, and then join in the laughter to show what decent chaps they are. The games of snobbery, being no longer hermetic, have lost much of their point. Our arrogances have become tentative. Looking back, we think we notice the rot setting in at least a century ago. By Kipling's day, we can discern, England's authority was palpably on the wane; already reality and its symbols failed to correspond. When the process became easily recognizable it was far advanced. Sir Winston Churchill was by 1940 a splendid anachronism, by 1945 an unacceptable one. The lessons of popular folklore, which may affect our day-dreams more than we realize, add to our discouragement. In one familiar plot, the ageing champion boxer (England?), to save his silver trophies from the pawnshop, decides to stage a comeback. Alas, some merciless contender half his age knocks him all around the ring. The champion, while the tell-tale blood trickles from the corners of his mouth, may perhaps vindicate himself with a final tremendous punch; if so, it will be his last one. We know, regretfully, that the wise money will be on Sonny Liston.

BUT IF, as I believe, our trouble is hypochondria, we have frightened ourselves unnecessarily as hypochondriacs do. Much in English life is unlikeable and unsatisfactory, but there is nothing hopelessly wrong with us. In comparison with most societies of the world we are extremely well off—economically, politically, socially. The point is that where we once exaggerated our prowess, our freedom of will, we now exaggerate our incapacity, our pre-destined downfall. Certain fashions in social analysis encourage the tendency. For example: METAPHORS FROM BIOLOGY. Though these are not used by sophisticated social scientists, they continue to grip our imagination. Yet why *should* we believe that human societies are in fact comparable to living organisms—moving in the same inevitable sequence from youth and maturity to senility and death? The relevance of such a metaphor is so broad as to be meaningless, though it may be employed in order to warn or scold us. Otherwise it tells us nothing: it has no predictive value.

GENERALIZING FROM RECENT CIRCUMSTANCES. Our collective memory is amazingly short, and so is that of our social analysts. Thirty years ago, the fall in the birth-rate of Western Europe and the United States was a serious problem. The phenomenon was examined and explained; the figures were plotted, and confidently extrapolated. Now we have forgotten that the problem existed. Ten or even five years ago France was commonly regarded as the Sick Man of Europe, a country with insoluble problems which were being tackled in all the wrong ways. Today it is not France's disasters but her economic achievements that impress us. Ten or even five years from now we may be offered plausible and authoritative explanations for Britain's remarkable recovery during the 1960s. In each case the commentator would be able to draw upon authentic historical evidence to strengthen and to dignify his argument.

WHOLESALE CHANGE deliberately planned and willed is, we have been taught, inevitably catastrophic. The thorough absorption of this lesson is indeed one reason why we are excessively timid. We respect the actual integrity of the human being but in consequence underestimate the potential of human energy and intelligence. Yet we recognize that *some* degree of planned change is feasible and desirable. In reckoning things up we ought to see that we have been lucky, and ought to share our luck with the rest of the world. If we stay alive, this is a good time to be alive. We may have given up our power with too-great psychological haste: at least we are not barmy. We are ready for change, even if puzzled what to do next. The puzzlement makes the headache feel more acute than formerly.

But we know that decisions can no longer be deferred, that the snoozing and the languor and the equivocations are over—that it is time to transform our policies and politics, schools and universities, courts and prisons, décor and architecture, cookery and customs, commerce and industry, images and identities: the whole fabric. It is time the invalid arose, like that temporary and redoubtable Victorian malingerer-reformer, Harriet Martineau, and addressed herself—being, after all, no fool—to the business of the world outside the sick-room.

Sex on these Islands

Alan McGlashan

RESPECT FOR THE PAST and for the value of continuity is our leading national characteristic, and it is by no means a mere matter of politics. The Labour Party clings as tenaciously to its early image of the cloth-capped, neckerchiefed Working Man, as does the Tory Party to its nostalgic vision of Merrie England. There is in fact nothing the English dislike so much as making a clean break. In many ways this attitude serves us well, since belief in the value of continuity gives power to endure; and endurance, as the history of every legendary hero testifies, is the prime heroic virtue.

But no human virtue is without its defect. Confronted with a challenge which demands a real break with tradition, the English are driven to call into play a less attractive expedient which, however, has the benefit of Platonic sanction: Saving Appearances. When we cannot have continuity of tradition we settle blandly for the appearance of it. For this purpose we have perfected an appropriate technique—lifting a corner of the national carpet and delicately sweeping under it the offending dust. The late Victorians and Edwardians developed an amazing virtuosity in this manœuvre, especially in regard to sexual dust, though they also became adept at the disposal of other kinds, such as factory conditions and child labour. The result was a smooth and deceptively attractive society.

The impact of Freudian ideas on this complacent Edwardian world was salutary in many ways, but not in all: the truth does not always set you free. When it is truth on a mechanistic level it can tighten your chains . . . as in Sweden, where the dissemination of detailed sexual information, combined with an exceptionally permissive social attitude towards pre-marital sex experience (and incidentally an unrivalled economic security) coincides with the second-highest youthful suicide rate in the world. The dust-concealing technique, for all its hypocrisy, carried the implication of an accepted moral code which it was reprehensible—and dangerous—to flout. When, with the advent of Freud, the carpet was lifted right up and the dirt unmistakably revealed, when the cupboards were thrown open and the skeletons came rattling out, the English community rather lost its head. It behaved as individuals sometimes do when too suddenly confronted with proof that their established moral attitudes are largely a sham: it became first shocked; then, in the 1920s, feverishly licentious; and finally, after the further brutal revelations of a second World War, disillusioned and apathetic.

Freud broke the Tables of Chalk on which the Victorian moral code was engraved. Now it is quite possible, *pace* the professional moralists, to live wisely without a moral system— but only if in its place there is a numinous ideal which draws a man ineluctably towards itself. Unfortunately in the concepts of Freudian mechanistic psychology there was no place for noumena and none for ideals: life was presented as a strictly self-regulating system of which the basic activating force was the sexual drive. It is now clear that Freud seriously over-played the phallic aspect—but the original impact of this doctrine gave a refreshing release to the long-pent natural impulses that stifled beneath the Edwardian frock-coat. At the same time, inevitably, it provided a sudden uplift of philosophical respectability to the gross materialism that underlay much of the Edwardian piety. The explosion of 1914–18 accelerated this process. It became possible and indeed fashionable openly to defy not only the rigid moral code but also all values that were not utilitarian. In *avant garde* circles immediately following the Great War idealism became a dirty word, and was brushed under the Bloomsbury carpets with all the eye-deceiving legerdemain that the previous generation had shown over sex.

ENGLISH YOUTH, observing with mixed astonishment and delight this *volte face* of their seniors, plunged gaily enough into the sexually permissive society which was thus created. Petting parties became the adolescent rage, illegitimate birth-rates bounded, early divorce rates soared. The decades of the 1920s and 1930s were the honeymoon period of the 'Freudian Liberation'. But with the advent of the second World War, and during its course, sexual licence became accepted among adolescents of all classes to a point at which it began to lose its revolutionary appeal; and suddenly the permissive atmosphere became, to youth's surprise, yawningly tedious.

Adolescence needs to rebel; and sex as an effective gesture of rebellion had been ruined. Their seniors were sexually laxer than they themselves were, and far better at it. Other gestures had therefore to be found, and so began to appear, as a socially significant phenomenon: the juvenile delinquent, the now obsolescent Teddy Boy, and the current Rocker. Unlike the period-costumed Teddy Boy, the Rocker owes nothing to the past. Black-leather-jacketed and suède-booted, he is uncompromisingly of his time; he dresses not to attract, but to shock; and spends up to £5 a week at his hairdresser, not to impress the girls, but as a mark of leadership and a narcissistic outlet, sweetly reinforced by the horror it creates among the Squares. Youthful vitality still pours itself out, as it must, in brash rebellion, but has found new and curiously anti-social channels. Sex, to a surprising number of English adolescents, is old hat; although naturally they continue to practise it, sexual freedom is casual and secondary—no longer a symbol of revolt. Many teenagers are a little shocked at their seniors' preoccupation with the subject. Others, constitutionally incapable of being shocked, are exasperated by the importance adults seem to accord to an activity which the teenager takes as a matter of routine, almost as a matter of hygiene.

Such detachment could be Olympian, and even admirable; but when it arises in an adolescent without sense of direction and devoid of inner resources, when the vacuum left in the psyche by the disappearance of Eros is filled with ever louder and cruder and emptier images, when finally the gun and the cosh come to represent unconsciously the lost virility of the male: the significance of this detachment becomes frighteningly clear; as also its connection with the deepening malaise of a society (and in particular a popular press) that has lost touch with Eros. For Eros is the archetypal force that alone keeps sanity and warmth alive in human hearts, and sex in its appointed place.

These groups of disillusioned juveniles, though important as indices of the direction the English community is taking, are of course only a small and over-publicized part of the total picture. Among the adult population there are numerous and capacious pockets of resistance where the traditional English attitudes persist—social milieux where sexual licence is still hidden, forbidden, and exciting; authoritarian structures like the Legislature, the Public Schools, and the Courts of Law, where the old drape-the-statues approach to sex is as unobtrusively active as ever.

IN RECENT YEARS Parliament has produced a collector's piece in this respect. The Street Offences Act of 1959, banning prostitutes from the streets and parks, may, on balance, have been sound legislation. Be that as it may, it would be hard indeed to find a more perfect example of the national tendency to sweep unpleasant things out of sight, off the streets, that is, and into the ambiguous little advertisements in newsagents' windows, and into the blameless pages of the London Telephone Directory.

Less obvious, but of far more consequence, is the Legislature's quietly repressive treatment of homosexuality. But this issue, of unsuspected importance to the psychological health of the English, is involved with the influence of that remarkable anachronism, the English Public School, which must first be considered.

The most resourceful and persistent under-the-carpet operator of our time is undoubtedly the Public School System. It is indeed becoming difficult to walk on its carpet at all owing to the number and size of the inconvenient facts concealed beneath it. The System has incontestable virtues, but they belong to the past. The types it produces are no longer at home, no longer 'with it' in the contemporary world, and unless fortunate enough to find refuge in Government Service, have a great deal of agonizing reappraisal to face before they can fit in with current requirements. But the major defect of the System lies surely in its bitter, thin-lipped refusal to face the physiological facts of adolescent sexual development.

Physical sex is an instinct, and like other basic instincts—like hunger and the will to survive—it springs into activity at the moment of birth, and dies only with the dissolution of the body. Its goals and modes of satisfaction vary enormously at different stages of the individual's growth, but it is never inactive. There is a physiological time for all things: a time for interest in our own mind and body, a time for interest in the minds and bodies of our comrades, a time for interest in the minds and bodies of women. Not that this is the whole of a young male's life; under normal conditions it is only a small part of it. But it is a healthy and valid part, and should be lived through with as little interference as possible.

In contrast to this, the 'sex theory' of the Public School System—modified, fortunately, by occasional schoolmasters of insight and imagination, who are nevertheless, like the boys themselves, pinned down by the 'theory'—is that physical sex has nothing to do with normal boys, whose aims and satisfactions should be fully met by work and violent exercise. Where adolescent interest in sex appears, it is regarded as a weak self-indulgence or a dangerous perversion, to be exorcized by the classical method of the Inquisition—moral persuasion, promoted by the whip, forced confession, and public execution.

The distortion such an approach causes in the emotional and sexual development of an adolescent needs no emphasis: the System would seem to be ingeniously devised for this very purpose. The half-dozen years of a boy's life which the Public School claims, are the critical years when the inevitable homosexual component present in every normal male is physiologically and psychologically at its peak. The segregation of the sexes involved in Public School life inevitably reinforces and exaggerates this factor. Having in this way stimulated the homosexual phase, the System savagely represses it, surrounding the whole phenomenon—which in unmolested adolescence tends to be expressed in a platonic passion as pure and selfless as anything this world affords—with a guilty and furtive aura of sin, obloquy, birchings, and expulsions. Just in case a boy, driven off by fear and anguish from this perfectly normal phase of his development, should turn back to himself for sexual expression, the System has devised the well-known technique of admonitory talks, in which an embarrassed housemaster throws out veiled hints (veiled, and all the more frightening in their allusiveness) of the completely imaginary dangers involved, ranging from failure at work and sport to permanent impotence and insanity. Thus prepared for mature sex experience, the Public School boy at eighteen is returned to the continuous company of women from which he has been intermittently segregated since childhood.

To UNDERSTAND and value his own feminine side and—what follows from this—to achieve a full and deep relationship with a woman is, after such conditioning, needlessly difficult. That it occurs at all is proof of the almost miraculous recuperative power of the psyche. Moreover, this matter may not be one of merely domestic concern. Apart from all the private unhappiness, it is not impossible that one factor in our lagging national productivity is due to the same cause; due, that is, to the loss of vital executive energies involved in the heartbreaks, marital miseries, and gnawing inner tensions afflicting so many of the British managerial classes—as a result, in part at least, of their school-induced *gaucheries* towards women.

To RETURN to the attitude of the law and the Legislature towards homosexuality, this may now be considered in a wider context. Parliament, the Law Courts, and the Public School System have almost identical reactions to this problem—which is scarcely surprising, since a Public School is the educational background of the majority of politicians and of most, if not all, senior legal administrators. There is also in the reactions of all three institutions to homosexual conduct a period flavour which is curiously reminiscent of the late-Victorian attitude to extramarital sex: that in properly constituted individuals it does not exist; or if it does exist, it should not; that if condemned and punished severely enough it will probably cease to exist; and that if in spite of all this it is still there, at least let it be dismissed as summarily as possible. Under the carpet with it—and above all let there be no discussion.

That this should be the accepted standpoint of three major institutions in a community whose current degree of sexual licence has never been equalled since Restoration times, is one of those fascinating things about the English that makes the rest of Europe look at us in a kind of marvelling silence. But this paradox is rather more than a harmless source of amusement to others; it points straight to the heart of what is psychologically sick in the English attitude to sex: we 'sin', but with a bad conscience. We are oppressed by our sexual freedoms. The hollowness of the powerful taboos imposed by the Victorians has been publicly demonstrated, but since the demonstration was based on a mechanistic ethically neutral philosophy, nothing has taken the place of the lost taboos, and we are left without guidance, wandering in a Waste Land of withered certainties; for most of us have always required a strong and established set of rules to live by. Plainly what is needed is the construction of a new code of conduct consonant with our new insights and dawning convictions. But this kind of fundamental re-thinking is exactly what England, in its passion for compromise, instinctively rejects—and with this rejection is lost for the time being the possibility of an honest and integrated sexuality. We half-enjoy the new freedoms, but carefully maintain institutions, based on a now discredited moral code, to punish ourselves remorselessly for doing so. On any sexual issue our national judgment is ambiguous and vacillating, often combining by this means the maximum of human unhappiness with the minimum of help.

THIS IS pre-eminently the case with homosexuality. Admittedly one of the law's primary functions is to protect society and to promote its stability; and it could be said that the homosexual impulse constitutes a risk to social stability as at present organized. This might give at least a social sanction to deterrent punishment of this deviation—*if it worked*. But manifestly it does not work. Not only is homosexuality a far greater problem among men, where it is a major crime, than among women where virtually it is not; but also the very threat of such punishment opens wide the door to what is perhaps the least defensible of all crimes: blackmail. The number of cases of blackmail that are reported to the police is for obvious reasons a very small percentage of the amount that actually occurs. But of this small number of cases reported to the police in England and Wales in the years 1950 to 1953 inclusive, no less than 45% were connected with homosexual activities.

When at last a courageous and unbiased examination of this unresolved problem was made, in the Wolfenden Report, its conclusions were at once and unanimously regarded by all political parties as electoral poison, and its recommendations hastily shelved as high as possible out of reach. The only part, a very minor one, of the Report which was put into effect was, significantly enough, the Street Offences Act of 1959 which, as we have seen, was a law to ensure that little prostitutes, like little Victorian girls, should be neither seen nor heard. The Street Offences Act had an instant appeal and was passed amid a chorus of public approbation.

Let us face this fact: the harsh and illiberal treatment of the homosexual in English Courts of Law, condoned by the embarrassed silence of priest, professional, and layman, is the direct result of an unwillingness to make a clean break with out-moded ways of thought. This act of moral cowardice is a source of conscious or unconscious guilt in ourselves and of bad faith towards others. It is psychologically crippling.

WHAT HAS BEEN sketched so far is a general impression of the prevailing sex-attitudes in English social life. Fortunately there are active influences of an opposite kind, but their effectiveness is, as yet, scarcely perceptible. Genuine attempts however are made from time to time to present the objective facts about sex on these islands rather than to 'save appearances'. The Wolfenden Report is one outstanding instance, and the recent Report of the Religious Society of Friends another, as are many of the activities of the Howard League for Penal Reform. The Quaker Report is, in fact, a remarkably clear-sighted and courageous document, as may be gathered from its final paragraph dealing with pre-marital sex experience, '*which*', says the Report, '*is not*

such a sin. Where there is genuine tenderness and openness to respon-
sibility and the seed of commitment, God is surely not shut out.' The
importance of this statement lies in its manifestation of a sincere
desire on the part of a deeply religious group to lighten the sense
of guilt attaching to a natural and universal impulse. Theologians assure us that a sense of guilt is necessary to human beings:
and this may well be, though it is disputable. But if there must
be guilt, it would perhaps be a good idea to save it for the real
sins of the nation. *e.g.* apathy, complacency, etc.

It might be well, for example, if a little more guilt were
generated about the English community's attitude towards that
unsavoury subject, criminal abortion. The persistence with
which this problem has for many years been quietly hidden
from the public is almost unbelievable, in view of its sheer size.
Estimates of the number of women each year who have illegal
abortions vary from 50,000 to 100,000, the statistical vagueness
being due to the fact that it is difficult to see clearly under a
carpet. Even at the lower figure, it represents a pretty sizeable
pool of human misery, sickness, and death. To this ugly but
urgent situation the response of both Church and State is a
simple turning away of the head. In the words of a recent review of the subject, the problem is 'ignored as much as possible
in official quarters, and regrettably the Churches do not extend
to it a Christian charity. . . .'

As to the adequacy of police action, it is perhaps sufficient to
quote from an article in the current *Howard Journal*: 'In 1939
the Interdepartmental Committee on Abortion estimated that
54,000 illegal operations took place in England and Wales
annually; other more recent estimates put the figure considerably higher; yet the number of women brought to trial in
England and Wales in 1960 and 1961 was 34 and 40 respectively.' They were dealt with under a 100-year-old law, the
Offences against the Person Act, 1861, the severity of its
punishments being such that in practice they are now never
imposed. The Act is still in force. In 1961 a Private Member's
Bill, the Medical Termination of Pregnancy Bill, to reform this
antiquated law, 'was introduced in Parliament but was "talked
out" before a vote could be taken'.

Clear thinking and honest action on this subject would

certainly be spiritually painful and electorally dangerous. But it is surely overdue.

DISMAYED BY THE complex tangle of contemporary thoughts and feelings about sex (and not only about sex, for we are in almost as big a muddle over hanging and corporal punishment), inevitably the cry goes up from certain quarters—abolish these pernicious freedoms! Back to the old strict moralities, the relentless severities of social condemnation; within this rigid framework youth was happier on the whole, less burdened. . . . Is there something in it? The trouble is, we cannot go back, however passionately some may wish to. Such nostalgic dreaming as is doomed as that of the small girl whom I found one day sitting alone, wrapped in concentrated thought. When I asked what she was doing she replied, 'I am playing hide-and-seek by myself. I have just hidden something and now I am trying hard to forget where I put it.' It is precisely what we are doing with the Wolfenden Report, the Quakers' Report—and many other things.

THE SUGGESTION *that delinquency represents a failure to achieve a social life organized round sexual interest is advanced by Dr. T. C. N. Gibbens, senior lecturer in forensic psychiatry at London University, in a preliminary report of a psychiatric investigation of Borstal boys published today.*

'We read much about delinquent areas, delinquent subcultures, and why delinquents join gangs, but less about why the delinquent does not have girl friends like most of his non-delinquent contemporaries and organize his social life around them,' he says.

Criminologists had considered 'broken homes' and 'maternal deprivation' systematically, but few attempts had been made to relate sexual behaviour and development to criminal behaviour. It was found that 46 per cent of the boys had no experience of heterosexual intercourse; 37 per cent had occasional experience, and 17 per cent were promiscuous. Four per cent of the boys admitted to homosexual interests, but 25 per cent had known or suspected homosexual tendencies. The vast majority of boys said they did not drink or seldom did so.

THE TIMES

Against the Stream

Elizabeth Young

THE THOUGHTFUL British parent of adequate means can often be seen straddling the horns of the great national independent dilemma; shall he send his child to a public school? There is a strongly worded Right-wing myth that middle-class parents make great sacrifices to send their children away to boarding-school, and that this is so much in the national interest, it ought to be tax free. There is also the evident fact that the parents who do send their children away don't care too much about the State schools their children aren't going to, and that this is *not* in the national interest.

The present compromise is that children of well-off middle-class families do mainly go to public schools, but without tax relief. Meanwhile the State schools improve only slowly, the public schools prosper and build golf courses, and the nation's children go on being educated to fear and despise each other ever after.

This compromise will have to be re-negotiated fairly soon: what are the advantages and disadvantages of the public school system?

THERE ARE TWO WAYS to make the comparison: first, from the point of view of the parent who has to make an individual and immediate choice and must compare public schools with what else is now available, and second from that of society in general which has to decide whether the present roughly dual system is good, or whether the price we pay for it isn't too high.

To start with the individual.

Most public school boys have been to a preparatory school

and have been abstracted from normal home life at the age of seven or eight. All are taken away at thirteen. The assumed advantages of the preparatory school are that it 'cuts a boy away from his mother's apron strings', and that it teaches him to live in collectivity better because it begins to teach him sooner. On the other hand, there is no evidence that it is bad for a boy to live with his father and mother till he is thirteen, or even for that matter till he is eighteen. Those who cry out that 'the family is the basic unit of society' and that it is being 'disrupted' might even come to feel that this system which makes parents childless for much of the year is indeed a disruption. A more certain disadvantage is that it places the boy in a society where there is no alternative to homoxexual affection and where he is beaten or expelled if he expresses it. His first meeting with sex takes place under an artificially heavy cloud.

The public schools have a higher pupil-teacher ratio because they are able to pay their teachers more, and often to give them more amenities, than any but a handful of State schools. This means that a moderately intelligent boy—or girl: but the whole system is less pronounced on a girl's side—has a better chance of getting to a university (and particularly to Oxford or Cambridge) from the better public schools than from all but the same handful of State schools. On the State side, the comprehensive schools (which are probably the only solution to the problem) are only just beginning to send pupils to the universities: it is not yet possible to compare their achievement with that of the other schools. The competitive distortion of the system deriving from the paucity of university places is another question; but so long as it lasts the public schools will have their attraction for those who want their children to be successfully considered 'university material'.

THE PUBLIC SCHOOLS, being for the most part country boarding-schools, can through sheer lack of interruption be at the business of education fourteen hours a day. Family quarrels, long hours of travelling, the opposite sex, all these distractions are avoided. Others—school quarrels, petty indignities, 'traditions', the same sex—are of course introduced, but on balance the total of distraction is probably reduced. So it is that the public schools can cultivate so much mild and liberal eccentricity in their sixth forms. In a grammar school you never hear the strains of de Saumarez major's tuba floating through the rosegirt cloister at eleven on a summer evening. And certainly it is thus that that *nonpareil*, the English gentleman, is programmed and produced.

The programme, except for the rich or for those who get it as part of the perks of their job or swing it with the tax inspectors via grandfather's covenant, requires financial sacrifice. The sacrifice is not only the parents', it is the whole family's. The boy who is enabled to play the tuba at eleven in the evening will have fewer amenities at home, fewer foreign holidays, more of the nervousness that skimping for something which is or is believed to be an essential always brings.

The better chance of Oxford or Cambridge is not the only purchase. The other is the class stamp, and this perhaps weighs more with non-professional parents. In practice, only public school boys become officers in the Brigade of Guards. In practice, 'knowing the right people', being 'one of us' or 'our sort', is a convenience in the higher reaches of the City and the Foreign Service. So much is a commonplace of observation, pride, and resentment. Which brings us to the social aspects of the choice: to purchase these presumed advantages for one's child assumes a belief in the changelessness, past and future, of the kind of society we live in. Where, in practice, are young public school men most in demand now? If that is their only or main qualification, probably for decorative use in the front office of a prestige-minded firm, or behind the counter at Harrods. The middle-aged, self-made father who recalls that things would have been different for him thirty years ago if he had been a Wykehamist, and sends his son to Winchester, is calculating on a fifty-year social standstill. He is probably also mistaking the nature of his own success.

Because the price of 'starting out on the inside' is debility and general castration which derive from the imposition of backward-looking and segregationist outlook. 'Backward-looking': only last week a public school boy told me he had urged something on his headmaster, and had been told it would be the first time it had been done, and 'there are no first times at ——

School'. 'Segregationist': the younger clerks at the Foreign
Office, that essential extension of the public school, divide the
people there into 'chaps' (Executive Branch) and 'gnomes'
(Administrative Branch); the older ones talk in a relaxed way of
'wogs' and 'frogs' and 'niggers'. This is where the personal and
the public dilemmas overlap. Where the British middle classes
do achieve warmth of family life, vigour, and seriousness of
intellectual achievement, a sense of pleasure, and a sense of
beauty untinged with 'spiritual' and poovish aestheticism, they
do so not because but in spite of those elements in public school
life which are special to it.

THESE ELEMENTS ARE conservatism, and segregation by class
and by sex. The political parties now vie in declaring that if this
country is to survive and move it must become more adventur-
ous, more inventive and appreciative of invention, more in
touch with the world as it is. These are the qualities which the
public schools discourage and disparage. When a 'decision-
maker' lacks these qualities, as many do, the cause may be either
his having been at a 'good' public school, or at a 'bad' public
school which apes the good ones, or a bad grammar school
which apes what it supposes to be either. In their most precise
and active form public school values flourish best in four or five
great schools, but they percolate through the system, and as
they do so they tend to lose whatever is good in them, the
inculcation of solid public virtues, and leave only the acrid
residue.

Is IT POSSIBLE to bridge the gap, heal the wounds, and purge
the distempers? Perhaps we are now all too instinct with the
sense of division to mend ourselves, but we have no alternative
but to try; as Michael Young has said, babies are creeping
socialists. . . . (And so, under the banner of liberty, equality, and
sibling rivalry, are most young children.) Merging the public
schools into a comprehensive system would be complicated,
slow, and painful; but not merging them is already inflicting on
us complication, pain, and lethargy.

If some of the public schools gather up their skirts and skip
across the sea to Ireland they will at least be that much closer to

the capital base in the Bahamas. One need not take very seriously the argument that a comprehensive fee-less system is an intolerable infringement of an Englishman's freedom to spend his money as he likes. The Englishman gave up his freedom to buy his way to heaven centuries ago; he gave up his right to buy himself a commission in the army, to buy himself a private bill of divorcement, and each time gained more freedom than he lost. These things were and are too important to be left to the chance ownership of money.

It is now in education that the buyable element is cancerous on the system as a whole, just as indulgences and scandalous officers were in their day. Education, which used to be a class luxury, is now a necessity for the whole of our society.

What we need is a single system of schools, which would include all our children, not just most, with their teachers paid what they need in salary and amenities to assure them dignity and independence. Streaming should be tentative and remediable, as it is, for instance, under the French system of the *cours d'observation*. Schools where children go until sixteen or eighteen must be for teaching them as human beings, as members of society, not merely as 'university material' or as 'tomorrow's labour force'. Professional and vocational training is logically subsequent to this education; religious training and instruction cannot be extraneous to it, and (as we don't have anti-clericalism) should be, in so far as it exists, part of it. Implicit in the system should be the knowledge that although it is of marvellous interest where someone comes from, how he speaks and dresses, and who his cousin is, it is of absolutely no importance.

The Tragedy of Being Clever

John Vaizey

WOLVERTON is a mid-nineteenth-century railway town in Buckinghamshire, halfway between Oxford and Cambridge. There are hundreds of small hideous terrace houses in livid brick, a few chapels and railwaymen's clubs, humped in the flat countryside around the railway workshops, and one of the most dangerous road bridges in the country. It is a prosperous Southern edition of the squalid Northern industrial town. The failure to rebuild it is somehow indicative of what is wrong with our country. Poised as it is, midway between the university cities, and on the main line to London, with the M.1 only a few miles away, Wolverton seems like something out of *Fanny by Gaslight*. God knows what the North must be like, you feel, if Wolverton is like this.

But as you drive in from Oxford, a handsome new building stands on the right of the road in well laid-out grounds. Its elegant restrained lines—characteristic of the Bucks County Council architectural department—are a hundred years, and a million miles of aesthetic attainment, from the neighbouring town. It is the Wolverton College of Further Education.

It must have *some* effect—more than a billion pounds of educational building since the war, almost a tripling of university places, a sextupling of higher education, a hundred thousand more teachers, a rise of about eighteen months in the leaving age—it must all do something.

Before the war the educational system in England was sluggishly backward. Tawney's prose stands as a permanent memorial to the squalor and neglect of the nation's schools by the pre-war governments. In twenty years a lot has been done.

The really significant changes are easy to enumerate. The grammar schools, taking the most able children, are becoming seven-year schools with most of their pupils going on to eighteen. The 'Secondary Modern' schools, catering for two-thirds of the population, are developing courses for children over fifteen. The differences between the grammar school child and the 'secondary modern' child are being eroded. There has been an increase in technical education and in science teaching. Expenditure on education has gone up by probably three times (in real money-value terms) between 1938 and 1963.

So a flow of educational talent, in place of the former trickle, should have been beginning to transform British industry and British society. Why has it not done so? Partly because of the chronic shortage of places in the universities and other institutes of higher education. Partly because the class-barriers in England are not only gruesome but actively inhibit economic growth. Education ought to offer one of the ways—probably the only main way—to overcome these barriers. At present, in many respects, it reinforces them. The way it does so is simple. At every point—selection at eleven, selection at eighteen—more people are trying to squeeze through narrow gateways; those who pop through join the happy few who are there by birth— and *hey presto!* a few more recruits for the class system are available.

THE DEGREE TO WHICH social class has limited the development of talent can hardly be exaggerated. The number of able people in the universities could probably be at least tripled in the next two generations, with no lowering of standards, even in the judgment of the most conservative psychologists. Certainly the expansion which has taken place between 1920 and the present has been accompanied by a substantial improvement in the quality of the typical student. But—'the relationship of the provision of places to the distribution of ability is to the point of arbitrariness', writes Jean Floud. 'Social selection disguised as academic selection is a process at work in all schools. By the time children reach the threshold of secondary education at the age of eleven, those drawn from certain social groups have as a whole already begun to outstrip scholastically those from families at the other end of the scale, and the same process is continued among those selected from grammar schools during their time there.'[1]

There is now overwhelming evidence that the flow of talent from the working class—and from girls of all classes—is seriously inhibited by the inadequacy and over-selection of our schools; and that this process tends to entrench class divisions. The pressure from the rising birth-rate will increase the problem. It used to be a convenient statistic to remember that the number of births per year in England and Wales was about 650,000. It is now over 800,000—and a million births a year is not unthinkable. In common with all of Western Europe (except Ireland) this population explosion is creating a demand for more places in education which is putting pressure on the system and increases the difficulties of giving opportunities to people from the working class.

Recently the National Union of Teachers has called attention to the anachronistic, indeed primitive, character of many of our school buildings—although those in the new suburban areas are, of course, magnificent. The size of classes is still too big. There are some primary schools where the typical class is between forty and fifty. There are many secondary schools with nearly thirty children in the class. By contrast, in the typical fee-paying school a class of over twenty is rare. If we could get anywhere near to a situation where most children are taught by well-qualified teachers in reasonably small classes in pleasant buildings, it would effect a tremendous unleashing of talent. The interest that parents are now taking in the education of their children has outgrown the rate at which schools are being improved. If the two could be yoked together the change could be dramatic.

ANOTHER PROBLEM is apprenticeship. In this country, compared with many others abroad, the system of giving skills to young people who leave school at fifteen or sixteen is chaotic. The apprenticeship system has been very much under attack and is in need of substantial changes. Unless this is done, we shall

---

[1] *Ability and Educational Opportunity* (O.E.C.D., Paris, 1962), p. 107.

perpetuate the division between a limited class composed of those of high talents and high training 'creamed off' by the grammar schools, and a large number without adequate education or training, just unable to play their part in modern economic life at all competently. This fact, of course, diminishes the efficiency and effectiveness of a whole range of British industries to a great extent. Just try and get your car mended— or your house repaired—and you feel the effects. You cannot rely in England, in the way that you can in America, on the person of mediocre qualifications to tackle problems with that resourcefulness which only an adequate training can provide. Incompetence, bred by the wrong kind of education and training, is at the root of the British tradition of 'muddling through'.

WHAT IMPRESSED me most about France whenever I have lived there for any length of time is the difference between their educational system and ours. Partly there is more of it—a French child can go to a nursery school, and stay on at school till sixteen; partly it is less divisive. They don't have the caste-divisions of public schools, grammar schools, and the rest. That apart, there is a difference in the intellectual quality of French life—the status of the school, of the *professeur*, or the *normalien*, is an achieved status, achieved by intellectual competition; whereas here you feel that the occasional chap who has popped through the class-barrier is still a conspicuous phenomenon.

Generally speaking, the French attach more importance to education than we do. Since the war, their efforts have been heroic. Instead of facing the ordeal of the eleven-plus, every child at the age of eleven goes into a two-year 'cycle of observation' to help him and his parents choose the right course. Well over half the boys and girls choose the *Lycée* which prepares for university. The rest go into professional schools of various types, (including a three-year course of all-round individual apprenticeship). The universities will have half-a-million students in 1970. The whole organization of this expansion, which has been superb, has taken place against a background of phenomenally rising birth-rates. It seems that, earlier than the British, the post-war French decided to reorganize education effectively and well. Why?

Their historical legacy is more favourable. We have a dead-weight of neglect, partially alleviated in 1870, partially alleviated further in some places after 1918, but still, in 1944, the education system effectively divided the nation. The French have not had our truly astonishing and overt class (and sex) discrimination in public schools. Their best schools are in the cities, while ours are mostly isolated in the countryside. The town is an equalizing element in society. So, incidentally, was the army. Proust served in the ranks (which no men of his middle-class background would have done at that time in England, even had there been conscription) after he had been to a *Lycée* which was open to all. Intellect was the ladder most must climb. Here it was breeding tempered by wealth that secured advancement; there it had to be, at school at least, decently obscured.

One would not wish, in many respects, to emulate the French. But their professionalism, their cultivation of the arts, their day-to-day competence, their fundamental civilization, are just what we would wish to see here—and all that is admirable in their culture stems from the fact that ever since the Revolution, education has been one of their primary concerns.

In this country the sheer inadequacy of the greater part of the educational system is combined with snobbery, the hallmark of the traditional English school. It is the *un*importance of education which is the most striking characteristic of English social history.

OUR FEELINGS about universities tend to lag behind the facts. The 'new students' that you meet in Wigan or in Loughborough are far more like our pupils in Oxford than the 'undergrads' of popular tradition; and the Oxford don is—surely—far more like his Loughborough counterpart than he would care to admit. The same kind of house, the same kind of car, the same—dare one say it—kind of family. And to most of them this job is just a job—an attractive and interesting job—but a job, all the same. So I find most articles about universities too high-flown. In the daily round of teaching, writing, and sitting on committees, the high philosophical tone is really out of place; and by asserting too much about the nature of the university, we run the risk of attracting derision. Pompous dons seem ludicrous.

But I would not want to push the doctrine of ordinariness too far. We all believe, I suppose, that in *our* day Oxbridge had its golden age.

I read economics at Cambridge. Keynes was recently dead, but the intellectual excitement of being taught by his immediate successors—Joan Robinson, Richard Kahn, Nicholas Kaldor—was overwhelming. They created a new subject before our eyes. And to see these people, with scholars of equal distinction from other subjects—Dr. Leavis, say, or G. E. Moore—on the streets of Cambridge, in that clear light and revered beauty, was an experience that was all the greater for the prevailing sense of intimacy. Some would be great—writers or scholars, perhaps—while others would run the Civil Service, the stage, or the newspapers. This sense of being in daily contact with incipient distinction was a very real one, and even stronger, I suppose, in Oxford than in Cambridge. We had Thom Gunn; they had Ken Tynan.

I can understand how little one would want to change it, and how hard it is to believe that it has, in fact, all changed. When I was up, the undergraduates were war-veterans, with wives and children, and they belonged to the Labour Club. The Young Conservatives from minor public schools arrived with the end of petrol rationing.... Now they are eighteen again and are the post-C.N.D. grammar school boys who know it all. Change happens—among dons and students and in the subjects they study.

We know why change will continue. Nobody will be able, in the long run, to deny entrance to the thousands of new applicants. Meanwhile, the admissions policy discussions are endless and futile; you can't create places for students by juggling with examination papers.

There are the new subjects to be catered for. Microbiology is the supreme present example. How difficult it is to get them in. Take a minor one from economics. I tried—successfully—to establish the 'economics of education', on American money. I paid my own fare to America to get it. Now I do research on other international funds. My colleagues in sociology can tell a similar tale. Yet N.E.D.C. and others say they need the facts they won't pay for. Small wonder the dons emigrate.

It is these two key shortages—places in higher education and research funds—that deny a fair crack of the whip to girls and to working-class boys, and make the country short of 100,000 schoolteachers, thousands of social workers, and immeasurable numbers of engineers.

But is expansion enough? (It is so tedious that we still have to argue about the *need* for expansion—let us take it as read.) Won't it be too late and too dim? In our endless committees, with our tired administrators, can England cope? Who was responsible for architectural monstrosities like the Courtauld? The chaos of admissions is the latest case. The dons seem to believe that the new Oxbridge admissions schemes are desirable and fair and nobody seems to care that taken together the new schemes mean a process of continuous examination and form-filling for many months for the candidates, with all the bad results on the schools that Crowther has written about. In case after case we have known the facts for years. They set up the Crowther Committee to tell us at interminable length what Tawney had said thirty years before. Now we all wait, with bated breath, for the Robbins Committee to tell us what we all should have known (and some of us did) ten years ago. Why do we have to wait for the endorsement of the front-men to accept something (not, of course, that we will do anything about it)? English public life seems to consist of the sanctification of banality.

Will fast economic growth cure this loss of nerve? When we have more resources, will the expansion be so big that able people will be able to rise to the top without getting dead-beat in the process, like most of the present crew? Or is it something more profound? Is our economic failure, our political failure, our social failure—this total failure of nerve and inventiveness —something like the collapse of Spain, of Austria-Hungary? The signs are there—moral corruption in the Government, seedy self-deception in the Civil Service—and the while we respectable white-collar workers carry on making up self-defeating admission schemes of unimaginable complexity. Of course, we need great Victorian administrators again—or rather great American administrators—but we are caught in an endless circle. For the universities produce the administrators, who produce the children, who fill the universities, who produce the . . .

Small wonder they emigrate.

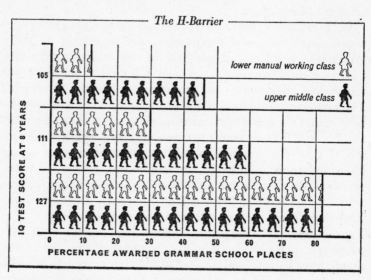

The H-Barrier

A 'National Survey of Health and Development of Children', which has been in progress since 1946, is going to be published shortly. It was conducted by Dr. J. W. B. Douglas, Director of the Medical Research Unit, London School of Economics, and covered a sample of more than 5,000 British schoolchildren. The conclusion which emerges from the survey (as reported by Thomas Pakenham in *The Observer*) is that 'the 11-plus examination and our selective educational system itself are seriously biased in favour of middle-class children and against virtually all those from poorer families . . .'

Our diagram shows in the first place (*top*) how the system operates on children whose abilities are slightly above average (I.Q. 105) at the age of eight. From this group only 12 per cent of the children from the lower classes are subsequently admitted to grammar schools compared to 46 per cent from the upper-middle classes.

The next pair of rows shows that among children of high ability (I.Q. 111) at the age of eight, 30 per cent of lower social background, 60 per cent of higher social background gain admission to grammar schools. Only the exceptionally gifted (I.Q. 127 and above) succeed in passing what one might call the 'H-barrier' (the 'dropped h').

The system works against the working-class child in two main ways: (*a*) Lack of encouragement from ill-educated parents, and bad primary schools, lead to a decline of the child's I.Q. between eight and eleven; (*b*) Where there is a shortage of places in grammar schools 'the examiners may believe that they are assessing the children on ability; but where the pinch occurs, a freshly scrubbed middle-class face may be as important as a good academic record'.

Postscript: The Manager and the Muses

ERRATUM

The publishers regret that owing to pressure of time in the production of this book what appears as Appendix 5, 'Towards a New Society: Profile of an Élite', ought to have been printed before Mr. Koestler's postscript which is partly based on the results of this inquiry.

1 The Vanguard

THE PROFILE which emerges from the pages of *New Society* is not a wildly inspiring one. It shows an earnest, sober, bland face, given to no nonsense. It reflects a mentality which is certainly progressive in the sense of giving education and technical training top priority, followed by 'firm economic leadership' and 'improved transport'; it is opposed to hanging, to racial discrimination, and the public schools; it favours divorce by consent, greater social equality, and 'a more sympathetic approach to criminal behaviour'. But the most remarkable feature in the portrait of this new élite group seems to me that, in spite of its indifference to Europe, the Commonwealth, and foreign affairs; in spite, that is to say, of its apparent isolationism and insularity, it is virtually indistinguishable from the image of its opposite numbers on the Continent of Europe. Four years ago I tried elsewhere to describe that 'Silent Generation' (as opposed to the noisy minority of Beats and semi-delinquents whose exhibitionistic antics monopolize the public's attention):

The face of the silent generation is uncommitted and non-committal. Its features provide no clues to individual character and temperament, but they already bear the professional stamp of the future manager, engineer, business man, or career woman. The girls mostly look like competent private secretaries and equally competent future mothers, whose family planning will be made dependent on the availability of baby-sitters. They drink mostly fruit-juices, Coca Cola, an occasional glass of beer—even in France where the sight of a young man sipping pineapple juice through a straw would have been unimaginable before the war. Sex is still a fascinating topic, but no longer a subject for verbal intercourse. Pre-marital sex is considered a normal expedient while waiting for the proper flat and income to settle down. The silent ones are far from deaf, but the stale slogans and anaemic values of their elders leave them cold. They know that the crusading generation of the 'thirties, the generation of their parents, was chiefly responsible for bringing about the present state of the world. They do not hate us for it, they are merely bored with us. They are indifferent to politics, not much interested in literature and the arts, and as immune against ideologies as we in the 'thirties were prone to them. They seem to have no aspirations except getting on in their profession, marrying early and going on holidays in the family car. Thus this super-historical age has produced a generation which seems to live outside History. Under the parabolic orbits of inter-Continental missiles they have peacefully settled down to cultivate their little gardens.

The affinities between these new societies, which grow silently all around us like grass under last year's rotting leaves, seems to me very striking. There are, of course, differences; Aldermaston, for instance, has caught on nowhere else in Europe. But in general there are more similarities than dissimilarities between the regional variants of this emergent generation of a new type of European.

Just as young Englishmen do not care tuppence—or two per cent, to be exact—about the past splendour of empire, so the young Germans, Italians, and Frenchmen do not give a damn about nationalism, frontiers, and tribal rivalries. The Germans, of course, want their torn country and torn families reunited, but that is no longer nationalism in the traditional sense. The French are grateful to de Gaulle for having saved them once more from a national calamity, but listen to his declamations on *Gloire* with the same affectionate amusement as the English listened to the more baroque flourishes of Churchillian rhetorics. (What a pity, but also how understandable, that these two great eighteenth-century *revenants* hated each other's guts.)

In a word, nationalism in Western Europe is dead, ideologies are on the wane, poverty is on the way out. The new structure which is taking shape is the society of managers, technocrats, official planning, chromium, motels, and motorways—everything that Henry Fairlie dislikes, and some of which I dislike just as heartily. But fortunately, this is only part of the picture. The new Europe is not Huxley's Brave New World, nor Orwell's 1984—as some of our intellectuals see it darkly through a jaundiced eye. The truth is that the arts and the crafts in Europe flourish today as they never flourished before.

The wonders which the Renaissance produced were accessible only to a chosen few—there were no photographs and no reproductions. Besides, the Renaissance was essentially a one-way movement, fanning out from the Italian peninsula. Contemporary Europe, on the other hand, is in a process of cultural cross-fertilization, the winds blowing from all directions of the compass. From the north come Scandinavian films, glassware, porcelain, furniture; from the west English and American literature; from Italy and France theatre, films, novels, ceramics, architecture, industrial design; even from oppressed Russia and Poland we got Pasternak and Andreizef, Leningrad composers, Moscow ballet, Warsaw films. (I keep mentioning films because they represent both the worst and also perhaps the best in twentieth-century art.) A new crop of novelists is maturing in Germany and Switzerland; an Icelander and a Sicilian have won Nobel Prizes in literature. There is an explosion of creativity all over the Continent, of which only muted echoes reach our islands.

2 The Rearguard

SOME YEARS AGO I wrote a kind of homily against the 'French 'flu'—the nostalgic palpitations and watery eyes which mere mention of the name of a Paris metro station used to produce in English *littérateurs*. Now the pendulum has swung in the opposite direction. Henry Fairlie is certainly an extreme case, yet his doubt 'whether we have much to learn from the French' is nevertheless characteristic. Let me make one or two modest suggestions. We could, for instance, learn from France to have a Minister of Culture with Cabinet rank; second, to appoint to that post a novelist; third, to give him a lavish budget of the size which enabled Malraux to subsidize the National Theatres on an unprecedented scale, and to have the façades of the historical buildings in the capital scrubbed white and restored to their virginal splendour.

We could perhaps also learn from our neighbours how to prevent wastage of the gross national product in intelligence and creativity. The present number of university students in Great Britain is 117,000. The number of university students in France last year was 260,000. By 1970 this country hopes to have 170,000 university students. The French estimate for the same year is 500,000. Said the elephant to the mouse: My, aren't you small. Said the mouse to the elephant: Yes, just lately I've not been well at all. . . . It may also be worth mentioning that French academic fees are extremely low; that more than half of the French students are exempt from paying them; and that more than 30 per cent benefit from scholarships which cover both their academic fees and living expenses.[1]

The reason why I am mentioning all this is not to sing the praises of France, but to explode the absurd fallacy that economic growth at the rate of 6 per cent *per annum*, as compared to our 2 per cent, must be bought at the price of neglecting the arts; that more exports mean less culture; that expert knowledge is incompatible with gracious living; that we must choose between *either* good management of our affairs *or* the cult of the muses.

NEEDLESS TO SAY, excessive emphasis on the material aspects of existence, on efficiency and competition *über alles*, can be soul-destroying—as some aspects of American or German civilization have drastically shown. But an effete aestheticism, soaked in nostalgia for the past and spiced with arrogance, can have similar effects. One of the few techniques at which the rearguard of Old Struthonians are real experts is a kind of semantic sleight of hand, performed by inventing spurious alternatives, and hypnotizing the public into accepting them: *either* efficiency *or* aesthetics, either Keynes or E. M. Forster, either washing machines or Horace. Here, for instance, is

[1] British figures supplied by the Ministry of Education, French figures by the French Embassy; the 1970 estimate is unofficial—see John Vaizey's article, page 219.

Simon Raven (whom Mr. Fairlie quoted with such approval) performing that stage magician's trick:

> While long-established English institutions tend to be illogical and wasteful, the values which they promote, however limited in their scope, are morally and aesthetically far superior to anything which the new world of admass tastes and applied science can show. If I care to spend my day writing Latin verses or watching cricket, as opposed to selling some beastly machine or rubbishy gimmick over a fat expense account luncheon, who is to say I am not the better man for it? . . . What it amounts to, then, is that the cure proposed (more and more technical efficiency, professionalism at all levels, smart sales-talk for our products) is far worse than the disease diagnosed (complacency, nepotism, charm, the amateur spirit). But, 'if we don't take the cure we shall die', *i.e.*, we shall go broke. Myself, I am beginning to think this might be a very good thing, if only because it would mean an end of those hatchet-faced middlemen guzzling up smoked salmon in Quaglino's. What is wanted is less industry and more Horace, who points out that the surest way of being happy is to make the best of what you've got. All this talk of production and competition has gone on so long and so loudly that people have forgotten what they're competing for. The answer is six foot of earth, and that pretty quickly; once you get that into your head, it is clear that Latin verses are every bit as relevant—or irrelevant—as money-grubbing or Sputniks, and make far less noise and smell. . . .

OSCAR WILDE once picked up one of those varnished skulls which at the time people used to keep in their libraries, and exclaimed: 'Death, how Gothic—life, how Greek! . . .' There is something definitely Gothic about our would-be Greeks. Horace was only a Roman, but, given to Latin precision, even he would have known that satellites do not smell, and that the only sound they produce as they orbit through soft stillness and the night is Pythagoras's Harmony of the Spheres. *'There's not the smallest orb which thou behold'st/But in his motion like an angel sings'*: this passage in the *Merchant* actually refers to Astronomy (on which Lorenzo lectures Jessica). The Elizabethans were deplorably science-minded, and fascinated by Dr. Gilbert's lodestones. One must bury one's head in lots of sand indeed to become deaf to the poetry of these miraculous little gadgets ploughing through the hoary deep towards Mars or Venus in search of other forms of life. Have we become so impoverished in fantasy that Lucian's dream of sailing to the moon has lost its appeal for us? Are we so deafened by the rival slogans of Engineers and Eggheads that we have forgotten the Renaissance ideal of *l'uomo universale*? Is there any evidence that the popularity of the Motor Show has diminished the popularity of the Flower Show?

It all hangs together by invisible threads: loss of imagination, intellectual affectations, the cult of ineffectuality, economic stagnation, waste of talent, waste of energy, fear of change. These are the foxes that spoil our vines; we can either deny that they exist, or pretend that they are nice little doggies, or get rid of them. No bloody massacre is needed to chase them away, not even more sweat and toil. Need it be said that efficiency and good management mean less sweat, less toil, higher productivity, and more *joie de vivre*? The Germans are planning to introduce the five-day week in all major industries; the French, the Belgians, the Swiss do not work longer hours than we do; they do not rush madly about nor have they given up their relaxed mid-day meals with wine—not even in favour of our gracious Grecian black-sweet tea with sausage rolls. How embarrassing that one should have to keep harping on the obvious; but how else is one to wind up a discussion which started with the ringing assertion of the Englishman's sacred 'right to be inefficient'—meaning the right of civil servants, company directors, and trade union bosses to rule us inefficiently? And how are we to combat that peculiar emotional climate in which words like Washing Machine, Blueprint, Technocrat, Efficiency, and even Plastic Bags and Detergents, have been turned into hate-slogans and negative fetishes?

3 The Other Rearguard

I HAVE BEEN paraphrasing the arguments of Goronwy Rees, Andrew Shonfield, Michael Shanks, Austen Albu, *et al.* Broadly speaking, they agree that the future will be decided between the new élite of the Silent Generation, and the powerful rearguard of Old Struthonians of all persuasions, from Blimps to trade union bosses. This leads to that other formidable phalanx of the rearguard, the British working class, and its trade unions, whose structure and mentality were analysed by John Cole, Michael Shanks, and Aidan Crawley.

What they said brought to mind two vivid memories. First, a scene in *Modern Times* where Charlie Chaplin, after several hours spent at the moving assembly belt going through the same sequence of three or four jerky motions, keeps on repeating them like a wound-up automaton after the belt has stopped moving. The second is a televised interview with two young Merseyside workers, occasioned by one of those demarcation disputes about who should drill the holes. Asked by the interviewer why they were opposed to young people learning more than one skill, to acquiring more knowledge, flexibility, and all-round understanding of the production process in which they were engaged, the two lads rigidly, stubbornly, repeated: 'Because that would lead to unemployment. We don't want to be pushed about. We remember 1929. . . .'

They did not, of course, remember 1929, only what their elders had told them, and their union leaders had taught them. It was the sacred doctrine that the man who lays the cold-water pipes must not be allowed to lay the hot-water pipes, the man who makes the cable must not be allowed to make the casting for the cable, a doctrine which holds up as an ideal the narrowing of man's potentialities, his rigid specialization on a single, mechanized, automatic routine—his reduction to a Chaplinesque robot. Chaplin's nightmare has become the boilermaker's wish-dream.

There is no English word for *abrutissement*—the blunting of talents and sensibilities to a chronic state of bemusement and brutishness. Our archaic system of apprenticeship, preparing for a rigidly demarcated existence (the equivalent of a life-sentence to a single type of job), seems to be expressly designed to produce that *abrutissement*, or Borstal mentality, which Alan Sillitoe has so shatteringly exposed. But there is another important factor which contributes to the massive inertial resistance of the British working class: the doctrine of non-competitiveness, a series of unwritten but constantly reiterated Maxims of Life. Go slow or you are letting your mates down and we shall all be landed on the dole. If you seek betterment or promotion you are breaking rank and will be sent to Coventry. It's a mug's game, mate, and you are in it for life unless you hit the pools; so you had better do as we do and go slow and make the best of it. . . . It is a religion apart, like Buddhism, with its sacred rites (the cult of the tea-break), its sacred taboo (competitiveness), its Powers of Light and Darkness (Them and Us), and its (four-letter) equivalent of the sacred syllable *OM*. I read recently about an elderly worker whose job was polishing metal rods and who refused to slow down—because he simply couldn't force himself to do so—with the result as above. About the effects of all this on the national economy no more need be said; what needs pointing out is the psychologically demoralizing effect on the young workman of this process of conditioning not to work to full capacity in the natural rhythm of his muscles, not to take a pride in his job, not to have ambitions in life—a kind of deliberate castration of the human spirit. Once more we find the ideal of the *l'uomo universale* reversed—on the other side of the barrier. 'The most striking conclusion', wrote Geoffrey Gorer, discussing a recent book on the life of coalminers, 'is how remarkably little high wages and secure employment have modified old habits and ways of life.'

During the first years of the war, thousands of slum children were evacuated to the country. Then a small booklet, *Our Towns —A Close-up*, by Margaret Bondfield, told an incredulous and shocked nation that the majority of these children had nits in their hair, that a fair number were not house-trained, and that others had never had a hot meal. That, thank God, is a thing of the past; but there prevails the same nation-wide ignorance today about the social and mental climate in industrial working communities. I hate picking again at Mr. Fairlie, but it is surely symptomatic if a brilliant political writer asserts that our class differences are 'more imagined than real' and that they 'scarcely matter a whit'.

LET ME MAKE two additional points which I think have not been given sufficient emphasis in this number. First, one specific and indeed unique feature of the British industrial scene is not the total volume of strikes, but their often grotesque, frivolous, and fratricidal causes—fratricidal because they are motivated by demarcational or wage-differential jealousies. The second, even more important, point arises out of a comparison between Communist influence on industrial relations in Britain and in the rest of Europe. In the early post-war period, Italy and France were on the verge of civil war, and the Communists were the strongest single force both in the trade unions and in Parliament. Today in both countries they still hold a sizeable number of Parliamentary seats; but the trade unions have split into Socialist, Christian, and Communist unions, and the latter, by being forced into the open and having to compete with the other two, can no longer pursue purely disruptive policies. In this country the opposite happened. Alone among the countries of Europe, Communist influence in the unions and on the shop floors increased instead of decreasing with growing prosperity, and has for the first time become a serious problem in the nation's life.

4 Death of an Ostrich?

BOTH REARGUARDS—'theirs' and 'ours', whichever side you are on—have their gaze turned backward and inward. They are riveted on the past; and they refuse to see what is happening in the rest of the world.[1]

[1] Three of our authors reported independently on the traumatic shock which a British trade union delegation suffered from its foolhardy venture of visiting Sweden—and realizing that it is possible for employers, workers, and Government to co-operate.

The historical origins of these attitudes have been discussed by several of our authors. On the one side, memories of the Tolpuddle Martyrs and of the hunger marches, a feeling of weakness and insecurity, of suspicion and resentment. On the other side, the cult of the 'Amateur and Gentleman', the taboo on expertise, the distrust of the too-clever and too-keen—attitudes whose origin can be traced back to the merging of feudal and mercantile traditions, the amalgamation of the values and tastes of landed gentry and *entrepreneurs*. Karl Marx was a shrewd observer; though he was revolted by the child labour in English factories and the condition of the working classes in general, he nevertheless thought that England was the only country in Europe where a social revolution might be effected by peaceful and legal means. One of the considerations that led him to this conclusion was, as he somewhat wryly remarked, that the British bourgeoisie instead of liquidating their aristocracy, had married their daughters.[1]

Most European countries went through a series of social revolutions in 1789, 1848, 1918, and 1945, which abolished or eroded the social and educational class-barriers to a considerable extent. This country was spared these bloody upheavals, but at a price which now makes itself increasingly felt. Instead of flames coming out of the roof, it saw the rafters crumbling with slow dry rot. It preserved its anachronistic class structure, and its micro-structure of sub-castes within the classes, as unique in the Western world as are its weights, measures, and currency.

It remained untouched not only by social revolution, but also by foreign invasion. This again turned out a blessing at a price. Physical devastation by air bombardment cannot be compared in its psychological effects to the experience of being invaded and ruled by alien soldiery. You cannot be a pacifist when your home, your wife or sister, and your self-respect are *literally* at stake. The conscientious objector is an ethical luxury-flower which could only grow on a safe island. Aldermaston is

[1] Marx's illustrious pupil, Vladimir Ilyich Lenin, came to a similar conclusion. When he read in a newspaper about a strike in England in the course of which the striking workers had actually won a soccer game against the police, he declared that the English would never make a revolution and clamped down on the subsidy for the British C.P.

another product of innocence and inexperience which found no imitators elsewhere. The youth of Europe is just as anxious as our marchers are to avoid war; but it has learned that pacifism, like love, is a game which needs two to play it.

THE ACCENT in this issue, as said at the beginning, was on diagnosis rather than on therapy (or on flattery—when a physician is asked to examine a person's liver, he does not report that the patient has dimpled cheeks and a winning smile). Nevertheless, some tentative suggestions have emerged, ranging over the whole field: from the reform of Parliament to the reform of the trade unions and the reform of the educational system.

My personal inclination is to give priority to the last-mentioned item. It is our out-dated educational system, out-dated in almost every respect—11-plus, streaming, curriculum, segregation by class and sex—which perpetuates the iniquities of the past. It tears the nation apart and provides, generation after generation, a new crop of unwilling combatants for the cold class war. Equal opportunities for equally gifted children regardless of the status of the parents seems to me the basic axiom of social justice on which a free society must be built.

All who collaborated on this issue (with one abstention) are agreed on the need for radical changes. Their explicit or implied proposals for reform seem to be neither too timid not Utopian. Perhaps the common element in the intentions and attitudes of this very heterogeneous team can be summed up in the short prayer of a community which feels, more urgently than others, the need for a new departure.

> God grant me the serenity to accept the things I cannot
> change;
> The courage to change the things I can;
> And the wisdom to know the difference.

It is a prayer repeated at the end of each meeting of Alcoholics Anonymous; its source is unknown.

A. K.

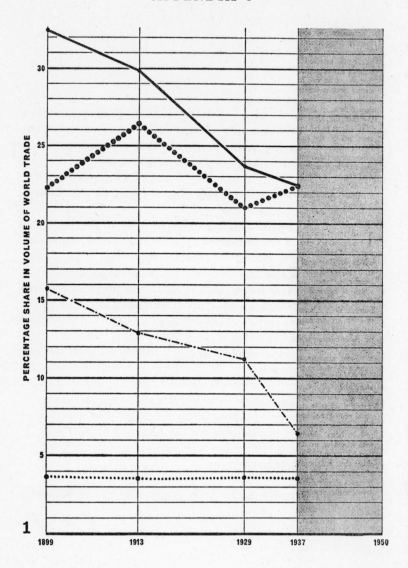

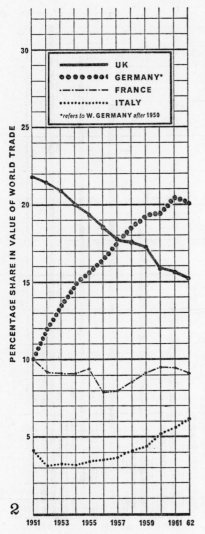

2

PERCENTAGE SHARE IN VALUE OF WORLD TRADE

UK
GERMANY*
FRANCE
ITALY
*refers to W. GERMANY after 1950

1951 1953 1955 1957 1959 1961 62

Britain's declining share in world trade

APPENDIX 1 AND APPEN-
DIX 2 DIAGRAMS illustrate
the steady decline of
Britain's percentual share in
world trade (LEFT) from the
turn of the century to shortly
before the outbreak of the
second World War; and the
rapid decline (RIGHT) in the
course of the last ten years.
The diagram on the left
is based on H. Tyszynski's
classic study;[1] the sharp
breaks are due to the fact
that his figures refer only
to the years which are in-
dicated. The unsettled war
years and immediate post-
war years are blacked out.
The sharp drop in the
German trade share is, of
course, due to the division
of Germany.

Appendix 3 and Appendix
4 diagrams refer to exports

[1] 'World Trade in Manufactured Commodities 1899–1950' in *The
Manchester School of Economic and Social Studies*, Vol. XIX, No. 3, September,
1951. The right-hand diagram is based on *National Institute Economic Review*,
No. 23, February, 1963, table 23, p. 76.

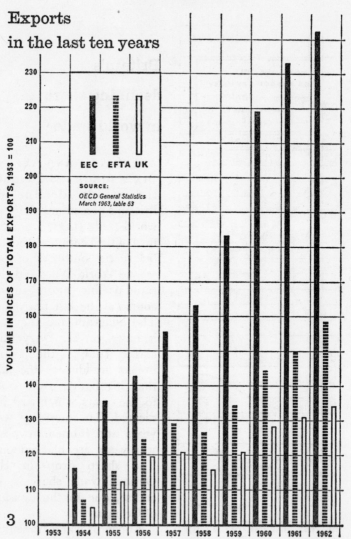

Exports in the last ten years

VOLUME INDICES OF TOTAL EXPORTS, 1953 = 100

EEC EFTA UK

SOURCE:
OECD General Statistics
March 1963, table 53

and industrial production. The left-hand diagram shows that in the last ten years the volume of our exports increased in round figures by less than 40 per cent, that of the Common Market by more than 140 per cent. Even the EFTA countries have done better than the United Kingdom.

The last four years

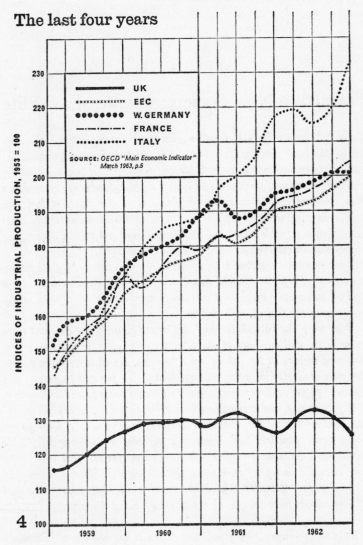

Finally, our industrial production in the course of the last four years (RIGHT-HAND DIAGRAM) shows an almost flat curve, whereas the steep rise in the production curves of the Common Market and its three biggest member-countries reflects the 'economic miracles' which they have jointly and severally experienced.

APPENDIX 5

Towards a New Society: Profile of an Élite

NEW SOCIETY (*which, together with the* New Scientist, *represents one of the most imaginative ventures in British journalism since the war) recently sent out a remarkable questionnaire. It contained twelve groups of questions formulated in a highly sophisticated way; the answers often involved choices in terms of priorities, lesser evils, ethical and utilitarian judgments. To fill in the questionnaire conscientiously must have taken a sizeable chunk out of the week-end; yet no less than 7,344 readers sent in complete answers (May 9th and 13th, 1963).*

This enormous response is in itself highly significant. 'Questionnaire answering', Professor Donald MacRae remarked in his comments, 'is a kind of surrogate voting, and all voting involves an attempt to stamp reality with the seal of one's desires.'

Who were the voters? By AGE *(in round figures) 70 per cent were under forty, and one-half of the total under thirty. By* SEX, *men outnumbered women at the rate of seven to three. By* OCCUPATION *24 per cent were students (including post-graduates), 14 per cent professors and teachers, 19 per cent were managers, 11 per cent came from Civil Service, local government, and nationalized industries, 11 per cent were professional men, and another 11 per cent social workers. In other words, some 40 per cent were in 'practical life', another 40 per cent in academic life. This would make an almost perfect balance—except for the fact that 'there were virtually no replies from working-class people'. (Here is something to ponder for optimists who keep assuring us that paperbacks and evening courses have brought in a new era of Enlightenment.)*

THE FIRST GROUP *of questions referred to the concept of 'Britain's greatness'. The reader was asked which, in his opinion, were the main factors that (a) had contributed most to Britain's greatness in the* past *and (b) will be most important 'for the kind of greatness which will be open to Britain in the* future'. *In the answers referring to the past, the top factors named were 'economic strength' (68 per cent), 'military* power' (*50 per cent*), *and* 'Empire' (*50 per cent*)*; whereas* 'educational standards' *and* 'welfare of the people' *came out bottom with 7 per cent and 2 per cent respectively. But, in judging the factors which will make for* future *greatness, the criteria were reversed.* 'Educational standards' *and* 'achievements in arts and science' *now came top with 71 per cent and 44 per cent respectively, whereas* 'military power' *and* 'Empire' *had slid to the bottom with a paltry 2 per cent to each.*

Another group of questions asked which institutions were consistent and which were not 'with the kind of Britain you want'. *The most massive* nays *were aimed at* 'capital punishment' (*80 per cent*)*; next came the* 'independent nuclear deterrent' (*76 per cent*). *The most massive* ayes *went to:* 'divorce by consent of both parties' (*75 per cent*) *and* 'Government direction of industries' (*70 per cent*). *The pros and cons were most evenly* balanced *on* 'unrestricted immigration' (*46 per cent pro, 52 per cent against*) *and on* 'limitation in the national interest of the right to strike' (*46 per cent pro, 53 per cent against*). *The public school system was rejected by almost two-thirds of the voters* (*64 per cent against, 35 per cent for*).

However, it also came to light that to hold an opinion on any of these points did not necessarily mean that the person felt strongly about it. When the readers were asked to rate, in order of importance, 'the tasks of any British Government (irrespective of party) in the next few years', *a different picture emerged. Abolition of capital punishment did not figure at all on the Governmental agenda, nor divorce by consent, although these had scored the most votes. Even more surprising, although 76 per cent had voted against the independent nuclear deterrent, only 9 per cent mentioned nuclear disarmament as an* 'important task'. *First in importance came* 'massive investment in education and technical training' (*32 per cent*) *and* 'improved transport' (*18 per cent*). *Bottom of the list were* 'strengthening of the Western alliance' (*4 per cent*), 'continued efforts to establish links with the Common Market' (*3 per cent*), *and* 'strengthening relations with the Commonwealth'—*a whole 2 per cent.*

WHICH OF OUR INSTITUTIONS *are in the most urgent need of radical reform? According to* New Society *readers the trade unions* (*27 per cent*)*, industrial management* (*23 per cent*)*, the House of Commons* (*17 per cent*). *The National Health Service came out best: only 6 per cent thought it in need of radical reform.*

Another group of questions asked readers to evaluate the most striking changes in the British way of life since the last war. Top rank was given to 'greater social equality' (58 per cent) and 'a healthier attitude to sex' (38 per cent). But an extremely poor view was taken regarding improvements in the personal sphere. Only 10 per cent thought that there was now 'a happier pattern of family relationships' and only 5 per cent thought that we had 'a gayer approach to life'.

So far there had been little indication of international-mindedness; but there was another surprise to come. The readers were asked which of the following 'external influences on British culture' they considered on the whole harmful or beneficial. It transpired that the only Bad Influence from abroad was 'Hollywood'; the others were all Good Influences:

	HARMFUL	BENEFICIAL	NEITHER
	%	%	%
American films and TV programmes	70	5	23
The growing popularity of foreign holidays	1	86	12
Political refugees from Europe	4	61	34
Italian design	4	56	38
West Indian immigrants	13	32	53

Finally, emigration: 42 per cent of the subjects had considered emigrating. The countries they had in mind were New Zealand, Australia, Canada, the U.S.A., and Sweden. The advantages they thought they would gain by emigrating were mainly improved standards of living, better working conditions, and—this is the only interesting point—50 per cent thought that they would be living in a more congenial social system.

HERE, THEN, ARE *some 7,000 people specifically concerned with social and moral problems who play (or will play) a significant part in the nation's life, and their answers project a surprisingly sharp profile of a new academic-managerial élite. The answers were analysed in considerable detail by Professor R. P. Kelvin. Here are some of the conclusions which emerged from his analysis:*

'Seventy per cent of the replies denied that Britain was still "a great power" and 79 per cent chose "individual happiness" as more important

than national greatness in a conflict between the two. And yet there was some nostalgia for greatness. Forty-two per cent would have been glad to think Britain great, and the rest were indifferent to greatness rather than hostile to it.

'*A majority (54 per cent) felt that Britain could never be "wholly European"; 45 per cent regretted this, but 31 per cent were glad.*

'*Taking the replies as a whole, the pattern is quite consistent; home affairs are regarded as far more crucial and urgent than foreign. The extent and consistency of the emphasis on domestic matters is perhaps a little surprising in this predominantly middle-class and highly educated group. It suggests an "inward-looking" approach, almost a desire to withdraw from undue involvement with the rest of the world; it suggests (at least) a latent isolationism of which the people in this group are probably aware and which, on principle, most of them would probably reject.*

'*This pattern is not due to xenophobia. Except for the hostility to American films and TV programmes, the other foreign influences suggested were considered beneficial rather than harmful. Nor does the pattern suggest any actual rejection of the rest of the world, but rather a relatively low level of willingness to take an active role in its affairs. This is presumably closely connected with the changed criteria of "greatness". Whatever the period people had in mind considering the past, the tendency was to think of greatness in terms of Britain's position vis-à-vis other countries, e.g., in terms of economic strength, military power, empire. Future greatness, however, is seen to lie in essentially domestic achievements, e.g., educational standards, achievements in arts and science. The difference between these two sets of criteria is fundamental. To use an analogy (and only an analogy), if one were to personify Britain, the change is akin to a change of personality from extrovet to introvert. (This does not imply that Britain is a nation of introverts!) The greatness, the happiness, the self-confidence with which people are concerned and identify themselves are seen to depend on the standards and achievements attained within the community rather than on the position of Britain in relation to the world at large. These feelings probably stem from the realization of the new status of Britain compared with Russia and the United States; but in their extent they suggest an over-reaction to this change. And this in turn would imply, at a conjectural level, that re-creating the self-confidence necessary for wholehearted involvement in world affairs may depend largely on the prior solution of domestic problems. . . .*

'*On the industrial side there was a strong demand for firm leadership rather than* laissez-faire *policies on economic problems. Seventy per cent thought Government direction of industry consistent with the British way of life and a sizeable minority (46 per cent) seem to question the fundamental right to strike. Most replies denied that there was an inevitable gulf between the interests of management and labour.*

'*The over-all results show three important features: the desire to maximize human resources; the unambiguous preoccupation with domestic rather than foreign affairs; and the fundamental change in the traditional concept of greatness.*'

Contributors

Austen Albu, M.P.—born in 1903—educated at Tonbridge School and Imperial College of Science and Technology, where he took an engineering degree. After several years as Works Manager for a light engineering firm, he went to Germany in a senior position with the Control Commission, returning to England in 1948 when he was, for a short time, Deputy-Director of the British Institute of Management before being elected Labour Member of Parliament for Edmonton.

Since entering the House of Commons, he has spent a great deal of his time trying to persuade the leaders of both parties of the need for technological change in British industry and for higher standards in technical education. In recent years these efforts seem to have begun to have had some effect. He is a member of the Board of Governors of the Imperial College of Science and Technology and of Battersea College of Advanced Technology and has recently written a book entitled *The Young Man's Guide to Mechanical Engineering* (Hamish Hamilton) to encourage young men to become engineers. . . .

John Grigg (formerly Lord Altrincham): 'I was born in 1924. My family on both sides was markedly political. At Eton I was Captain of the Oppidans (not much of a distinction, though shared by Shelley). At New College, Oxford, after the war was an Exhibitioner. Meanwhile had been in the army (Grenadier Guards). Between 1948 and 1960 (when it ceased publication) was concerned with editing the *National Review*, known after 1950 as the *National and English Review*. Contested Oldham West as a Tory in the general elections of 1951 and 1955. In the latter year my father died and have since been excluded from democratic politics. Since 1960 have been a weekly columnist for *The Guardian*. Published, in 1958, *Two Anglican Essays*. Disclaimed peerage July 31st, 1963. I now live and write under the name of John Grigg.'

John Cole: 'Born in Belfast in 1927; went to a council primary school and Belfast Royal Academy. Entered journalism on leaving school in 1945, and worked on the *Belfast Telegraph* for eleven years, finally as Political Correspondent. Joined the *Manchester Guardian* in 1956, worked in Manchester for eighteen months, and liked the North of England. . . . Moved to London as Labour Correspondent of *The Guardian* in 1957, and liked the South of England. Even liked the English, but still feel sufficiently unintegrated after seven years to study them with ostentatious detachment. . . . Have an obsession about the English obsession about class. Believe, gloomily, that it will never change.'

Cyril (Vernon) Connolly: 'Born 1903 of Anglo-Irish and West Country antecedents; educated Eton (Scholar) and Balliol College, Oxford (Scholar); began to write for the *New Statesman* and when twenty-three to work for Logan Pearsall Smith, founded and edited *Horizon* (1939–50), joined *Sunday Times* 1951, author of *Rock Pool, Enemies of Promise, Unquiet Grave.* . . .'

Aidan Crawley: 'Born in a vicarage in Benenden, Kent. Specialized in History and Cricket at Harrow, in Cricket and Horses at Oxford. Became a journalist but resigned over a fiat that nothing objectionable about Mussolini or the Emperor of Japan should appear in the journal for which I worked. . . . Joined the auxiliary Air Force and the Labour Party in the same year. Prisoner of war for four years. . . . Became Labour Member of Parliament, married in 1945. Disillusionment with socialism enlarged by study of industrial relations. Resigned from Labour Party 1956; joined Conservatives 1957. As writer and television commentator toured the Western world, making special studies of India, the Middle East, and Africa. . . . Re-elected to Parliament as a Conservative (West Derbyshire) 1962. . . .'

Marcus Cunliffe: 'Born in Lancashire (1922). Military education sketched out at Sandhurst, Catterick, etc.: drastically re-sketched in Normandy, Holland, Germany. . . . Higher learning sought at Oxford (Oriel), then at Yale on a Commonwealth Fellowship. Have taught since 1949 at Manchester University, where I hold a chair of American History and Institutions. . . . Books I have published include *Literature of the United States* (Pelican) and a biography of George Washington. Books I intend to publish are concerned at least in part with the United States. My wife is a New Yorker. America, in other words, is a second country (France would come third). . . . Am tempted to emigrate but may well stay put. Britain is the place I am fondest of and most exasperated by. . . .'

Henry Fairlie was born in 1924, and educated at Highgate School and Corpus Christi College, Oxford. After working on *The Observer* and *The Times*, he freelanced mainly as a political journalist. Among his well-known polemics was the first recorded shaft against *The contemporary* 'Establishment'. He is a regular contributor to *Encounter*.

Dr. Alan McGlashan (M.C., M.R.C.S., L.R.C.P., D.P.M.) has been a practising psychiatrist for twenty-five years. He was born in 1898, educated at Epsom College and Clare College, Cambridge. His publications include *St. George and the Dragon* (1931) and many articles in *The Lancet, The Listener*, etc. . . .

John Mander: 'Born London, 1932. An English upper-middle-class education—prep. school, public school, Trin. Coll. Camb.—takes time to live down, liberal parentage notwithstanding (mother, writer; father, Liberal M.P. and opponent of Chamberlain's appeasement policies). After Cambridge, slight feeling of nausea at Restoration England of mid-fifties led to sustained effort to "be a foreigner" (see Alastair Reid, June *Encounter*). Lived one year teaching and writing in Munich; three years in Berlin. 1959–60: *The Writer and Commitment*—essays about literature and politics. 1960–62: staff member of *New Statesman*. Writing for *New Statesman* on German political scene leads to book on Berlin crisis (Penguin Special: *Berlin, Hostage for the West*), disaffection from editorial line, resignation. . . . Autumn, 1962: in India for *Encounter* during Indo-Chinese hostilities. Recently published: a study of Britain's hitherings and ditherings in foreign policy, *Great Britain or Little England?* (Penguin, and Secker & Warburg). Since March, 1963, Assistant Editor of *Encounter*. . . .'

Malcolm Muggeridge, born 1903, educated at Selhurst Grammar School and Cambridge. 1927–30, lecturer at the Egyptian University, Cairo. 1930, on the editorial staff of the *Manchester Guardian*, and later for a year their correspondent in Moscow, and another year Assistant Editor of the Calcutta *Statesman*. Served during the war in East and North Africa, Italy, and France. Was the *Daily Telegraph*'s Washington Correspondent (1946–47) and Deputy Editor (1950–52). 1953–57, Editor of *Punch*. His books include *Winter in Moscow, The Thirties*, and *Affairs of the Heart*. . . .

Goronwy Rees: 'I was born at Aberystwyth, in Cardiganshire, in 1909. Many years later I returned there for a brief and unhappy experience as Principal of the University College of Wales. I was educated at the High School for Boys, Cardiff, and at New College, Oxford; in 1930 I was elected to a Fellowship at All Souls. Joined the army as a gunner, ended in Germany as a Staff Officer attached to the Political Adviser to the Commander-in-Chief. After the war, I published a novel, *Where No Wounds Were*, worked in an engineering firm, and was for a time Estates Bursar of All Souls. Recently have devoted myself to writing. Anyone who wishes to know more about me may read it in a book of autobiography, *A Bundle of Sensations*, which was published in 1960. . . .'

Hugh Seton-Watson (born 1916, Professor of Russian History, University of London, since 1951): 'My interest in international politics was mainly aroused by my father, R. W. Seton-Watson, diplomatic historian and specialist in Central European and Balkan politics. It was further stimulated at Winchester, whose climate I remember as one not in the least of conformism, but rather of free and critical argument. It was extended by studying, and later by teaching, Politics (P.P.E.) at Oxford, and by travelling in Europe, the Middle East, North America and, only briefly, to South Africa and the Far East. . . .'

Michael Shanks: 'I was born in 1927, and educated at a West of England public school and later at Balliol College, Oxford, which I entered as a would-be philosopher and left as an economist. I worked on *The Economist* and the *Financial Times*, which I joined in 1953. First book, *The Stagnant Society* (Penguin, 1961). Second book, *Britain and the New Europe*, with John Lambert (Chatto & Windus, 1962). Other publications include *The Lessons of Public Enterprise* (Jonathan Cape, 1963), which I did for the Fabian Society, and a number of pamphlets: *How to Export, Incomes Policy and the Professional Employee*, etc. . . .'

Andrew Shonfield: 'I have been writing from a very early age and have never had an ambition to do anything but write. But although I have greatly enjoyed newspaper journalism and have been fairly successful at it—becoming first foreign editor of the *Financial Times* and later economic editor of *The Observer*—the things that I have really wanted to write have usually been done outside normal working hours, mostly late at night or on holiday. I have published two books, one on British economic policy and the other on the problem of the underdeveloped countries. At the age of forty-four,

I gave up newspaper work and was appointed Director of Studies at the Royal Institute of International Affairs. . . .'

John Vaizey: 'Born in London in 1929 and educated at L.C.C. elementary and grammar schools. A Scholar of Queens' College, Cambridge, and read Economics. . . . Radical views expressed in *Scenes from Institutional Life*; intellectual side is presented in such books as *The Economics of Education* and *The Costs of Education*. After a period in the University of London, am now Fellow and Tutor of Economics at Worcester College, Oxford. . . .'

Elizabeth Young: educated: International School, Geneva, Downe House, Somerville College, Oxford; three years lower deck W.R.N.S.; five children—four of school age being educated by London County Council. Has written: *Old London Churches* (architectural history—with Wayland Young); *Time is as Time Does* (poems); three Fabian pamphlets, *The Socialist Imagination, Disarmament: Finnegan's Choice* (both with Wayland Young), and *Nations and Nuclear Weapons*. Reviews books on architectural and Arms Control topics. Was secretary of the British Tibor Dery Committee; is secretary of the Hawksmoor Committee.